CHINESE HERBAL PATENT FORMULAS

A Practical Guide

With Appendices on American Made
Chinese Herbal Products

by Jake Fratkin

with a special chapter by
Subhuti Dharmananda, Ph.D.

Institute for Traditional Medicine
Portland, Oregon

This book is dedicated to my teachers:

Dr. Ineon Moon
Dr. Guo, Zhen-gang
Dr. Pak-leung Lau

This volume would not be possible without the help and support of Dr. Subhuti Dharmananda. He has contributed many valuable suggestions and corrections; this book would have been very different without his input. I am inspired by Subhuti's clarity and knowledge, and especially his dream that Chinese herbs can benefit the health and well-being of people throughout the world.

I am also deeply indebted to Alan Lau of Mayway Trading Company, San Francisco, for his generosity and kindness in supporting this project.

I would like to thank the following for their contributions:

Guo, Zhengang, M.D., O.M.D.
Pak-leung Lau, O.M.D.
Lisa Lau
Joy Smedley (Zhou, Zuo-hua, D.Ac.)
Mary Jonaitis
Fred Taub, N.D.
Laura Lewis
Winnie Adams
Carol Conlon, C.A.
Jenny Boehm
Rick Posmantur, N.D.
Kevin Kronick
Miles Roberts, C.A.
Kathy Shields

and the wonderful Chinese herb shops of San Francisco, Vancouver, Seattle, Victoria and Chicago.

CHINESE CITIES WITH HERBAL MANUFACTORIES
represented in this volume

*   major manufacturers

1	HARBIN, Heilongjiang	
2	CHANGCHUN, Jilin	
3	FUSONG, Jilin	
4	LIAOYUAN, Jilin	
5	BEIJING	*
6	TIANJIN	*
7	HANDAN, Hebei	
8	JINAN, Shandong	
9	QINGDAO, Shandong	
10	LANZHOU, Gansu	*
11	XIAN, Shaanxi	
12	CHENGDU, Sichuan	
13	CHONGQING, Sichuan	
14	YICHANG, Hubei	
15	HANYANG, Hubei	
16	ZHENJIANG, Jiangsu	
17	CHANGZHOU, Jiangsu	
18	SUZHOU, Jiangsu	
19	SHANGHAI	
20	HANGZHOU, Zhejiang	
21	KUNMING, Yunnan	
22	GUIYANG, Guizhou	
23	CHANGSHA, Hunnan	
24	NANNING, Guangxi	
25	GUILIN, Guangxi	
26	YULIN, Guangxi	
27	WUZHOU, Guangxi	
28	GUANGZHOU, Guangdong	*
29	HONG KONG	
30	AMOY, Fujian	

TABLE OF CONTENTS

Group 1:
Pills For Problems Due To Exogenous Wind-Invasion

1 Antelope Horn And Fructus Forsythiae
    Febrifrugal Tablets
2 Bi Yan Pian
3 Chuan Qiong Cha Tiao Wan
4 Ganmaoling Tablets
5 Huang Lien Shang Ching Pien
6 Ling Yang Shang Feng Ling
7 Refined Sang Chu Gan Mao
8 Sang Chu Yin Pien
9 Tablet Bi-Tong
10 Yin Chiao Chieh Tu Pien (Superior Quality)
11 Yin Chiao Chieh Tu Pien - Tianjin
12 Yin Chiao Chieh Tu Pien - Beijing
13 Zhong Gan Ling

Group 2:
Patents For Cough, Phlegm And Labored Breathing

Group 2-A: Pills

14 Bronchitis Pills (Compound)
15 Bronchitis Tablet
16 Chi Kuan Yen Wan
17 Ching Fei Yi Huo Pien
18 Chuan Ke Ling
19 Clean Air Tea
20 Erh Chen Wan
21 Fritillaria Extract Sugar-Coated Tablets
22 Ma Hsing Chih Ke Pien
23 Ping Chuan Pill
24 Pulmonary Tonic Pills
25 Tung Hsuan Li Fei Pien
26 Zhi Sou Ding Chuan Wan

Group 2-B: Syrups

Group 3:
Pills To Remove Internal, Toxic And Damp Heat

Group 3-A:
Pills To Remove Internal And Toxic Heat

Group 3-B:
Pills To Remove Damp-Heat

55   Armadillo Counter Poison Pill
56   Chien Chin Chih Tai Wan
57   Ji Gu Cao Pill
58   Lidan Tablets
59   Lidian Paishi Tablets
60   Li Gan Pian - Liver Strengthening Tablets
61   Specific Drug Passwan
62   Yudai Wan

Group 3-C:
Fevers In Infants And Young Children

63   Bo Ying Pills
64   Hou Tsao San
65   Hui Chun Tan
66   Pao Ying Tan
67   Po Ying Tan (Pills) Babies Protector
68   Tao Chih Pien (For Babies)

Group 4:   Pills, Liniments And Plasters For Removing Wind-Damp

Group 4-A: Pills

69   Chen Pu Hu Chien Wan
70   Du Huo Jisheng Wan
71   Feng Shih Hsiao Tung Wan
72   Guan Jie Yan Wan
73   Hong She Pills
74   Kai Yeung Pill
75   San She Tan Chui Feng Wan
76   Specific Lumbaglin
77   Ta Huo Lo Tan (Chinese Old Man Tea)
78   Ta Huo Lo Tan (Beijing)
79   Tian Ma Hu Gu Wan
80   Trisnake Itch-Removing Pills
81   Tu Zhung Feng Shi Wan
82   Xiao Huo Luo Dan

Group 4-B:
Plasters For External Application

83 Anti-Rheumatic Plaster
84 Kou Pi Plasters
85 Musk Rheumatism-Expelling Plasters
86 Shang Shi Zhi Tong Gao:
    Plaster For Rheumatic Pains

Group 5:
Products For Blood Stagnation, Bleeding And Pain

Group 5-A: Pills

87 An Tai Wan (For Embryo)
88 Chin Koo Tieh Shang Wan
89 Corydalis Yanhusus Analgesic Tablets
90 Fargelin For Piles
91 Gastropathy Capsules
92 Hsiung Tan Tieh Ta Wan
93 Prostate Gland Pills
94 Tienchi Ginseng Tablet
95 Tienchi Powder Raw
96 To Jing Wan
97 Yunnan Paiyao
98 Wei Te Ling "204"
99 Zhi Wan

Group 5-B:
Pills For Heart Congestion, Angina And Stroke

100 Dan Shen Tablet Co.
101 Kuan Hsin Su Ho Wan
102 Guan Xin Su Ho Capsules
103 Maodungching Capsules
104 Ren Shen Zai Zao Wan
105 Su He Xiang Pills: Styrax Pills
106 Tsai Tsao Wan
107 Yan Shen Jai Jao Wan

Group 5-C:
Patents For External Application

Group 6:   Pills For Promoting Digestion And
Relieving Congestion At The Center

Group 7:
Pills And Extracts For Tonifying And Nurturing

Group 7-A:
Pills And Extracts To Tonify Qi

140 Central Qi Pills - Bu Zhong Yi Qi Wan
141 Deer Tail Extract
142 Extractum Astragali
143 Ginseng Royal Jelly Vials
144 Jian Pi Su
145 Peking Royal Jelly
146 Shen Qi Da Bu Wan

Group 7-B:
Pills And Extracts To Nourish Blood

147 Angelica Tea
148 Butiao Tablets
149 Eight Treasure Tea
150 Essence Of Chicken With Tang Kuei
151 Imperial He Shou Wu Jit
152 Kang Wei Ling
153 Pai Feng Wan - (White Phoenix Pills)
154 Rehmannia Glutinosa Compound Pills
155 Shou Wu Chih
156 Shou Wu Pian
157 Sugar Coated Placenta Tablets
158 Tabellae Tang Kuei
159 Tang Kwe Gin
160 Tienchi Powder Prepared
161 Wu Chi Pai Feng Wan:
     White Phoenix Pills (Condensed)
162 Wu Chi Pai Feng Wan - Tientsin Formula
163 Yung Sheng He Ah Chiao - (Famous Ass Glue)

Group 7-C:
Tonics For Deficiency Of Yang

164 Anti-Lumbago Tablets
165 Ba Wei Di Huang Wan
166 Bowsun Wan
167 Ching Chun Bao - Recovery Of Youth Tablet
168 Chin So Ku Ching: Golden Lock Tea
169 Duzhong Bu Tian Su
170 Gejie Bu Shen Wan
171 Golden Book Tea
172 Hailung Tonic Pills
173 Kang Gu Zeng Sheng Pian
174 Kwei Ling Chi
175 Nan Bao Capsules
176 Sea Horse Herb Tea
177 Tabellae Chuang Yao Tonic
178 Xiong Bao

Group 7-D:
Tonics For Deficiency Of Yin Or Fluids

179 Ba Xian Chang Shou Wan
180 Cataract Vision-Improving Pills
181 Da Bu Yin Wan
182 Dendrobrium Monilforme Night Sight Pills
183 Eight Flavor Tea
184 Kai Kit Pill
185 Lycium And Chrysanthemum Tea
186 Rehmannia Tea
187 Restorative Pills
188 Six Flavor Tea
189 Smooth Tea
190 Tso-Tzu Otic Pills
191 Yeuchung Pills

Group 7-E:
General And Combination Tonics

192 Alrodeer Pills
193 Angelicae Longana Tea
194 Essence Of Chicken With Ginseng
195 Gejie Ta Bu Wan
196 Ginseng Polygona Root Extract
197 Ginseng Tonic Capsules
198 Jen Shen Lu Jung Wan
199 Jen Shen Lu Jung Wan (Condensed)
200 Ren Shen Yang Ying Wan
201 Shih San Tai Pao Wan
202 Shen Kue Lu Jung Wan
203 Shen Yung Pai Feng Wan
204 Ten Flavor Tea
205 Tzepao Sanpien Extract
206 Wan Nian Chun Zi Pu Ziang
207 Yang Rong Wan (Ginseng Tonic Pills)

Group 8:
Pills To Calm Shen (Restlessness And Insomnia)

208 An Mien Pien
209 An Sheng Pu Shin Wan
210 Cerebral Tonic Pills
211 Cinnabar Sedative Pill
212 Ding Xin Wan
213 Emperor's Tea
214 Healthy Brain Pills
215 Pai Tzu Yang Hsin Wan
216 Shen Ching Shuai Jao Wan
217 Tabellae Suan Zao Ren Tang
218 Tze Zhu Pills

Group 9:   Pills To Control
Endogenous Liver Wind And Hypertension

Appendix 1:

East Earth Herb Company
Turtle Mountain / Dragon Eggs
Formulated By Bill Brevoort

Jade Pharmacy
Formulated By Ted Kaptchuk, OMD

242 Compassionate Sage - Heart Spirit
243 Dynamic Warrior - Kidney Yang
244 Prosperous Farmer - Spleen Qi
245 Quiet Contemplative - Kidney Yin
246 Relaxed Wanderer - Stagnant Liver Qi
247 Wise Judge - Lung Yin And Qi

Appendix 2:

Nature's Sunshine Constitutional Therapy
Formulated By Subhuti Dharmananda, Ph.D.

248 Tiao He - Bupleurum And Peony 12 Combination
249 Bu Xue - Dang Gui And Peony 16 Formula
250 An Shen -
Fushen And Dragon Bone 16 Combination
251 Yang Xin - Biota And Zizyphus 18 Formula
252 Xiao Dao -
Agastache And Shenqu 16 Combination
253 Wen Zhong - Ginseng And Licorice 18 Formula
254 Xuan Fei - Pinellia And Citrus 16 Combination
255 Fu Lei -
Astragalus And Anemarrhena 16 Formula
256 Qu Shi - Alisma And Hoelen 16 Formula
257 Jian Gu -
Eucommia And Achyranthes 18 Formula
258 Qing Re -
Forsythia And Schizonepeta 18 Formula
259 Bu Yin -
Rehmannia And Ophiopogon 16 Formula
260 Jie Yu -
Bupleurum And Cyperus 18 Combination
261 Sheng Mai -
Astragalus And Ganoderma 18 Formula

Appendix 3:

Health Concern's Chinese Traditional Formulas Formulated By Subhuti Dharmananda, Ph.D.

262   Astra Eight
263   Astra Garlic
264   Cir-Q
265   Ease Plus
266   Ease 2
267   Motility 1
268   Motility 2
269   Nasal Tabs
270   Rejuvenate 8
271   Resp
272   Stomach Tabs
273   Astra 18
274   Astra Diet Tea

Alphabetical Index Of Products

PREFACE

This book is an easy-access desk reference for the selection of Chinese patent formulas commonly available in North America, as well as domestically produced products made from imported Chinese herbs.

I have written it for the benefit of health practitioners trained in traditional Chinese medicine as well as for the many individuals who have used or who wish to use Chinese patent formulas found in the Chinatowns of North America, Australia, New Zealand and Europe.

Practitioners of traditional Chinese medicine having a firm foundation in Chinese herbs will find this book useful. With an understanding of differentiation of syndromes, appropriate selection from the 274 patent formulas described in the book can easily be made. Also, the formulas can serve as models in the prescribing of raw herbs for your patients.

For acupuncturists with limited knowledge in herbal therapy, this book reviews the various Chinese patents in language common to both acupuncture and traditional herbal medicine. This allows the acupuncturist to make an informed and appropriate selection of a patent formula that can serve as adjunctive therapy. Reinforcing acupuncture treatments with daily ingestion of an appropriate patent can greatly benefit the patient.

Individuals who have been accustomed to frequenting Chinatown pharmacies, as well as health practitioners in western medicine, naturopathy, chiropractic and therapeutic massage, can also benefit from this volume in the selection of various herbal patent formulas. If one is unfamiliar with the language peculiar to traditional Chinese medicine (TCM), refer to the short glossary of the terms used, found in the back of the book. Also, there are various English language volumes available which explain the language and mechanisms of TCM, including *The Essentials of Chinese Acupuncture*, Kaptchuk's *The Web That Has No Weaver*, as well as Teeguarden's *Chinese Toxic Herbs*. (See Recommended Reading).

This book came about for two reasons. Most importantly, people in the English speaking world should know about Chinese herbal patent formulas. They are of significant benefit in a variety of health complaints, without side effect (when used properly), and relatively inexpensive. Many of the prescriptions have been in use for hundreds of years, and have proven themselves in clinical application. The patent formulas discussed in this book are commonly used and prescribed in mainland China to the benefit of vast numbers of people. Their safety and efficacy are well accepted in that country.

Secondly, there is a paucity of written information regarding the application, or composition, of the formulas. Many products available in North America from the People's Republic of China contain informational inserts in English, but they seldom discuss the application in terms appropriate to traditional Chinese medicine. Indications may or may not be included, and often they are misleading; furthermore, the listings of the ingredients in English are often confusing or erroneous.

The purpose of this text is to provide clear indications for the uses of the commonly available patent fomulas. I have organized the products according to traditional therapeutic categories, describing their energetic functions as well as the common symptoms which they treat. I have tried to accurately list the ingredients with percentage dosages.

USING CHINESE PATENT FORMULAS

Chinese patent formulas are quite effective. Often, patents are used alone in acute problems at recommended package doses with remarkable effect, particularly colds, trauma, fever and pain. In chronic problems of deficiency (*qi*, blood, *yin*, *yang*, etc.), they are often the therapy of choice.

Patents may be given alone, or in combination. For example, dizziness due to deficiency of liver blood with accumulation of spleen damp or stomach phlegm can be treated by combining SHOU WU PIAN (156) to nourish liver blood with ER CHEN WAN (20) to resolve stomach phlegm.

Patents are usually taken at least thirty minutes before or after meals, with a glass of water or tea. Exceptions to this are noted with the individual patents. **When taste permits, they are best absorbed if chewed.**

With the exceptions of tonics, which can be taken for extended periods of time, patents are generally administered only as long as the energetic imbalance they are treating manifests symptoms, or signs of the pulse or tongue. Once the energetic imbalance changes, use of the patent formula must be reevaluated, and either changed or discontinued. This is especially true for conditions exhibiting heat, cold, damp, phlegm or stagnation, as well as for the exogenous invasions of colds and flus.

The patents are valuable as adjunctive therapy to acupuncture, chiropractic, and therapeutic massage. These treatments are often limited to once weekly; daily ingestion of an appropriate patent will allow healing to take place at an accelerated pace.

For practitioners having the use of raw Chinese herbs, reviewing the patents encourages consideration of new ideas in herbal prescribing. Patents also allow the traditional herbalist to administer substances not usually decocted in teas, including borneol, musk gland, gallstone, etc.

INCREASING DOSAGES

As primary therapy, doses recommended in the book (which are the dosages suggested by the manufacturers), are the recommended maintenance dosages. It is not uncommon to increase this dosage by 30 to 100%, especially in acute or early treatment, taking into consideration the parameters of the ingredient herbs, and a reasonable appraisal of the individual's condition. In acute stages, frequency of dosing is usually increased, often up to every two hours for the first day. Dosages are reduced for children.

A NOTE ON THE PRODUCTS SELECTED

The patent formulas selected are commonly available in North America. Products with the same name are often manufactured by different factories. I have listed the manufacturers names for the products chosen, and ingredients and dosages are for that manufacturers' product. Products of the same name, but from different factories, may have different ingredients or dosages. In fact, they may be completely different prescriptions. If you order by Chinese character name, you may recieve a significantly different product. The only way to control this is to specify the manufacturer.

For the most part, this book lists patents that have been made in mainland China, rather than Hong Kong or Taiwan. (Where Hong Kong products have been used, it will say so). This was done because China has a good reputation for quality assurance in their products, and because their products are labeled in both Chinese and English. Many Hong Kong products are very good, but their labeling only in Chinese makes their use difficult for English speaking people.

Chinese herbal products made in the United States are discussed in the three appendices. The products mentioned are known to be of high quality in the selection and manufacturing processes.

THE ORGANIZATIONAL FORMAT

Each patent medicine is listed according to the English name found on the product itself. These names may be romanizations of the Chinese pronunciation, or its English name. Below this is written the pinyin romanization of the Chinese name of the product. Below this is a translation of the Chinese name into English, and finally, below, is the manufacturer of the particular product that is being reviewed.

The patents are organized in traditional therapeutic categories, within which they are listed in alphabetical order. For those wishing to know the Chinese characters for the products, there is an alphabetical listing in the back of the book based either on its English-name spelling, or on its pinyin-romanization spelling.

ORGANIZING BY CATEGORIES

The patents have been organized according to the traditional categories of pathology and therapeutics specific to Chinese herbal medicine. I have not given any discussion to these categories (other than some general contraindications), and if you are unfamiliar with them, good expositions have been written in Bensky and Gamble's *Chinese Materia Medica*, as well as Hsu's *Traditional Therapeutic Classifications of Chinese Herbs* (Bulletin of OHAI); see RECOMMENDED READING. In the absence of these, surveying the indications of a category's selections should give a good idea of its scope.

Patent formulas, as they have developed in China, seem to be strong in certain categories, and low or missing in others. The largest categories include general tonics, fevers and heat, cough and phlegm, and blood stagnation (including trauma).

A NOTE ON THE NAMING OF INGREDIENTS

We use a naming system for the herbs that has been developed at the Institute for Traditional Medicine. The Chinese herbs are in English, but based, with a few exceptions, on the Latin (pharmaceutical) names of the herbs. For example, Cortex Cinnamomi becomes CINNAMON BARK, Radix Astragali becomes ASTRAGALUS ROOT, and Pericarpium Citri Reticulata becomes CITRUS PEEL. This is done for the convenience of English-speaking people, without having to go through Latin as an intermediate language. At the same time, practitioners and students familiar with the pharmaceutical names will easily identify the herbs.

We have retained certain common names different than the pharmaceutical names for herbs in certain instances, including LICORICE ROOT (Radix Glycyrrhizae), GINGER RHIZOME (Rhizoma Zingiberis), and OX GALLSTONE (Calculus Bovis). Conversely, other common English names have been abandoned in favor of their pharmaceutical names, including MORUS (Mulberry) and TARAXACUM (Dandelion).

Where two or more plants have the same species, we refer to the more commonly used or named plant by species name and part used (Atractylodes Rhizome, Angelica Root). For other species members, we use the species name, plus its Chinese pinyin name, without the plant part (Atractylodes Cang Zhu, Angelica Dang Gui, Angelica Du Huo).

In the CROSS-REFERENCE INDEX OF HERBAL NAMES at the back, we list the English name (as is used in this book) with the pharmaceutical name, the Pinyin romanization of the Chinese names, the Wade-Giles romanization, and Dr. Hsu's English naming system. We did not include the Chinese characters for the individual herbs; these are readily available in Bensky and Gamble, American College's *Pharmacopedia*, Yeung, or Hsu's *Treatment by Chinese Herbs*. (see Recommended Reading).

CONTRAINDICATIONS

There are certain contraindications for the herbal products, and these are noted with each product where applicable.

Pregnancy is the most common reason for a product being contraindicated. These formulae usually break up stagnation and can threaten the fetus. Women who are pregnant should take Chinese herbal products under the careful supervision of an experienced and knowledgeable TCM practitioner.

Other contraindications should be considered for individual herbs within a formula. Familiarity with the Chinese materia medica is important here. Rhubarb Rhizome, for example, may cause diarrhea in weaker patients, and products containing it should be discontinued if diarrhea develops. Similarly, Ephedra Leaf, often found in formulae for wind-invasion, may cause nervousness or sleeplessness in weaker individuals, and should be used appropriately.

Contraindications also include the principle that most products should be given only for the condition for which it is indicated and discontinued once that condition has stopped or changed. Broad overview of contraindications for specific categories are noted at the beginning of each category, where applicable. These statements, however, are no substitute for a more thorough background in traditional Chinese pathology and therapeutics, nor for the advice of a practitioner.

MANUFACTURING

Chinese herbal farmers are famous for the care and attention given to the growing, harvesting and processing individual herbs and medicinal substances. Often, whole villages (or communes) of thousands of people will work together to cultivate medicinal plants. This is the basis of their income, and may have been so for hundreds of years. Modern intrusions are usually avoided so as not to endanger time-proven ways, and the quality of the plants is very good.

Similiarly, herb combining in the factories also exhibit care and attention. The cost of labor being so much cheaper than in North America, one can say that the cost of a product produced with the same effort in the United States might be many times the amount.

PACKAGING

Most herbal products come in glass bottles of 50 to 300 pills. These bottles usually are corked (beneath plastic twist caps), and covered in wax. A good way to remove the cork is to use a small sharp knife and etch a line around the rim of the cork; then poke with the knife to remove it. Also, corkscrews work well.

Certain *qi* tonics come in small glass bottles, equipped with glass cutters and straws. These are gradually being replaced with plastic or metal caps.

Other herbs come as very large soft balls, contained within wax covered plastic "eggs". After being removed from the "egg", these can be chewed and swallowed, cut into smaller pieces and swallowed, or dissolved in hot water.

OBTAINING CHINESE PATENT FORMULAS

If you are purchasing the formulas from domestic English-speaking distributors, using the English-language names will probably be sufficient. If you are purchasing from Chinese distributors or shops, you will probably have to order using the Chinese names or characters. The Chinese characters are listed in an appendix in alphabetical order according to their Pinyin name. Distributors are listed in the back.

A FINAL WORD

The products listed in this book are basically safe and without side-effects. (Contraindications are indicated with specific products). If you are new to the world of Chinese patent formulas, I encourage you to discuss their use with qualified practitioners. There are many wonderful products that can benefit your general health, or are important as emergency first-aid remedies. The tonics, particularly, may be used for extended periods to great beneficial effect. If you are an experienced practitioner of traditional Chinese medicine, I hope you will find this collection useful in your practice.

It is my deep belief that Chinese herbal therapy is an important and valuable aid to the health and well-being of all people. Using the patent formulas is an excellent way to benefit your health, and become acquainted with the fascinating world of traditional Chinese medicine.

CHINESE PATENT FORMULAS

a special chapter by Subhuti Dharmananda, Ph.D.

Chinese herbal medicine has become an acceptable form of therapy in the United States during the last six years, trailing by nearly a decade the adoption of acupuncture therapy. The transition from nearly complete ignorance about herbs to an unprecedented demand comes as a result of English language publications and courses. Such courses have been been offered for several years by Oriental Healing Arts Institute, American College of Traditional Chinese Medicine, San Francisco College of Acupuncture and Oriental Medicine, and the Institute for Traditional Medicine. These California organizations were spurred on by the large Chinatown populations of San Francisco and Los Angeles, where Chinese herb products first entered the country, and by their proximity to China itself.

Students and beginning pracitioners of Chinese herbology usually prefer to work with the crude herb materials, which are to be made into decoctions. These materials lend well towards enhancing the practitioners' ability to mix together any desired combination of herbs. Many people are immediately attracted to the natural beauty and quality of Chinese crude herbs. However, as the use of Chinese herbs as a therapeutic technique has gained broader acceptance in the United States, more and more patients are arriving at clinics from that portion of our population that refuses to deal with the odd smelling and foul tasting teas. Frequently, they demand access to pills, capsules or powders that are easy to take.

There has been some resistance to this type of preprocessed formula by practitioners trained in the West. This response has often stemmed from the lack of adequate knowledge of how the products have been produced, what range of formulas is available, and how to use them to best advantage. During six visits to China during the past decade, I have gathered information about the production methods and the practical application of prepared herbal products. I have actively promoted the use of concentrated extracts produced in Taiwan by Sun Ten

Pharmaceuticals and am impressed by their efficacy, but equally important, I had an opportunity to see the manufacturing process and the quality control behind the scenes. I am convinced that the product is as close to a traditional tea as one can conveniently get without making the tea personally. However, there are numerous valuable formulas which are not manufactured in Taiwan, but which are available as patent formulas from mainland China.

Books that serve as guides to the use of concentrated extracts from Taiwan have been available in English for ten years. Dr. Hong-yen Hsu has written books such as *How to Treat Yourself with Chinese Herbs*, *Commonly Used Chinese Herb Formulas with Illustrations*, and *The Way to Good Health with Chinese Herbs*. Until this volume by Jake Fratkin, no one has effectively catalogued the patent formulas from China. The absence of this kind of book has not had its roots in any lack of demand - Chinese herb practitioners and students have been begging for such a work for years. But there has been no one around with sufficient expertise coupled with the time and energy to commit to the project. Jake has taken the necessary time and effort to produce the required work, which is of excellent quality.

During my visits to China, I have toured several factories where these patent formulas are made, and visited the research institutes where many of the formulas are designed and tested. I can readily attest to the high quality of manufacturing practices employed at most of these factories, and the fact that clinical and laboratory research almost always supports the claims made for the products. I have published some of my observations in this regard in the *Journal of the Institute for Traditional Medicine*, Volume 2, #4.

ANIMAL PRODUCTS IN THE PATENT FORMULAS. Animal products are generally very potent in their effects because of the constituents include substances quite similiar to those found in our own bodies. Hence, for example, a hormonal compound in an animal drug may have one-third the potency of the related human hormone, while a plant component, such as steroidal glycoside, may have a potency of 1/100th that of the corresponding human hormone. Patent formulas frequently incorporate animal compounds in the treatment of heat and toxin, spasm and paralysis, blood stasis, and draft wet pain. Some examples are:

> Rhinoceros Horn (for blood heat)
> Bear Gallbladder (for blood heat)
> Ox Gallstone (for heat and spasm)
> Antelope Horn (for heat and spasm)
> Scorpion (for toxin and spasm)
> Earthworm (for spasms)
> Tiger Bone (for pain and spasm)
> Agkistrodon Pit Viper (for pain)
> Anteater Scales (for blood stasis)
> Cicada Skin (for wind-heat)

A few of the animal drugs are used primarily as *yang* tonics, such as:

> Gecko Lizard
> Deer Antler
> Cordyceps (worm plus fungus)
> Penis, Kidneys and Testes of various animals
> Human Placenta

Some persons may object to the use of animal drugs on the basis of a vegetarian philosophy. In such cases, a substitute formula can be picked that is lacking in animal drugs. Oyster Shell, Margarita Pearl, and Dragon Bone (the latter being a fossil and not truly an animal part) are usually not objectionable.

Products labeled to contain Rhinoceros Horn may not actually have Rhinoceros Horn. One can calculate from the product price and the limited supply of Rhinoceros Horn that it is not possible for most of the products to contain this rare and expensive item. Most likely, Water-Buffalo Horn is being used instead. Nonetheless, some of the more expensive items do contain Rhinoceros Horn.

Similiarly, products which list Tiger Bone on the label probably lack that item. The tigers are found in northern China and there are relatively few left. Bones of oxen, or domestic or wild cats other than tiger may be used. Both Rhinoceros Horn and Tiger Bone are restricted items in North America, and it is to our advantage as a community of concerned practitioners to refuse to utilize products which actually contain these substances.

WESTERN DRUGS IN CHINESE HERB PRODUCTS. In general, the Chinese do not mix western drugs with Chinese herbs in their patent formulas. They do combine western medical therapies with herbal therapies in their clinics, so the concept is not totally objectionable to them. The Tianjin factory recently produced a version of the very popular YINCHIAO CHIEH TU PIEN (#10) with the addition of three western drugs. Practitioners are cautioned to read the label carefully, since the difference between an herbal formula and an herb/drug mixture may not be evidenced in the name of the product, but only on the ingredient label. (Of the products listed in this book, only YINCHIAO (#10) contains western drugs. - Ed.)

There was a big stir a few years ago about an herb product for arthritis that contained cortisone or cortisone-like western drugs without it being labeled in English. It was not manufactured in mainland China. It is doubtful that the mainland Chinese herb factories incorporate western drugs without mentioning them in the label.

ARTIFICIAL COLORS IN CHINESE HERB PRODUCTS. In most cases, when an herb product is made entirely of concentrated extracts, it is sugar coated. The sugar coating preserves the ingredients and also prevents the pills from melting together. Many of the sugar coatings that the Chinese use are brightly colored, and they are obviously artificial colors.

DOSAGE. The dosage on the package is generally correct for obtaining the desired effect. For more rapid effects, one usually uses a dosage that is 50-100% higher. Thus, when using a therapy for long term and slow changes, follow the package directions, those that are stated in this book. When using the patent formula as a principle therapy, especially in acute conditions, use up to twice the dosage. In some cases, the package label or insert will mention this.

PRICE. Patent medicines vary widely in price based on:

> **Source**: each supplier may have a different mark-up.
> **Availability**: when scarce, the product price increases.
> **Ingredients**: products with Musk Gland, for example, are usually expensive.

Most bottles of patent formulas contain a 5 to 10 day supply. The price per bottle or box to the retail consumer or patient varies from $3.50 - $20. On the average, the monthly cost of using patent formulas is $16 - $35.

SECRET FORMULAS. While some formulations are kept entirely secret, such as YUNNAN PAI YAO (#97), many of the formulas do contain ingredients marked as "others", and, to an undetermined extent, many contain unmarked ingredients. It is common practice in Chinese medicine to mix a prescription with, as one ingredient, another formula. This other formula, which may comprise 10-30% of the whole, is what makes the product different than one of similar effect from another factory. The exact ingredients are kept secret to prevent duplication. This is the Chinese method of patenting a formula. Ingredients listed in this book reflect ingredients announced by the manufacturer.

REGULATION AND LEGAL STATUS. The labeling of patent formulas from China more often than not fails to comply with FDA (Food and Drug Administration) standards. Those that contain on their package or in their inserts indications for use (insomnia, headache, etc.) are technically unlicensed new drugs.

If the FDA feels the products will be used for medicinal effect, they can send back the shipments. Consequently, many of the patent formulas are smuggled into the United States and then sold to Chinatown shops and distributors. The price of the formulas is higher than it otherwise might be. In Canada for example, the patents are legally imported, and the prices there are considerably less than in the United States.

The FDA does not necessarily object to any of the ingredients. In fact, they have little information about the herbs. Most people in the FDA realize that Chinese herbs have been used in the U.S. for many years with virtually no consumer complaints.

Crude herbs are legally imported because, as crude materials, they are classified as foods. Formulas manufactured in the U.S. with imported Chinese herbs and labeled in compliance with FDA regulations are generally not harassed. I believe that we will have access to most Chinese patents for many years, and that as their popularity increases, there will be greater efforts by the Chinese manufacturers to work towards a legal status by relabeling, reformulating or meeting other specific requirements.

However, the value of this book should not be judged by whether or not the products it lists are available for use, or even whether or not the ingredients change slightly from one brand to the next. It is important in that it presents herbal combinations valued for their efficacy in China. Should some products vanish from the market, the knowledge of what combinations work, or have been used, will persist and continue to make its effects felt.

AMERICAN-MANUFACTURED CHINESE FOR-MULAS. There is a fast growing realization that Chinese herb formulas made in America, though more expensive than those produced in China, can solve certain problems associated with the patent formulas. Generally, American manufacturers leave out most of the animal agents, avoiding problems with endangered species and with objections from some consumers. The ingredients are fully listed (if not, the manufacturer faces stiff penalties). The supply is not interrupted as easily by the FDA, which more often exercises its power in importation rather than domestic distribution. Finally, the products can be formulated with the American consumer in mind, dealing with the type of health problems more common in our society.

Recognizing this trend, there are three appendices of American made products. The Turtle Mountain products are designed and manufactured by herbalist Bill Breevort. The Jade Pharmacy products are designed by Ted Kaptchuk. I designed the formulas of Nature's Sunshine Products and have also selected or formulated products distributed by Health Concerns.

My experience has been that the crude herbs made into teas, the concentrated extracts from Taiwan, the patent formulas from mainland China and Hong Kong, and the American made Chinese herb combinations are extremely valuable. We should be careful to avoid prematurely rejecting any herbal combination based on its form. When the formula is properly designed and the product is manufactured with care, it will satisfy the needs of practitioners and consumers alike.

Subhuti Dharmananda, Ph.D.   July, 1986

GROUP 1

PILLS FOR PROBLEMS DUE TO EXOGENOUS WIND-INVASION

NOTE: Wind invasions (colds, flus, sinusitis and acute headaches) should be differentiated as heat or cold, and treated appropriately. Patent formulas are very effective for wind invasions if administered immediately and in greater frequency then implied by the label. Other herbal patents that one may be taking should be discontinued during administration of pills for wind invasion.

1 ANTELOPE HORN AND FRUCTUS FORSYTHIAE FEBRIFRUGAL TABLETS
Ling Qiao Jie Du Pian
"Antelope Horn, Forsythia Fruit Relieve Toxin Tablet"
Tsinan People's Medicine Works; Jinan, Shandong

Dispels wind, removes heat, pacifies cough, and stops pain. Use for early stage of exogenous wind-heat or wind-cold attack (best for wind-heat attack). Symptoms include stiff shoulders, headache, sore throat, swollen glands, fever or chills, weak lungs, or aching feeling. Use during first two days of attack, while the invasion is still in the surface. This formula is identical to YINCHIAO CHIEH TU PIEN (10).

Bottles of 150 tablets. Take 4-6 tablets every four hours.

Forsythia Fruit	17.0 %	Licorice Root	8.6
Lonicera Flower	17.0	Schizonepeta Herb	8.0
Mentha Herb	11.0	Lophatherum Leaf	8.0
Platycodon Root	11.0	Soja Seed	8.0
Arctium Fruit	11.0	Antelope Horn	0.4

2   BI YAN PIAN

Bi Yan Pian
"Nose Inflammation Pills"
Chung Lien Drug Works; Wuchang, Hubei

Dispels wind-cold or wind-heat, reduces heat. Use for wind-heat or wind-cold invasion to the upper burner and face. Symptoms include sneezing, itchy eyes, facial congestion, and sinus pain. Useful in acute and chronic rhinitis, sinusitis and hayfever, nasal allergies, as well as general mucus congestion in the face. [If chronic, combine or follow with HSIAO YAO WAN (#123) to decongest and invigorate the liver].

Bottle of 100 tablets. Take 4-6 tablets, 3-5 x day.

Magnolia Flower	25.0 %	Forsythia Fruit	7.0
Xanthium Fruit	20.0	Angelica Root	6.0
Phellodendron Bark	7.0	Anemarrhena Rhizome	4.0
Licorice Root	6.0	Chrysanthemum Flower	4.0
Platycodon Root	4.0	Siler Root	4.0
Schizandra Fruit	4.0	Schizonepeta Herb	4.0

3 CHUAN QIONG CHA TIAO WAN

Chuan Qiong Cha Tiao Wan
"Ligusticum [with] Green Tea Mix Pill"
Shanghai Chinese Medicine Works; Shanghai

Classical formula to disperse wind-cold and stop pain. Primarily used for sudden headache due to exogenous wind-cold invasion; also nasal congestion, sinusitis and rhinitis, and wind-vertigo. Take with strong green tea to enhance the effect.

Bottles of 200 pills. Take 8 pills, 3-5 x day.

Mentha Herb	32.7 %	Notopterygium Rhizome	8.2
Ligusticum Rhizome	16.3	Licorice Root	8.2
Schizonepeta Herb	16.3	Siler Root	6.1
Angelica Root	8.2	Asarum Plant	4.0

4 GANMAOLING TABLETS
Gan Mao Ling Pian
"Common Cold Effective Remedy"
United Pharmaceutical Manufactory; Guangzhou, Guangdong

Dispel wind, sedate heat, detoxify pathogens (viruses). Excellent cold and flu remedy with symptoms of chills, high fever, swollen lymph glands, sore throat, stiffness of upper back and neck. Effective both in wind-cold and wind-heat invasions.

Bottle of 36 tablets. Take 3-6 tablets, 3 x day. For prevention of colds: 2 tablets, 2-3 x day for 3 days.

Ilex Root	34.3 %	Vitex Fruit	13.0
Evodia Fruit	21.7	Lonicera Flower	4.8
Isatis Root	3.0	Menthol Crystal	0.01
Chrysanthemum Flower	13.0		

Also available from Great Wall Brand, Tianjin with same name but different packaging: Tubes of 8 tablets, 12 tubes to the box.

Also available as SU XIAO GANMAOLING, from China Inner Mongolian Autonomous Region Drug Manufactory.

5 HUANG LIEN SHANG CHING PIEN
Huang Lian Shang Qing Pian
"Coptis Upper Clearing Tablets"
Tientsin Drug Manufactory; Tianjin

Dispels wind-heat, neutralizes toxic heat, and purges internal heat in the stomach and lungs. Primarily used for serious exogenous invasion to upper burner causing high fever, headache, sore throat, and ear infection. Beneficial for wind-heat in the skin, causing redness and itching, including hives. Can be used for endogenous heat in the stomach channel causing swollen gums, toothache, nosebleed, insomnia, and red eye. Useful for heat and damp-heat in lower burner causing constipation, diarrhea or concentrated scanty urine.

Tubes of 8 tablets, 12 tubes to a box, or in bottles of 20 tablets. Take 4 tablets, once per day.

CAUTION: Discontinue when heat symptoms subside or change. Lower dosage or discontinue if frequent loose stools develop. Prohibited during pregnancy.

Rhubarb Rhizome	25.%	Platycodon Root	6
Vitex Fruit	16	Scutellaria Root	6
Chrysanthemum Flower	12	Siler Root	3
Coptis Rhizome	8	Gypsum Mineral	3
Schizonepeta Herb	6	Ligusticum Rhizome	3
Angelica Root	6	Licorice Root	3

6 LING YANG SHANG FENG LING

Ling Yang Shang Feng Ling
"Antelope Horn Injured [by] Wind Efficacious-Remedy"
Tianjin Drug Manufactory; Tianjin

Dispels wind-heat, resolves toxic inflammation. Use for sudden and acute onset of wind invasion (flu and colds), with symptoms of sore throat, thirst, dry cough, fever with chills, aching shoulders, and headache. Use in first two or three days of attack, while the invasion is still in the surface. Excellent when main symptom is pronounced thirst with sore throat. Similiar in composition and application to # 1 and 10.

Take 4 tablets, 2 x day. Increase dosage in severe invasions.

Forsythia Fruit	22.5 %	Licorice Root	9.4
Lonicera Flower	22.5	Pueraria Root	3.7
Arctium Fruit	15.0	Trichosanthes Root	3.7
Schizonepetra Herb	11.3	Antelope Horn	.5
Lophatherum Leaf	11.3	Mentha Herb	.1

7 REFINED SANG CHU GAN MAO

Sang Ju Gan Mao Pian
"Morus, Chrysanthemum Common Cold Tablets"
Kwangchow Pharmaceutical Industry; Guangzhou, Guangdong

Based on the classical SANG JU YIN prescription, this formula dispels wind-heat invasion where slight cough or headache is prominent. Symptoms include fever, slight thirst, sore throat, and headache or aching joints. Can also be used in measles and influenza. Excellent remedy when the symptoms predominently affect lungs and face: coughing, sneezing, runny nose, congestion, watery eyes.

Bottles of 24 tablets. Take 4 tablets, 3-4 x day.

Morus Leaf	21.2 %	Forsythia Fruit	12.8
Armeniaca Seed	16.8	Chrysanthemum Flower	8.2
Platycodon Root	16.8	Licorice Root	6.8
Phragmites Rhizome	16.8	Mentha Herb Oil	6

8 SANG CHU YIN PIEN
Sang Ju Yin Pian
"Morus, Chrysanthemum Medicine Pill"
Tianjin Drug Manufactory; Tianjin

The same formula as SANG CHU GAN MAO (#7), but with different proportion of ingredients and different manufacturer. Use during the first two days of an exogenous wind-heat attack with slight dry cough, congestion in head, dry or sore throat, sneezing, runny nose, and watery eyes.

One dozen bottles of 8 tablets. Take 4 tablets, 2-4 x day.

Morus Leaf	19.8 %	Forsythia Fruit	11.9
Platycodon Root	15.9	Chrysanthemum Flower	7.9
Armeniaca Seed	15.9	Mentha Herb	6.3
Phragmites Rhizome	15.9	Licorice Root	6.3

9 TABLET BI-TONG
Bi Tong Pian
"Nose Open Tablet"
China National Chemicals Import & Export Corp; Guangdong

Dispels wind-heat, resolves phlegm, cools liver heat, and stops pain. Use in chronic rhinitis, acute and chronic sinusitis, hayfever and nasal allergies, with accompaning symptoms of sneezing, watery eyes, and facial congestion.

Bottles of 100 tablets. Take 4 pills, 3 x day.

Main ingredients:

Centipede	Pogostemon Leaf
Lonicera Flower	Menthol Crystal
Paeonia Root	Schizonetpeta Herb
Chrysanthemum Flower	Pig Bile

10 YINCHIAO CHIEH TU PIEN
(SUPERIOR QUALITY - SUGAR COATED)
Yin Qiao Jie Du Pian
"Lonicera, Forsythia Dispel Heat Tablets"
Tianjin Drug Manufactory; Tianjin

Expels toxic heat and wind-heat from exterior. Use for the first day or two of a wind-heat attack, exhibiting toxic heat symptoms (flu): swollen lymph nodes, sore throat, aching body, fever with chills, headache, sore shoulders, stiff neck. Promotes sweating. Excellent when taken immediately. Also useful for skin itching due to wind-heat, and allergenic skin reactions (hives).

Bottles of 20, 60 or 120 sugar-coated pills. Take 5-6 pills every 2-3 hours (the first 9 hours), then every 4-5 hours as needed. Discontinue by third day of wind attack.

Lonicera Flower	17.8 %	Soja Seed	8.9
Forsythia Fruit	17.8	Licorice Root	8.9
Arctium Fruit	10.7	Lophatherum Leaf	7.1
Platycodon Root	10.7	Schizonepeta Herb	7.1
Mentha Herb	10.7	Antelope Horn	.5

Note: Newer imports of this product have added three western chemicals. They are: Paracetamolum, Caffeine, Chlorpheniraminum. This version should be avoided.

11 YINCHIAO CHIEH TU PIEN
YIN CHIAO TABLETS - TIANJIN
Yin Qiao Jie Du Pian
"Lonicera, Forsythia Dispel Heat Tablets"
Tientsin Drug Manufactory; Tianjin

The same formula as above with similiar ingredients, but without Antelope Horn, western chemicals or the sugar coating. Use for the same indications as #10. Uncoated they are a bit dryer to swallow.

Boxes of 12 bottles, 8 pills to the bottle. Also bottles of 100 pills. Take 5-6 pills every 2-3 hours (the first 9 hours), then every 4-5 hours as needed. Discontinue by third day of wind attack.

Lonicera Flower	17.8%	Soja Seed	8.9
Forsythia Fruit	17.8	Licorice Root	8.9
Arctium Fruit	10.7	Lophatherum Leaf	7.1
Platycodon Root	10.7	Schizonepeta Herb	7.1
Mentha Herb	10.7		

12 YIN CHIAO CHIEH TU PIEN - BEIJING
FRUCTUS FORSYTHIA ANTIDOTAL TABLETS
Yin Qiao Jie Du Pian
"Lonicera, Forsythia Dispel Heat Tablets"
Peking Tung Jen Tang; Beijing

Dispels wind-heat, resolves toxic invasion. The same name as the above two products (#10, #11), but with a simpler formula. Use for common cold or flu with fever, sore throat, muscle aching, and dry cough.

Boxes of 12 vials, with 8 tablets. Take 2-4 tablets, 3 x day.

Lonicera Flower	20.%	Schizonepeta Herb	10
Forsythia Fruit	20	Platycodon Root	10
Mentha Herb	10	Starch and binders	30

13 ZHONG GAN LING

Zhong Gan Ling
"Valuable Cold Efficacious-Remedy"
Meizhou City Pharmaceutical Manufactory; Guangdong

Dispels wind-heat, reduces toxic heat, promotes sweating. Use for acute wind invasion causing severe cold or flu. Symptoms include sudden onset of high fever with sore throat, swollen lymph nodes, aching limbs, headache, and cough. Similiar to GANMAOLING TABLETS (#4).

Bottles of 48 tablets. Take 4-6 tablets, 3-4 x day.

Ilex Root	27.%	Artemesia Qing-hao	7
Pueraria Root	27	Gypsum Mineral	4
Verbena Leaf	18	Notopterygium Rhizome	3
Isatis Root	14		

ALSO APPLICABLE for Wind Invasions:

25   TUNG HSUAN LI FEI PIEN: cough due to wind invasion
79   TIAN MA HU GU WAN: wind headache
125   HUO HSIANG CHENG CHI PIEN:
        wind to stomach (stomach flu)
130   PILL CURING: wind to stomach (stomach flu)
258   QING RE: wind-heat
265   EASE 1: wind invasion in the Shaoyang stage
269   NASAL TABS: sinusitis

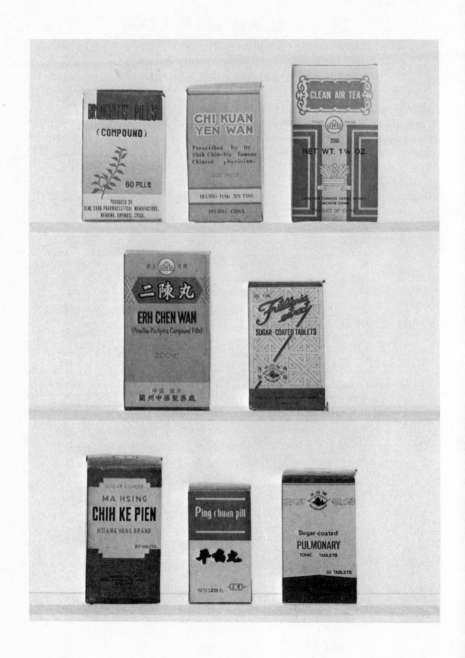

GROUP 2

PATENTS FOR COUGH, PHLEGM, AND LABORED BREATHING

GROUP 2-A: PILLS

14   BRONCHITIS PILLS (COMPOUND)
Fu Fang Qi Guan Yan Wan
"Medicinal Compound Bronchitis Pills"
Qing Shan Pharmaceutical Manufactory;
Nanning, Guangxi

Resolves cough, phlegm and labored breathing due to deficiency of lung *qi* with retention of phlegm. Useful in acute and chronic bronchitis, chronic asthma, and cough and phlegm brought on by exogenous invasion.

Bottles of 60 capsules. Take 2-3 capsules, 3 x day.

Polygonum Hu Zhang	67.%
Mahonia Root	16.
Eriobotrya Leaf	17.

15 BRONCHITIS TABLET
Zhi Qi Guan Yan Pian
"Resolve Bronchitis Tablet"
National Changsha Pharmaceutical Works; Changsha, Hunnan

Resolves phlegm-heat, stops cough, facilitates breathing. Use for acute bronchitis with profuse or sticky yellow phlegm, and for cough due to heat or phlegm.

Take 5 tablets, 3 x day.

Ardisia Plant	41.7%	Earthworm	12.5
Scutellaria Root	20.8	Licorice Root	12.5
Ephedra Leaf	12.5		

16 CHI KUAN YEN WAN
"Bronchitis, Cough, Phlegm, Labored Breathing Pills"
Beijing Tung Jen Tang; Beijing

Moistens dryness, resolves phlegm-heat and phlegm-damp, tonifies lung *qi*, Use to treat dry cough with sticky phlegm due to heat in the lung and trachea, with labored breathing. Also appropriate for chronic phlegm-damp in the lungs, including bronchitis and asthma.

Bottles of 200 pills. Take 20 pills, 2 x day.

Eriobotrya Leaf	28.%	Peucedanum Root	4
Codonopsis Root	16	Polygala Root	4
Jujube Fruit	12	Aristolochia Fruit	2
Morus Leaf	8	Citrus Gan Pi	2
Ginger Rhizome	8	Schizandra Fruit	2
Fritillaria Bulb	8	Tussilago Flower	2
Armeniaca Seed	6		

17 CHING FEI YI HUO PIEN

Qing Fei Yi Huo Pian
"Clear Lungs Restrain Fire Tablet"
Tientsin Drug Manufactory; Tianjin

Removes heat from lungs and liver, clears phlegm-heat and toxic heat, moistens lungs and throat. Use for lung heat with phlegm aggrevated by liver fire, with symptoms of yellow phlegm (profuse or sticky), dry or raspy cough, sore throat, fever, concentrated urine and constipation. Also useful for mouth sores, bleeding gums due to heat, and toothache.

Tubes of 8 tablets, 12 tubes to a box. Take 4 tablets, 2-3 x day.

CAUTION: Discontinue after heat symptoms subside. Reduce dosage or discontinue if diarrhea develops. Prohibited during pregnancy.

Scutellaria Root	21.%	Platycodon Root	12
Rhubarb Rhizome	18	Sophora Root	9
Gardenia Fruit	12	Anemarrhena Rhizome	9
Trichosanthes Root	12	Peucedanum Root	7

18 CHUAN KE LING

Chuan Ke Ling
"Asthma Cough Efficacious-Remedy"
Fu Sung Pharmaceutical Works; Fusong, Jilin

Tonifies lung *qi*, resolves phlegm, stops cough. Use for labored breathing with cough, with or without productive phlegm. Useful for chronic asthma, bronchitis, or emphysema.

Bottles of 100 tablets. Take 3-4 tablets, 2-3 x day.

Platycodon Root	35.%	Armeniaca Seed	25
Licorice Root	30	Pig Bile	10

19 CLEAN AIR TEA
Qing Qi Hua Tan Wan
"Clear Qi, Expel Phlegm Pills"
Lanzhou Fo Ci Pharmaceutical Factory; Lanzhou, Gansu

A classical prescription for resolving phlegm-heat in lungs, throat and sinuses. Useful in the treatment of bronchial congestion, sinus congestion and asthma when there is expectorated phlegm or nasal discharge. Useful in sticky phlegm, including chronic asthma or emphysema. Not appropriate for early stage of wind-invasion.

Bottles of 200 pills. Take 6 pills, 3 x day.

Pinellia Rhizome	16.7%	Citrus Ganpi	11.1
Arisaema Rhizome	16.7	Citrus Xiangyuan	11.1
Trichosanthes Seed	11.1	Armeniaca Seed	11.1
Scutellaria Root	11.1	Poria Fungus	11.1

Also available as PINELLIA EXPECTORANT PILLS from the same manufacturer.

20 ERH CHEN WAN
Er Chen Wan
"Two Chen Pill"
Lanchow Chinese Medicine Works; Lanzhou, Gansu

Classical formula to dissolve phlegm, resolve spleen-damp, regulate *qi* and harmonize the center. Use in cases of excessive phlegm congestion in stomach, lung or face, as well as symptoms brought about by food retention in the stomach. Symptoms include nausea and abdominal fullness, dizziness and vertigo, alcoholic hangover, phlegm-damp in the lungs. [Can be combined with TIANMA AND SHOU WU (223) for dizziness due to phlegm and liver fire.]

Bottles of 200 pills. Take 8 pills, 3 x day.

Pinellia Rhizome	44.%	Licorice Root	22
Poria Fungus	22	Citrus Peel	11

21 FRITILLARIA EXTRACT SUGAR-COATED TABLETS
Chuan Bei Jing Tang Yi Pian
"Fritillaria Essence Sugar-Coated Tablets"
Handan Pharmaceutical Works; Hebei

Resolves cough due to phlegm-heat or phlegm-damp, calms lungs, pacifies breathing. Can be used in acute or chronic cough where phlegm (profuse or sticky) is a component. Useful in bronchial asthma aggrevated by climatic changes.

Bottles of 60 tablets. Take 3-6 tablets, 3 x day.

Fritillaria Bulb	21. %	Platycodon Root	15
Polygala Root	20.	Citrus Peel	15
Schizandra Fructus	17.	Licorice Root	12

22 MA HSING CHIH KE PIEN
Ma Xing Zhi Ke Pian
"Ephedra, Armeniaca Stop Cough Tablet"
Siping Pharmaceutical Works; Jilin

Sedates lung heat, removes wind to clear the surface, resolves cough and phlegm. Use for dry cough or labored breathing due to heat or wind-heat in the lungs. Symptoms may also include fever, swollen lymph glands, and sore throat.

Bottles of 80 tablets. Take 4 tablets, 2-3 x day.

Platycodon Root	22.%	Licorice Root	12
Armeniaca Seed	15	Honey	11
Citrus Peel	12	Talcum Mineral	11
Gypsum Mineral	12	Ephedra Leaf	5

23 PING CHUAN PILL
Ping Chuan Wan
"Calm Asthma Pill"
Sing-kyn Drug House; Guangzhou, Guangdong

Tonifies *qi*, stops cough, resolves phlegm, tonifies kidneys. Use for cough and difficulty in breathing due to weak kidney rooting of the lungs, with systemic deficiency of *qi*. Useful in chronic asthma, emphysema, and chronic bronchitis.

120 pills per bottle. Take 10 pills, 3 x day.

Codonopsis Root	15. %	Ficus Leaf	10
Armeniaca Seed	15	Citrus Peel	9
Licorice Root	10	Cynanchum Rhizome	8
Elaeagnus Fruit	10	Gecko Lizard	5
Morus Root-bark	10	Cordyceps Fungus	5

24 PULMONARY TONIC PILLS
Li Fei Tang Yi Pian
"Benefit Lungs Sugar-coated Tablets"
Handan Pharmaceutical Works; Hebei

Tonifies lung *qi* and *yin*, resolves phlegm, sedates heat. Use in chronic lung weakness with heat, with symptoms of dry cough and sticky phlegm.

Bottles of 60 pills. Take 5 pills, 3 x day.

Bletilla Rhizome	27.%	Lily Bulb	8
Stemona Root	15	Licorice Root	6
Kadsura Root	13	Cordyceps Fungus	5
Oyster Shell	11	Phrynium Leaf	5
Eriobotrya Leaf	10		

25 TUNG HSUAN LI FEI PIEN
Tong Xuan Li Fei Pian
"Open, Drain, Put-in-order Lungs Tablet"
Tianjin Drug Manufactory; Tianjin

Dispels wind, relieves heat, resolves phlegm, stops cough. Use for cough due to wind-invasion, or asthma. Resolves phlegm in thick or watery nasal discharge. Also helpful in relieving wind symptoms of headache, fever and chills, sneezing and general aching.

Boxes of 12 vials, each with 8 tablets. Take 4 tablets, 2 x day.

Licorice Root	28.4 %	Tussilago Flower	6.8
Perilla Leaf	15.7	Citrus Peel	5.7
Peucedanum Root	14.5	Pueraria Root	3.8
Aurantium Fruit	12.7	Lily Bulb	3.8
Platycodon Root	8.6		

26 ZHI SOU DING CHUAN WAN
Zhi Sou Ding Chuan Wan
"Stop Cough, Calm Asthma Pill"
Tientsin Drug Manufactory; Tianjin

Calms cough, sedates lung heat, resolves phlegm-heat, dispels wind, facilitates breathing. Use for acute or chronic cough with labored breathing related to asthma or bronchial phlegm congestion.

Bottles of 150 pills. Take 10 pills, 2 x day.

Main ingredients:

Licorice Root	25 .%	Ephedra Leaf	1
Armeniaca Seed	19	Others	40
Gypsum Mineral	15		

ALSO APPLICABLE for cough and phlegm:

Lung Phlegm:
231   LUNG DISPERSING WATER
254   XUAN FEI
271   RESP

Cough due to deficiency of lung *qi* and *yin*:
227   WHITE MONKEY - LUNG
247   WISE JUDGE
255   FU LEI
259   BU YIN

For phlegm-heat conditions infants and small children:
64   HOU TSAO SAN
65   HUI CHUN TAN
66   BAO YING TAN

For cough due to spleen damp and phlegm:
128   TABELLAE LIU JUN ZI

For nasal congestion:
2   BI YAN PIEN
9   TABLET BI-TONG
269   NASAL TABS

For morning sickness:
202   SHIH SAN TAI PAO WAN

GROUP 2-B: SYRUPS

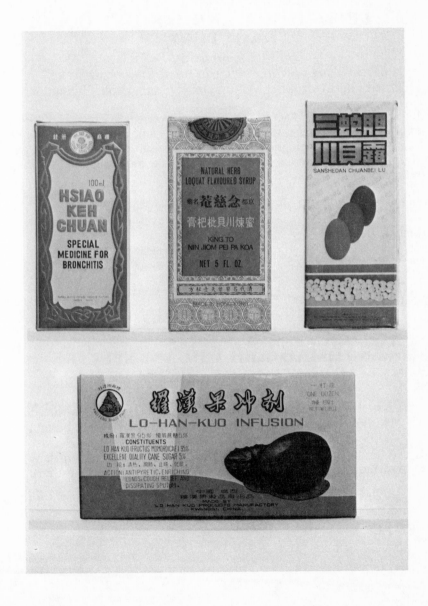

GROUP 2-B: SYRUPS

27 FRITILLARIA AND LOQUAT COUGH MIXTURE
Zhi Ke Chuan Bei Pi Pa Lu
"Treat Cough [with] Fritillaria [and] Eriobotrya Syrup"
United Pharmaceutical Manufactory; Guangzhou, Guangdong

Syrup for chronic and acute cough due to a variety of causes, including exogenous wind attack, weakness of lung *qi*, deficiency of lung *yin* with heat, and sticky phlegm. Use to allay cough and resolve phlegm. Helpful in emphysema, asthma and labored breathing. Safe during pregnancy.

Bottles of liquid, 150 ml. Take 1-3 teaspoons, 3-4 x day.

Main ingredients:

Fritillaria Bulb	13.3 %	Mentha Herb	3.3
Eriobotrya Leaf	10.0	Platycodon Root	3.3
Stemona Root	5.3	Syrup	60.8
Armeniaca Seed	4.0		

28 HSIAO KEH CHUAN: SPECIAL MEDICINE FOR BRONCHITIS
Xiao Ke Chuan Zhuan Zhi Qi Guan Yan
"Dispel Cough [and] Asthma Specific [to] Treat Bronchitis"
Harbin Chinese Medicine Factory; Harbin, Heilongjiang

Syrup for cough due to exogenous cold, phlegm, weakness of lung or kidney. Indicated in acute and chronic bronchitis, cough and asthma.

Bottles of 100 ml. Take 7-10 cc, 3 x day with water.

Main ingredient: Rhododendron Root

29 LO HAN KUO COUGH JUICE
Luo Han Guo Zhi Ke Lu
"Momordica Fruit Stop Cough Syrup"
Yulin Drug Manufactory; Yulin, Guangxi

Syrup to resolve phlegm-heat with deep cough; moistens lungs to relieve thirst. Use in acute phlegm and cough conditions.

Bottles of 100 ml. Take one spoonful (10 ml.) 3-5 x day.

Momordica Fruit	60.%	Armeniaca Seed	6
Fritillaria Bulb	26	Glehnia Root	6
Polygonatum Rhizome	8		

30 LO HAN KUO INFUSION
Luo Han Guo Chong Ji
"Momordica Fruit Instant Medicine"
Kwei-feng Trade Mark, China National Native Produce and Animal By-Products Import and Export Corporation, Kwangsi Chuang Autonomous Region Branch; Guangxi

Mormordica Fruit (*Luo Han Guo*) soothes the lung and resolves phlegm, cough, and labored breathing. Pleasant to the taste and easy to prepare. This product is dissolved in hot water to make a tea.

Boxes of 12 small boxes, each with two doses. Take one cube at a time, and dissolve in one cup of hot water. Take 3-6 times per day.

Mormordica Fruit	95 %
Sugar	5

31 NATURAL HERB LOQUAT FLAVORED SYRUP
Mi Lian Chuan Bei Pi Pa Gao
"Honey Refined Fritillaria, Eriobotrya Syrup"
Superior Brand; Hong Kong

Syrup for chronic and acute cough due to exogenous attack, weakness of lung *qi*, deficiency of lung *yin* with heat, and sticky phlegm-heat. Use to allay cough and resolve phlegm, including sinus congestion. Helpful in emphysema and acute bronchitis.

Bottles of 5 oz, 10 oz, and 25 oz. (10 or 25 oz recommended). 1 tbsp, 3 x day. Children: 1 tsp, 3 x day.

Main ingredients:

Fritillaria Bulb	Platycodon Root
Eriobotrya Leaf	Pinellia Rhizome
Citrus Peel	Armeniaca Seed
Mentha Herb	Ginger Rhizome
Trichosanthes Seed	Honey
Licorice Root	Sugar

32 SAN NUNG SI PEI PA KOA: PIPACAO SYRUP
Mi Lian Chuan Bei Pi Pa Gao
"Honey Refined Fritillaria, Eriobotrya Syrup"
United Pharmaceutical Manufactory; Guangzhou, Guangdong

Same Chinese name as NATURAL HERB LOQUAT FLAVORED SYRUP, with slightly different composition. Syrup for chronic and acute cough due to exogenous attack, weakness of lung*qi*, deficiency of lung *yin* with heat, and sticky phlegm-heat. Useful in bronchitis, emphysema, and sinus congestion.

Bottles of 5 oz, 10 oz, and 25 oz. (10 or 25 oz recommended). 1 tbsp, 3 x day. Children: 1 tsp, 3 x day.

Main ingredients:

Fritillaria Bulb	Pinellia Rhizome
Adenophora Root	Mentha Herb
Schizandra Fruit	Tussilago Flower
Citrus Peel	Sugar

33 SAN SHE DAN CHUAN BEI YE
San She Dan Chuan Bei Ye
"Three Snake Gallbladder [with] Fritillaria Liquid"
United Pharmaceutical Manufactory; Guangzhou, Guandong

Resolves phlegm, clears heat, stops cough. A liquid extract for chronic or acute cough with phlegm, including bronchitis, emphysema, or asthma. Valuable for stubborn phlegm.

Box of 6 glass vials, each 10 cc. Remove plastic cap and take through accompanying straw. Take 1-2 per day, with water.

Fritillaria Bulb	51.7 %	Snakegall Trio	13.8
Armeniaca Seed	34.5		

34 SNAKE GALL AND LOQUAT EXTRACT
San She Dan Chuan Bei Pi Pa Gao
"Three Snake-Gall Fritillaira [and] Eriobotrya Syrup"
Wuzhou Drug Manufactory; Guangxi

Sedates heat, moistens lung, replenishes *yin*, dissipates phlegm. Use for treating lung fire causing cough, phlegm-heat (sticky or profuse), hoarse throat, dry mouth, or sputum with blood. Use for acute bronchitis or pneumonia.

Bottles of 7 oz. Take 1 tblspn, 3 x day.

Fritillaria Bulb	20.0 %	Lotus Seed	7.5
Snake Gall Trio	15.0	Rehmannia Root	7.5
Eriobotrya Leaf	15.0	Jujube Fruit	7.5
Asparagus Root	10.0	Scrophularia Root	7.5
Ophiopogon Root	10.0		

GROUP 3

PILLS TO REMOVE INTERNAL, TOXIC, AND DAMP HEAT

NOTE 1: All patent medicines listed in Group 3 contain fire-purging herbs. Many of these are drying, and can damage stomach fluids if taken for long periods of time. Administer these products only as long as fire and heat symptoms are evident, then discontinue. Caution is advised in pre-existing heat in spleen or stomach, or pre-exisiting deficiency of stomach *yin*. Reduce dosage or discontinue if diarrhea or abdominal cramping develop.

GROUP 3-A
PILLS TO REMOVE
INTERNAL AND TOXIC HEAT

NOTE 2: For products containing OX GALLSTONE, RHINOCEROS HORN, MUSK GLAND or BORENOL CRYSTAL: Use for short time only, administering the product once or twice. Do not use in coma following excessive sweating, vomitting, or hemorrhage, or if person is in shock with sweating, cold limbs, etc. In these cases, revive with formulas to warm the center and tonify *qi*.

NOTE 3: Synthetic substitutions similiar biochemically but not of animal origin may have been substituted for the following products: OX GALLSTONE, MUSK GLAND, and TOAD SECRETION. Common domestic animal substitutions may have been substituted for the following substances: RHINOCEROS HORN, TIGER BONE, and BEAR GALLBLADDER.

35 AN KUNG NIU HUANG WAN
An Gong Niu Huang Wan
"Peaceful Palace Ox Gallstone Pill"
Beijing Tung Jen Tang; Beijing

Clears toxic heat, cools liver fire and calms internal wind, opens orifices (senses). Use for high fever with restlessness, anxiety, vertigo, constipation, muscle spasms, delerium, loss of consciousness, or convulsions. Efficacious in high fevers in children, including measles.

Prohibited during pregnancy.

Boxes of 1 pill. Adults - one pill, 1-2 x day.
Children under 6 years - 1/2 pill. Under 2 years, 1/3 pill.

Caution: See NOTE 2 and 3 at head of chapter. This product lists Rhinoceros Horn, a prohibited substance in North America.

Ox Gallstone	20.%	Margarita Pearl	10
Rhinoceros Horn	20	Musk Gland	5
Coptis Rhizome	15	Honey Binder	15
Curcuma Root	15		

36 CHUAN XIN LIAN -
ANTIPHLOGISTIC PILLS
Chuan Xin Lian Kang Yan Pian
"Penetrate Heart, Repeatedly Fight Heat Pills"
United Pharmaceutical Manufactory; Guangzhou, Guangdong

Purges toxic heat, cools the blood, resolves inflammations, soothes the throat. Use for acute throat inflammations with swollen glands and fever, including strep infections. Beneficial in viral infections causing fever (measles, flu, hepatitis); also, for toxic furuncles, mastitis, and abscesses.

Bottles of 60 pills. Take 3 pills, 3 x day, for one or two days.

Andrographis Leaf	50.%	Taraxacum Plant	25
Isatis Root	25		

37 COMPOUND PILLS OF BEZOAR AND MUSK
Xi Huang Wan
"Rhinoceros and Ox Gallstone Pills"
Sichuan Chengdu Traditional Chinese Pharmaceutical Factory; Chengdu, Sichuan

Sedates liver fire and wind, purges toxic heat, cools blood heat, relieves inflammations, opens heart orifice, resolves stagnation of blood and phlegm in the blood vessels, calms *shen*, breaks up stagnant blood. Use for acute fevers and infections, fever with delerium or coma, and inflamed or abscessed lesions. Can be used as emergency remedy in stroke or heart attack. This formula is based on a classical formula which originally used Rhinoceros Horn; Musk Gland has been substituted.

Prohibited during pregnancy.
Caution: See NOTE 2 and 3 at head of chapter.

Packets of 2 vials. Take contents of one vial, 1-2 x day.

Main ingredients:

Musk Gland	Frankincense Resin
Ox Gallstone	Myrrh Resin

38 HERBAL TORTOISE JELLY

Yao Zhi Gui Ling Gao
"Medicine Made [from] Tortoise [and] Smilax Rhizome Syrup"
Wuchou Manufacturing Chemist; Wuzhou, Guangxi

Dispels toxic heat, nurtures *yin* and blood, promotes tissue regeneration. Use internally for inflamed or infected skin lesions, including abscesses, carbuncles and furuncles, or chronic inflammed dermatoses. Also for painful lesions of urinary tract or gastro-intestinal tract.

Bottles of 300 g. of honey based syrup. Take straight, hot or cold, or with water. Adult: 1/4 to 1/2 bottle, 2-3 x. Children: half adult dosage. Bottle should be kept refrigerated after opening.

Main ingredients:
Golden Coin Tortoise   Lonicera Flower
Smilax Rhizome   Desmodium Leaf
Rehmannia Root   Tribulus Fruit
Licorice Root

39 LARYNGITIS PILLS
Hou Yan Wan
"Larynx Inflammation Pills"
China Szechuan Provincial Pharmaceutical Factory;
Chengdu, Sichuan

Clears toxic heat, sedates internal heat, resolves phlegm-heat, calms agitation and disturbed *shen*. Used primarily to resolve laryngitis due to heat. Also applicable for acute tonsillitis, acute mumps, or sore throat. Similiar in prescription and application to LIU SHEN WAN (#41). Not appropriate for sore throat in early stage of wind invasion. [If strep infection is involved, combine with CHUAN XIN LIAN (#36).]

Small boxes of 3 vials, each with 10 pills. Take 3 x day internally as follows:

> Children to 1 year old: take 1 pill.
> Children 1-2 years old: take 2 pills.
> Children 2-3 years old: take 3-4 pills.
> Children 4-8 years old: take 5-6 pills.
> Children 9-15 years old: take 8-9 pills.
> Adults: take 10 pills.

Externally: Crush 5-10 pills in vinegar and apply to throat.

Prohibited during pregnancy.
Caution: See NOTE 2 and 3 at head of chapter.
Caution: Toad Secretion is toxic. Limit and monitor use. This product lists Rhinoceros Horn, a prohibited substance in North America.

Borax Mineral-salt	30.%	Margarita Pearl	7
Coptis Rhizome	28	Bear Gallbladder	7
Rhinoceros Horn	10	Ox Gallstone	5
Toad Secretion	10	Musk Gland	3

40 LIEN CHIAO PAI TU PIEN
Lian Qiao Bai Du Pian
"Forsythia Defeat Toxin Tablet"
Tianjin Drug Manufactury; Tianjin

Sedates heat, dispels toxic heat, relieves wind-heat in the exterior. Use for acute inflammations and infections, including ulcerated abscesses and carbuncles with pus; fever due to local or systemic toxic infection; and skin itching with rash and redness.

Boxes of 12 vials, 8 tablets to a vial. Take 2-4 tablets, 2 x day.

Prohibited during pregnancy.

Forsythia Fruit	13.8%	Paeonia Chi Shao	10.3
Lonicera Flower	13.8	Rhubarb Root	13.8
Siler Root	10.3	Scutellaria Root	10.3
Dictamnus Root-bark	10.3	Gardenia Fruit	10.3
Cicada Skin	7.0		

41 LIU SHEN WAN
Liu Shen Wan
"Six Spirits Pill"
Shanghai Chinese Medicine Works; Shanghai

Clears toxic heat, sedates internal heat, resolves phlegm-heat, calms agitation and disturbed *shen*. Use for a variety of severe heat problems including acute tonsillitis, acute mumps, or sore throat; also high fever and with delerium. Has the same applications as LARYNGITIS PILLS (39). Not appropriate for sore throat in early stage of wind attack; best remedy for sore throat due to internal heat. [If strep infection is involved, combine with CHUAN XIN LIAN (36).]

Bottles of 10, 30 or 100 pills. Take 10 pills, 1-3 x day. (For children's dosages, see #39). Take whole; or crush 10 "seeds" in a half of glass of water, gargle and swallow. Externally: Crush 5-10 pills in vinegar and apply to throat.

Prohibited during pregnancy.
Caution: See NOTE 2 and 3 at head of chapter.
Caution: Toad Secretion is toxic. Limit and monitor use.

Main ingredients:

Ox Gallstone	Camphor Crystal
Mother-of-Pearl Shell	Toad Secretion
Borneol Crystal	Musk Gland

42 LUNG TAN XIE GAN PILL

Long Dan Xie Gan Wan
"Gentiana Purge Liver Pills"
Kwangchow Pharmaceutical Industry Co.
Guangzhou, Guangdong

Classical formula to purge heat from the liver and gallbladder, and damp-heat from the three burners. Use for upwards flaring of liver fire causing headache, red and burning eyes, ringing in the ears, sore throat, fever blisters on the mouth, scanty urine, or constipation. Use for damp-heat in liver or gallbladder causing leukorrhea, urinary tract infections, or itchiness in the groin. Helpful in oral and genital herpes; also hyperthyroid due to liver-gallbladder fire. Reduces liver heat due to stagnation of liver *qi* [combine with Xiao Yan Wan #123].

Bottles of 100 pills. Take 6 pills, 2 x day.

Gentiana Root	20.%	Angelica Dang Gui	9
Bupleurum Root	15	Scutellaria Root	9
Gardenia Fruit	9	Clematis Root	9
Plantago Seed	9	Rehmannia Root	9
Alisma Rhizome	9	Licorice Root	2

43 MARGARITE ACNE PILLS

Cai Feng Zhen Zhu An Chuang Wan
"Colorful Phoenix Precious Pearl Hide Skinboil Pill"
Guandong Fushan Manufactory Corporation; Foshan,
Guangdong

Clears heat, clears the surface, cools blood, dispels toxins, relieves swollen masses, promotes blood circulation. Use to treat acne, furuncles, skin itching and rashes, including hives. Excellent in adolescent acne.

Caution: Reduce dosage if diarrhea develops. Bottles of 30 pills. Take 6 pills, 2 x day.

Margarita Pearl	24.%	Lonicera Flower	12
Rehmannia Root	12	Phellodendron Bark	12
Adenophora Root	12	Rhubarb Rhizome	10
Scrophularia Root	12	Antelope Horn	6

(Also available as ACNE SWEEPING PILLS, bottles of 36 pills.)

44 MING MU SHANG CHING PIEN

Ming Mu Shang Qing Pian
"Bright Eyes Upper Clearing Tablets"
Tientsin Drug Manufactory; Tianjin

Dispels heat in upper burner, clears vision, sedates liver fire. Use for liver heat affecting the eyes, causing redness, itching, tearing, and swelling (conjunctivitis). Also useful for liver wind causing light-headedness and vertigo. Symptoms may also include concentrated urine, constipation and fever.

Boxes of 12 vials, each with 8 tablets. Take 4 tablets, 2 x day.

Prohibited during pregnancy.

Gardenia Fruit	30.0%	Forsythia Fruit	4.0
Angelica Dang Gui	20.3	Tribulus Fruit	4.0
Coptis Rhizome	6.4	Cicada Skin	4.0
Chrysanthemum Flower	6.4	Ophiopogon Root	4.0
Rhubarb Rhizome	6.4	Gypsum Mineral	4.0
Scutellaria Root	6.4	Plantago Seed	4.0

45 NIU HUANG CHIEH TU PIEN
BEZOAR ANTIPYRETIC PILLS
Niu Huang Jie Du Pian
"Ox Gallstone Dispel Toxin Tablet"
Tientsin Drug Manufactory; Tianjin

For toxic heat and real fire in liver, heart and stomach channels (upper burner) with congestion due to phlegm-heat. Symptoms include fever, inflamed throat or gums, red irritated eyes, earache, toxic swellings, delerium, toothache, headache, dizziness, and oral ulcers. Useful in children's fever. Do not use in deficiency heat syndromes.

Bottles of 8 or 20 tablets. Take 4 tablets, 2 x day.

Prohibited during pregnancy.
Caution: See NOTE 2 and 3 at head of chapter.

Rhubarb Rhizome	26.6%	Licorice Root	7.4
Gypsum Mineral	26.6	Borneol Crystal	4.2
Scutellaria Root	20.2	Ox Gallstone	1.0
Platycodon Root	13.8		

46 NIU HUANG CHIEH TU PIEN BEZOAR ANTIDOTAL TABLETS
Niu Huang Jie Du Pian
"Ox Gallstone Dispel Toxin Tablet"
Peking Chinese Drug Manufactory; Beijing

The same name as product #45 but with a more elaborate formula. Use for toxic heat and real fire in liver, heart and stomach channels (upper burner) with congestion due to phlegm-heat. Symptoms include fever, inflamed throat or gums, red irritated eyes, ear-ache, toxic swellings, delerium, toothache, headache, dizziness, and oral ulcers. Useful in children's fever. Do not use in deficiency heat syndromes.

Boxes of 10 vials, each with 8 tablets. Take 2 tablets, 2 x day.

Prohibited during pregnancy.
Caution: See NOTE 2 and 3 at head of chapter.

Lonicera Flower	20.0%	Angelica Root	8.0
Coptis Rhizome	14.0	Borneol Crystal	7.5
Scutellaraia Root	14.0	Mentha Herb	7.0
Gardenia Fruit	10.0	Ligusticum Rhizome	7.0
Rhubarb Rhizome	10.0	Ox Gallstone	2.5

47 NIU HUANG CHING HSIN WAN
Niu Huang Qing Xin Wan
"Ox Gallstone Clear Heart Pills"
(Beijing Formula)

The same Chinese name as NIU HUANG QIN XIN WAN (#49), but with a different formulation. Cools liver and blood heat, opens heart orifices closed due to heat and fever, fortifies *qi*. Symptoms include prolonged high fever with restlessness and anxiety, delerium, loss of consciousness, vertigo, convulsions, and constipation. Useful in children's fevers.

Boxes of 10 gummy pills, each wrapped in wax. Take 1 pill, 2 x day. Cut and form into smaller pills or dissovle in hot water and drink.

Prohibited during pregnancy.
Caution: See NOTE 2 and 3 at head of chapter. This product lists Rhinoceros Horn, a prohibited substance in North America.

Ginseng Root	10.%	Ligusticum Rhizome	6
Antelope Horn	9	Paeonia Root	5
Ox Gallstone	8	Rhinoceros Horn	5
Cinnamon Bark	8	Musk Gland	5
Donkey-Skin Glue	7	Licorice Root	5
Angelica Dang Gui	6	Honey Binder	20
Siler Root	6		

48 NIU HUANG SHANG CHING WAN
Niu Huang Shang Qing Wan
"Ox Gallstone Upper Clearing Pill"
Tientsin Drug Manufactory; Tianjin

Clears heat and toxic heat in upper burner, sedates liver fire. Use for systemic heat rising from liver causing headache, eye pain or redness, sore throat, toothache, and fever with thirst. Also for constipation and concentrated urine, and toxic skin boils.

Bottles of 50 pills. Take 10 pills, once per day.

Prohibited during pregnancy.
Caution: See NOTE 2 and 3 at head of chapter.

Rhubarb Rhizome	20.%	Borneol Crystal	5
Coptis Rhizome	15	Platycodon Root	5
Chrysanthemum Flower	15	Lotus Plumule	5
Angelica Dang Gui	15	Licorice Root	2
Ox Gallstone	10	Others	7

49 NIU HUANG QIN XIN WAN
BEZOAR SEDATIVE PILLS
Niu Huang Qing Xin Wan
"Ox Gallstone Clear Heart Pills"
Lanchow Chinese Medicine Works; Lanzhou, Gansu

Same name as formula #47, but with a smaller prescription. Cools liver and blood heat, opens heart orifices closed due to heat and fever. Symptoms include serious fever with restlessness and anxiety, delerium, loss of consciousness, vertigo, convulsions, and constipation. Useful in children's fevers.

Boxes of 10 gummy pills, wrapped in wax. Take 1 pill, 2 x day.
Cut and form into smaller pills or dissovle in hot water ane drink.

Prohibited during pregnancy.
Caution: See NOTE 2 and 3 at head of chapter.
Caution: Cinnabar, a natural substance, contains mercury, a heavy metal. Limit use to two or three days.

Coptis Rhizome	59.0%	Scutellaria Root	3.0
Ox Gallstone	30.0	Curcuma Root	2.5
Gardenia Fruit	3.5	Cinnabar Mineral	2.0

50 NIU HUANG XIAO YAN WAN
BEZOAR ANTIPHLOGISTIC PILL
"Ox Gallstone Dispel Inflammation Pill"
Soochow Chinese Medicine Works; Suzhou, Jiangsu

Relieves toxic heat, circulates blood and *qi*, stops pain. Use for fever, sore throat, inflamed and infected swellings (carbuncles and furuncles), toxic infections, and constipation.

Boxes of 10 bottles, each with 60 pills. Take 10 pills, 2 x day. For children, 5 pills, 2 x day.

Caution: See NOTE 2 and 3 at head of chapter.
Caution: Toad Secretion is toxic. Monitor and limit use.

Main Ingredients:

Mother-of-Pearl Shell	19.2%	Indigo Powder	7.9
Trichosanthes Root	19.2	Toad Secretion	5.8
Rhubarb Rhizome	19.2	Other	19.1
Ox Gallstone	9.6		

51 PEACEFUL TEA
Niu Huang Qing Xin Wan
"Ox Gallstone Clear Heart Pills"
Nanking Drug Manufactory; Nanjing, China

Same Chinese name as #48. Clears liver and blood heat, opens heart orifices, dissipates heart-phlegm, restores consciousness. Use for loss of consciousness or delerium due to fever, or for prolonged high fever with signs of restlessness, convulsions, tetany or cramping. Used for encephalitis and brain fevers. Useful in childrens fevers.

Prohibited during pregnancy.
Caution: See NOTE 2 and 3 at head of chapter.

Main ingredients:

Ginseng Root	2.5%	Ox Gallstone	.8
Paeonia Root	2.5	Rhinoceros Horn	.5
Cinnamon Twig	1.8	Borneol Crystal	.5
Poria Fungus	1.6	Musk Gland	.2
Angelica Dang Gui	1.5	Other Herbs	36.1
Goat Horn	.9	Binders	48.9

52   SAI MEI AN (Internal Formula)
Sai Mei An
"The Race [between] Rot and Peaceful Health"
Sei Mei An Medicine Factory; Chuanzhou

Reduces heat, stops pain, reduces hyperacidity. A specific remedy for duodenal and gastric stomach ulcers without bleeding, relying heavily on calcium and other mineral-salts to neutralize excessive stomach acid. Useful for irritations and inflammations to the stomach lining, with pain following meals.

NOTE: Products including seashells or minerals can damage spleen and stomach *qi* with long term use. Monitor and limit use.

Bottles of 50 pills. Take 3 pills, 3 x day.

Clam Shell	23.%	Borneol Crystal	10
Calcite Mineral	20	Stalacitite Mineral	10
Cockle Shell	20	Margarita Pearl	2
Stove Ash	15		

53 SUPERIOR SORE THROAT POWDER SPRAY

Shuang Liao Hou Feng San
"Extra Quality Throat-Wind Medicinal-powder"
Fitshan Hang Chun Medicine Factory; Guangdong
also, Meichou Medicine Factory; Guangzhou, Guangdong

Clears heat and inflammation due to toxic heat or wind-heat. Use for sore throat, mouth ulcers, and ulcerative skin lesions. Can also be used for inflamed sinuses and mid-ear infections. (This product is effective, but bad tasting.)

Bottles of powder (2.2 g.) in spray form.
For throat and mouth application, spray once, 3 x day.
For sinusitis, spray in nose, 5 x day.
For oozing mid-ear inflammations, wash with hydrogen peroxide and spray, once daily.
For ulcerative skin lesion, wash with strong tea, dry and spray, once daily.

Caution: See NOTE 2 and 3 at head of chapter.

Coptis Rhizome	30.%	Ox Gallstone	5
Borneol Crystal	25	Mother-of-Pearl Shell	5
Licorice Root	15	Indigo Powder	5
Sophora Root	15		

54 TZU-HSUEH-TAN
Zi Xue Dan
"Purple Snow Pellet"
United Pharmaceutical Manufactory, Guangzhou; Guangdong

Clears fire in blood and liver, opens the orifices (senses), sedates toxic heat, opens the channels. Use for acute and very high fever with delerium, convulsions, or coma. Do not use in fevers due to recent wind attack.

2 tubes to a package, each with 1.56 g; 10 packages to a box. Take 2 tubes per day.

Prohibited during pregnancy.
Caution: See NOTE 2 and 3 at head of chapter. This product lists Rhinoceros Horn, a prohibited substance in North America.

Mirabilite Mineral	14.3%	Licorice Root	5.7
Glauber's Salt	14.3	Saussurea Root	3.6
Magnetite Mineral	14.3	Rhinoceros Horn	3.6
Talcum Mineral	7.1	Antelope Horn	3.6
Gypsum Mineral	7.1	Aquillaria Wood	3.6
Cimicifuga Rhizome	7.1	Musk Gland	.8
Scrophularia Root	7.1	Caryophyllum Flower	.7
Calcite Mineral	7.1		

ALSO APPLICABLE for Internal and Toxic Heat:

5   HUANG LIEN SHANG CHING PIEN = heat in upper burner
17   CHING FEI YI HUO PIEN = heat in lungs and liver causing
      hot cough, toothache, etc.
91   GASTROPATHY CAPSULES = stomach heat causing ulcers
208   AN MIEN PIEN = liver heat causing insomnia
234   DETOX = liver heat, toxic heat
258   QING RE = wind-heat, toxic heat

For heat due to deficiency of *yin*, consider:
181   DA BU YIN WAN
183   EIGHT FLAVOR TEA
187   RESTORATIVE PILLS

GROUP 3-B
PILLS TO REMOVE DAMP-HEAT

55 ARMADILLO COUNTER POISON PILL
Chuan Shan Jia Qu Shi Qing Du Wan
"Anteater Scale Remove Damp, Clear Toxin Pill"
Fatshan United Pharmaceutical Works; Guangdong

Cools heat and dispels damp and wind-damp, promotes blood circulation, removes toxins. Use for damp-heat and toxic damp-heat conditions affecting the skin, characterized by itching, inflammation or pain. Applicable for various "weeping" eczemas, dermatitis, acne, hives, etc.

Bottles of 48 pills. Take 4 pills, 3 x day.

Anteater Scales	20.0 %	Chrysanthemum Flower	4.0
Jin Qian Turtle	10.0	Xanthium Fruit	3.0
Codonopsis Root	6.5	Ligusticum Rhizome	3.0
Rehmannia Root	5.0	Fritillaria Bulb	3.0
Ox Gallstone	5.0	Forsythia Fruit	2.5
Euphorbia Leaf	5.0	Arctium Fruit	2.5
Hydnocarpus Seed	5.0	Cnidium Fruit	2.5
Astragalus Root	5.0	Scutellaria Root	2.0
Dictamnus Root-Bark	4.0	Paeonia Root	2.0
Smilax Rhizome	4.0	Lonicera Flower	2.0

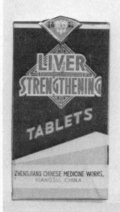

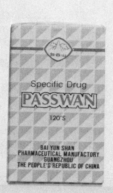

56 CHIEN CHIN CHIH TAI WAN
Qian Jin Zhi Dai Wan
"Thousand Pieces of Gold Stop Leukorrhea Pill"
Tianjin Drug Manufactory; Tianjin

Clears heat and damp, detoxifies, astringes damp discharge, regulates *qi* and blood, benefits kidney and uterus, stops pain. A special prescription for damp vaginal discharge (leukorrhea), due to deficiency of *qi* or blood, or heat in lower burner. Applicable to both hot or cold leukorrhea, as well as trichomonas and vaginal infections. Other symptoms include lower backache, fatigue, abdominal distension and pain.

Bottles of 120 pills. Take 10 pills, once a day.

Indigo Powder	16.%	Corydalis Rhizome	10
Codonopsis Root	12	Dipsacus Root	10
Oyster Shell	12	Atractylodes Rhizome	5
Saussurea Root	10	Fennel Fruit	5
Angelica Dang Gui	10		

57 JI GU CAO PILL
Ji Gu Cao Wan
"Abrus Leaf Pills"
Yulin Drug Manufactory; Yulin, Guangxi

Clears heat and damp-heat of the liver, nourishes and invigorates liver blood. Developed specifically for acute and chronic hepatitis with jaundice. Reportedly excellent results without side-effects In acute hepatitis, combine with LI GAN PIAN (#60). Also useful for dispelling liver heat due to stagnation, when combined with Hsiao Yao Wan (#123).

Bottles of 50 pills. Take 4 pills, 3 x day.

Abrus Leaf	40.%	Angelica Dang Gui	10
Snake-Gall Trio	15	Lycium Fruit	7
Salvia Root	15	Margarita Pearl	3
Ox Gallstone	10		

58 LIDAN TABLETS
Li Dan Pian
"Benefit Gallbladder Tablets"
Tsingtao Medicine Works; Qingdao, Shandong

Resolves damp-heat and toxic heat in the liver and gallbladder, harmonizes the middle burner. Developed specifically to treat acute and chronic gallstone inflammation. Used in China to dissolve and remove gallstones. Can be used for pathological excess in the Gallbladder Channel.

Bottles of 120 tablets. Take 6 tablets, 3 x day.

Scutellaria Root	30.%	Capillaris Leaf	10
Saussurea Root	16	Bupleurum Root	10
Lysimachia Leaf	10	Isatis Leaf	10
Lonicera Flower	10	Rhubarb Rhizome	4

59 LIDIAN PAISHI TABLETS
Li Dan Pai Shi Pian
"Benefit Gallbladder Discharge Stone Tablet"
Tsingtao Medicine Works; Qingdao, Shandong

Removes damp-heat, invigorates *qi* at the center, benefits liver and gallbladder, kills worms. This is an efficacious formula for the disintegration and removal of gallstones. Use to reduce inflammation in both the gallbladder and liver, or to promote bile secretion. Also used for ascariasis (roundworm) in the bilary ducts.

Bottles of 120 tablets.
For gallstones: 6-10 tablets, 2 x day.
For inflammation: 4-6 tablets, 2 x day. Take 10-15 days as a course of treatment, then wait 7 days before repeating second course.

Caution: If diarrhea develops, decrease dosage. Prohibited during pregnancy.

Lysimachia Leaf	16.%	Aurantium Fruit	10
Rhubarb Rhizome	16	Curcuma Root	10
Saussurea Root	16	Capillaris Leaf	7
Areca Husk	10	Mirabilite Minera	15
Magnolia Bark	10		

60 LI GAN PIAN - LIVER STRENGTHENING TABLETS
Li Gan Pian
"Benefit Liver Tablets"
Zhengjiang Chinese Medicine Works; Zhengjiang, Jiangsu

Reduces heat and damp-heat in liver and gallbladder, regulates bile. This is a recently developed patent formula to treat acute and chronic jaundice, hepatitis, and gallstones. It is a good adjunctive patent for products #57, 58, and 59.

Bottles of 100 tablets. Take 2-4 tablets, 3 x day, with meals.

Desmodium Leaf	70.%
Pig Bile	30.

61 SPECIFIC DRUG PASSWAN
Te Xiao Pai Shi Wan
"Specially Effective [Specific Drug] Discharge Stone Pill"
Mai Yun Shan Pharmaceutical Manufactory; Guangzhou, Guangdong

Resolves damp-heat in kidneys and bladder, counters crystalization, cools heat in small intestine, stops bleeding, stops pain, benefits kidneys, spleen, bladder and intestines. Use for acute and chronic urinary calculi in kidney, bladder or ureters.

Bottles of 120 capsules. Take 6-8 capsules, 3 x day.

Lysimachia Leaf	25.0%	Coptis Rhizome	5.4
Lygodium Fungus	20.0	Rhubarb Rhizome	5.0
Angelica Root	10.0	Millettia Niu Da Li	5.0
Andrograhpis Plant	10.0	Pseudoginseng Root	3.0
Cyathula Root	7.5	Succinum Resin	2.0
Ficus Root	5.5	Other	1.6

62 YUDAI WAN
Yu Dai Wan
"Heal Leukorrhea Pill"
Lanzhou Fo Ci Pharmaceutical Factory; Lanzhou, Gansu

Classical formula to clear damp-heat in the uterus and kidneys, tonify blood and *yin*, and astringe damp discharge. For damp-heat vaginal discharge (dark and odorous leukorrhea) with pre-existing deficiency of blood. Other symptoms include lower backache, fatigue, abdominal distension and pain.

Bottles of 100 pills. Take 8 pills, 3 x day.

Ailanthus Bark	46.9 %	Phellodendron Bark	6.2
Paeonia Root	15.6	Alpinia Rhizome	6.2
Rehmannia Root	12.5	Ligusticum Rhizome	3.1
Angelica Dang Gui	9.4		

ALSO APPLICABLE for liver and gallbladder damp-heat:

42   LUNG TAN XIE GAN PILL
234   DETOX

GROUP 3-C
FEVERS AND PHLEGM IN INFANTS

63 BO YING PILLS
Bao Ying Dan
"Protect Baby Powder"
Eu Yan Sang, Hong Kong

Reduces heat and fire, pacifies liver, calms *shen*, dispels wind-heat and phlegm-heat. A medicine formulated for a wide range of children's diseases involving heat, wind, or phlegm, for the symptoms of fever, coarse respiration, productive cough, stomachache, diarrhea, vomiting, restlessness, and night crying. May be given 2 x month as a preventive.

Tins of 6 vials of powder. Give the recommended dose once or twice per day. May be mixed with a favorite food (eg, apple-sauce) or powder may be placed on nipple.

Infants less than 1 month: 1/2 bottle
Infants to 3 years: 1 bottle
3 years to 10 years: 2-3 bottles

Caution: see Notes 2 and 3 at head of chapter.

Arisaema Rhizome	16.%	Bamboo Resin	7
Scorpion	12	Aconite Bei Wu Tou	7
Uncaria Stem	10	Margarita Pearl	4
Silkworm	10	Musk Gland	4
Siler Root	10	Borneol Crystal	3
Mentha Leaf	8	Ginger Rhizome	2
Cicada Skin	7		

64 HOU TSAO SAN

Hou Zao San
"Monkey Gallstone Powder"
United Pharmaceutical Manufactory; Guangzhou, Guangdong

Dispels phlegm and phlegm-heat, sedates fire, dispels wind, pacifies liver, opens heart orifices. Use for infant disorders characterized by sudden onset fever with phlegm, convulsion or fits, red face, coarse respiration, productive cough, diarrhea, vomiting, stomachache, restlessness, and night crying.

Boxes of 12 vials of powder. Mix with juice, water, or in applesauce, or powder may be placed on nipple.

Under one year: 1/2 bottle.
1-3 years, 1 bottle.

Caution: see Note 2 and 3 at head of chapter.

Licorice Root	15.3 %	Calamina Mineral	6.3
Snake-Gall Trio	11.2	Monkey Gallstone	4.5
Scorpion	8.0	Succinum Resin	4.5
Cardamon Fruit	7.7	Glauber's Salt	4.5
Asarum Plant	7.7	Alum Mineral-Salt	3.4
Gleditsea Fruit	7.7	Borax Mineral-Salt	3.4
Ox Gallstone	6.7	Musk Gland	1.8
Mother-of-Pearl Shell	6.7	Borneol Crystal	.7

65 HUI CHUN TAN
Hui Chun Dan
"Return to Spring Powder"
Hong Kong

Reduces heat and fire, disperses wind, clears phlegm, calms *shen*, opens and invigorates *qi* in the center. Use for infant disorders including fever, cough with phlegm, colds, fitfulness, measles, stomachache, vomiting, diarrhea, and difficult respiration.

Boxes of 10 bottles, each containing 3 pills.
Under 1 year: Take 1 pill, 3 x day.
1-5 years: Take 3 pills, 3 x day.
5-9 years: Take 5 pills, 3 x day.

Caution: see Notes 2 and 3 at head of chapter.

Arisaema Rhizome	10.%	Fritillaria Bulb	6
Mylabris Beetle	10	Citrus Seed	6
Aquilaria Wood	6	Cardamon Fruit	6
Gastrodia Rhizome	6	Silkworm	6
Inula Flower	6	Santalum Wood	6
Aurantium Zhi Ke	6	Licorice Root	4
Bamboo Resin	6	Musk Gland	2
Scorpion	6	Ox Gallstone	2
Catechu Resin	6		

66 PAO YING TAN

Zhu Po Bao Ying Dan
"Pearl Protect Baby Powder"
United Pharmaceutical Manufactory; Guangzhou, Guangdong

The same Chinese characters as *Bo Ying Pills* (#63), with similiar application but slightly stronger prescription. Use for a variety of children's diseases involving heat, wind, and/or phlegm, for the symptoms of fever, difficult respiration, productive cough, stomachache, diarrhea, vomiting and night crying. May be given 2 x month as a preventive.

Boxes of 10 wax-eggs, with paper-wrapped packets of loose powder. Give the contents of one wax-egg for mild cases, and two for severe cases, per day. Infants less than 1 month: 1/2 packet.

Caution: see Notes 2 and 3 at head of chapter. Caution: Scorpion is a toxic substance. Limit and monitor use.

Snake Gallbladder	12.9 %	Calaminia Mineral	5.7
Scorpion	9.7	Borneol Crystal	5.7
Gastrodia Rhizome	8.0	Cicada Skin	5.7
Silkworm	8.0	Bamboo Resin	5.7
Siler Root	8.0	Ox Gallstone	5.7
Uncaria Stem	8.0	Margarita Pearl	5.4
Succinum Resin	7.2	Musk Gland	4.3

67 PO YING TAN (PILLS) BABIES PROTECTOR

Ba Bao Zhu Po Bao Ying Dan
"Eight Precious Pearls Protect Baby Pills"
Po Che Tong Poon Mo Um; Hong Kong

Reduces heat and fire, pacifies liver, calms *shen*, dispels wind-heat and phlegm-heat. A medicine formulated for a wide range of children's diseases involving heat, wind, or phlegm, for the symptoms of fever, headache, coarse respiration, productive cough, stomachache, diarrhea, vomiting, restlessness, and night crying. Similiar to products #63 and 66.

Tins of 6 vials of powder. Give the recommended dose once or twice per day. May be mixed with a favorite food (eg, apple-sauce) or placed on nipple.

Infants less than 1 month: 1/2 bottle
Infants to 3 years: 1 bottle
3 years to 10 years: 2-3 bottles

Caution: see Notes 2 and 3 at head of chapter.

Uncaria Stem	18.8 %	Siler Root	6.3
Gastrodia Rhizome	12.5	Borneol Crystal	6.2
Silkworm	12.5	Succinum Resin	6.1
Arisaema Rhizome	10.0	Ox Gallstone	1.3
Typhonus Rhizome	8.8	Margarita Pearl	1.0
Cicada Skin	8.7	Musk Gland	.3
Scorpion	7.5		

68 TAO CHIH PIEN (FOR BABIES)
Dao Chi Pian
"Guide [away] Red Pills"
Tientsin Drug Manufactory; Tianjin

Clears heat, detoxifies, stimulates bowels, promotes urination. Use for heat in the stomach and intestine channels causing sore throat, mouth sores, swollen gums, fever, red eye, constipation, stomachache, and scanty dark urine.

Tubes of 8 tablets, 12 tubes to a box.
Take 2-4 tablets, 2 x day for children 1 to 7.
For infants less than 1 year, reduce dosage.

Caution: reduce dosage or discontinue if diarrhea develops.

Rhubarb Rhizome	32.%	Poria Fungus	9
Gardenia Fruit	26	Akebia Stem	9
Rehmannia Root	17	Other	7

ALSO APPLICABLE for children's fevers:

35   AN KUNG NIU HUANG WAN
45   NIU HUANG CHIEH TU PIEN
47   NIU HUANG CHING HSIN WAN

GROUP 4

PILLS, LINIMENTS, AND PLASTERS FOR REMOVING WIND-DAMP

NOTE: Synthetic substitutions similiar biochemically but not of animal origin may have been substituted for the following products: OX GALLSTONE, MUSK GLAND, and TOAD SECRETION. Common domestic animal substitutions may have been made for the following substances: RHINOCEROS HORN, TIGER BONE and BEAR GALLBLADDER.

GROUP 4-A: PILLS

69 CHEN PU HU CHIEN WAN
Jian Bu Hu Qian Wan
"Walk Vigorously [like] Tiger Stealthy Pill"
Beijing Tong Jen Tang; Beijing

Dispels wind-damp, strengthens kidney *qi* and *jing*, nourishes liver blood, benefits tendons and bones. Use for kidney weakness aggravated by wind and damp, causing problems in the lower back, legs, or gait. Appropriate for chronic arthritis, lumbago and sciatica.

Bottles of 200 pills. Take 20 pills, 2 x day.

Note: This product lists Tiger Bone, a prohibited substance in North America.

Chaenomeles Fruit	14.9 %	Angelica Dang Gui	10.3
Achyranthes Root	14.9	Ginseng Root	6.9
Tiger Bone	12.6	Honey Binder	30.1
Gentiana Qin Jiao	10.3	and other ingredients.	

70 DU HUO JISHENG WAN
Du Huo Ji Sheng Wan
"Angelica Du Huo and Loranthus Pill"
Min-Kang Drug Manufactory; Yichang, Hubei

Classical formula to dispel wind-cold and damp, tonify liver and kidney, and tonify *qi* and blood. Use for wind-damp in the joints, lower back, and knees, causing weakness, pain and stiffness. Conditions include chronic sciatica, arthritis and rheumatism. Also useful in injuries to lower limbs. Not recommended in hot conditions.

Bottles of 100 pills. Take 9 pills, 2 x day.

Caution during pregnancy.

Eucommia Bark	9.7 %	Cinnamon Bark	8.3
Codonoposis Root	9.7	Loranthus Twig	5.8
Rehmannia Root	9.7	Angelica Du Huo	5.8
Ginger Rhizome	9.7	Angelica Dang Gui	5.8
Poria Fungus	9.7	Licorice Root	3.9

71 FENG SHIH HSIAO TUNG WAN
Feng Shi Xiao Tong Wan
"Wind-Damp Dispel Pain Pill"
Tientsin Drug Manufactory; Tianjin

Clears wind-damp and wind-damp-heat, invigorates blood circulation, benefits kidney and liver, strengthens tendons and bone. Use for wind-damp rheumatism causing lower backache, chronic sciatica, or pain to joints, including fingers, shoulders, knees and hips.

Bottles of 100 pills. Take 10 pills, 2 x day.

Note: This product lists Tiger Bone, a prohibited substance in North America. See NOTE at head of chapter.

Siegesbeckia Leaf	15.%	Carthamus Flower	10
Clerodendron Leaf	15	Chaenomeles Fruit	10
Tiger Bone	15	Deer Ligament	10
Notopterygium Rhizome	15	Binders	10

72 GUAN JIE YAN WAN
Guan Jie Yan Wan
"Close Down Joint Inflammation Pills"
Chang Chow Jian Ming Medical Works; Changzhou, Jiangsu

Removes wind-damp (cold and hot) from *luo* channels and joints, for complaints of arthritis and rheumatism, cold sensation in limbs, and aching joints. Useful for periodic flaring of sciatic nerve, as well as rheumatoid arthritis.

Bottles of 300 pills. Take 8 pills, 3 x day.

Prohibited during pregnancy.

Erythrina Bark	20.0 %	Gentiana Qin Jiao	6.5
Atractylodes Rhizome	18.8	Cinnamon Bark	6.5
Coix Seed	18.8	Ginger Rhizome	3.2
Stephania Root	13.3	Ephedra Stem	3.2
Achyranthes Root	6.5	Angelica Du Huo	3.2

73 HONG SHE PILLS
Feng Shi Pian
"Wind-Damp Tablet"
Chung Lien Drug Works; Wuchang, Hubei

Dispels wind-damp, resolves cold. Use for acute wind-cold-damp attack into skin, muscle and joints, causing stiffness, pain and rheumatism. Useful for chronic joint pain due to injury.

Bottles of 24 pills. Take 2 pills once a day (only).

Prohibited during pregnancy.

Cinnamon Twig	20. %	Notopterygium Rhizome	10
Strychnos Seed	20	Achyranthes Root	3
Ephedra Leaf	16	Licorice Root	2
Eucommia Bark	16	Other	2
Siler Root	11		

74 KAI YEUNG PILL
Hua She Jie Yang Wan
"Pit Viper Dispel Itching Pill"
Hanyang Pharmaceutical Works; Hubei

Dispels wind-damp, relieves the surface, sedates heat, dispels toxins, and tonifies and circulates blood and *qi*. This formula counteracts skin itching, and is indicated for various pruritus and eczema diseases, dermatitis, fungal infection, and skin itching due to allergenic and drug reactions.

Bottles of 60 pills. Take 30 pills, 3 x day.

Caution during pregnancy.

Astragalus Root	10.%	Atractylodes Rhizome	10
Ligusticum Rhizome	10	Xanthium Fruit	5
Angelica Root	10	Siler Root	5
Agkistrodon Pit Viper	10	Rehmannia Root	5
Angelica Dang Gui	10	Black-Striped Snake	5
Ginseng Root	10	Cnidium Fruit	5

75 SAN SHE TAN CHUI FENG WAN
San She Dan Zhui Feng Wan
"Three Snake Gallbladder Dispel Wind Pill"
United Pharmaceutical Factory; Guangzhou, Guangdong

Disperses wind and damp, opens and invigorates the channels, nourishes liver *yin* and blood, benefits tendons and joints. Use for chronic and acute wind-damp invasions into muscles causing lower back or limb pain, stiff or creaky joints, and rheumatism. Effective for acute sciatic attack; also chronic spinal subluxations.

Take 10 pills, 2 x day.

Prohibited during pregnancy.

Gastrodia Rhizome	23.%	Arisaema Rhizome	6
Angelica Dang Gui	23	Snake Gall Trio	6
Silkworm Droppings	23	Citrus Seed	2
Earthworm	11	Other	6

76 SPECIFIC LUMBAGLIN
Te Xiao Yao Tong Ling
"Special Efficacy Lower Back Pain Pills"
Guangzhou Pharmaceutical Industrial Corporation;
Guangzhou, Guangdong

Strengthens waist and kidneys, tonifies *jing*, invigorates blood, removes blood stagnation, dispels wind and damp, relaxes tendons, activates *luo* channels to relieve inflammation, pain and achiness. Use for lower back pain, muscular strain, and sciatic inflammation.

Boxes of 24 capsules. Take 1-2 capsules, 3 x day.

Caution during pregnancy.

Main ingredients:

Eucommia Bark	Polygonum Shou Wu
Morinda Root	Angelica Root
Ligusticum Rhizome	Loranthus Twig
Carthamus Flower	Angelica Dang Gui
Achyranthes Root	Clematis Root
Gentiana Qin Jiao	Polypodium Rhizome

77 TA HUO LO TAN
CHINESE OLD MAN TEA
Da Huo Luo Dan
"The Greater Invigorate Luo Channel Pill"
Tientsin Herb Tea Manufactory; Tianjin

Activates blood circulation, disperses stagnant blood and phlegm, dispels wind and cold in the joints and *luo* channels, tonifies kidney *yin* and *yang*, invigorates *qi*. Use for joint pain, back pain, stiff muscles, and difficulty in walking or sitting. Use in serious and acute cases.

Bottles of 40 pills. Take 5 pills, 2 x day. Also, boxes of 10 large pills. Take 1 pill, 2 x day. Cut and form into small pieces. Can be chewed. Or dissolve in hot water and drink.

Caution during pregnancy.

See NOTE at head of chapter.

Ginseng Root	4.3%	Lindera Root	2.8
Siler Root	3.6	Saussurea Root	2.8
Clematis Root	2.8	Aquilaria Wood	2.8
Cinnamon Bark	2.8	Angelica Dang Gui	2.1
Notopterygium Rhizome	2.8	Caryophyllum Flower	1.4
Coptis Rhizome	2.8	Asarum Plant	1.4
Tortoise Plastron	2.8	Frankincense Resin	1.4
Polygonum Shou Wu	2.8	Citrus Qing Pi	1.4
Gastrodia Rhizome	2.8	Musk Gland	.7
Rehmannia Root	2.8	Honey Binders	53.0
		and other ingredients.	

78 TA HUO LO TAN (BEIJING)

Da Huo Luo Dan
"The Greater Invigorate Luo *Channel Pill"*
Beijing Tung Jen Tang; Beijing

A similiar prescription to the TA HUO LO TAN (#77), with the addition of Tiger Bone, Rhinoceros Horn, and Ox Gallstone. It has the same indications.

Boxes of 10 large pills. Take 1 pill, 2 x day. Cut and form into small pieces, then chew. Or dissolve in hot water and drink.

Caution during pregnancy.
Note: Rhinoceros Horn and Tiger Bone are prohibited sub-stances in North America.
See NOTE at head of chapter.

Ginseng Root	4.2%	Gastrodia Rhizome	2.8
Siler Root	3.6	Saussurea Root	2.8
Tiger Bone	3.0	Angelica Dang Gui	2.1
Notopterygium Rhizome	2.8	Asarum Plant	1.4
Cinnamon Bark	2.8	Caryophyllum Flower	1.4
Tortoise Plastron	2.8	Frankincense Resin	1.4
Polygonum Shou Wu	2.8	Citrus Qing Pi	1.4
Rehmannia Root	2.8	Rhinoceros Horn	1.0
Lindera Root	2.8	Ox Gallstone	1.0
Aquilaria Wood	2.8	Musk Gland	.7
Clematis Root	2.8	Honey Binders	47.4
Coptis Rhizome	2.8		

79 TIAN MA HU GU WAN
Tian Ma Hu Gu Wan
"Gastrodia, Tiger Bone Pill"
Dung Feng Chengdu Pharmaceutical Factory; Chengdu, Sichuan

Dispels wind, activates *qi* and blood, dissipates damp, relieves heat, tonifies kidney and liver, stops pain. Use for wind-damp invasion affecting muscles, bone, and lower back. Applicable for chronic and acute arthritis and rheumatism, and numbness or pain in extremeties. Also useful for exogenous or endogenous wind causing headache, dizziness, and nausea.

Bottles of 60 pills. Take 4 pills, 3 x day.

Note: This product lists Tiger Bone, a prohibited substance in North America.
See NOTE at head of chapter.

Main ingredients:
Gastrodia Rhizome
Ligusticum Gao Ben
Tiger Bone
Ligusticum Rhizome

Eucommia Bark
Angelica Root
Ginseng Root

80 TRISNAKE ITCH-REMOVING PILLS
San She Jie Yang Wan
"Three Snakes Dispel Itching Pills"
United Medicine Manufactory; Guangzhou, Guangdong

Dispels wind-damp, relieves the surface, removes heat, tonifies blood, circulates *qi* and blood, dispels toxins. Use for all kinds of skin itching conditions including pruritis, dermatitis, eczema, acne, and fungal infections. Also useful for leukorrhea.

Take 4-5 pills, 2 x day.

Caution during pregnancy.

Main ingredients:

Hubei Agkistrodon Viper
Agkistrodon Pit Viper
Black-Striped Snake
Astragalus Root
Atractylodes Rhizome

Cnidium Fruit
Ginseng Root
Ligusticum Rhizome
Paeonia Root
Ox Gallstone

81 TU ZHUNG FENG SHI WAN
Du Zhong Feng Shi Wan
"Eucommia Bark Wind-Damp Pills"
China National Chemicals Import and Export Corp;
Guangtung Branch

Strengthens bone and tendon, fortifies kidney and liver, tonifies and invigorates *qi*, nourishes, invigorates and warms blood, dispels wind-damp, and stops pain. Use for rheumatic aching of joints and lower back, including wandering joint pain (Bi syndromes), sciatica inflammations, and gout.

Contraindicated during exogenous wind attacks (flus and colds).

Prohibited during pregnancy.

Bottles of 60 or 120 pills. Take 4-6 pills, 2 x day.

Angelica Dang Gui	12.%	Achyranthes Root	8
Eucommia Bark	10	Gentiana Qin Jiao	8
Cinnamon Bark	10	Siler Root	7
Angelica Du Huo	10	Poria Fungus	5
Codonopsis Root	10	Asarum Plant	5
Loranthus Twig	10	Ligusticum Rhizome	3

82 XIAO HUO LUO DAN
Xiao Huo Luo Dan
"The Lesser Invigorate Luo Channel Pills"
Lanchow Chinese Medicine Works; Lanzhou, Gansu

Invigorates and clears the channels, activates *qi* and blood, benefits kidney *yang* to disperse cold. Relieves rheumatic pain, numbness or difficulty in moving joints, chronic lower back pain. If coexisting with deficiency, combine with tonic.

Bottles of 100 pills. Take 6 pills, 2-3 x day.

Contraindicated during pregnancy.

Aconite Root	21.2%	Earthworm	21.2
Aconite Bei Wu Tou	21.2	Pistacia Root	7.5
Arisaema Root	21.2	Myrrh Resin	7.5

ALSO APPLICABLE for kidney deficiency causing lower back pain:

164	ANTI-LUMBAGO TABLETS
169	DUZHONG BU TIAN SU
195	GEJIE TA BU WAN
267	MOTILITY 1
268	MOTILITY 2

GROUP 4-B
PLASTERS FOR EXTERNAL APPLICATION

83 ANTI-RHEUMATIC PLASTER
Jing Zhi Gou Pi Gao
"Essence [of] Manufactured Dog Skin Plaster"
Tientsin Drug Manufactory; Tianjin

A topical application for removing musculo-skeletal pain due to heat, invasion of cold, or obstruction of *qi* and blood in the surface channels. Use for chronic aching in muscles, joints and lower back. Also suitable for traumatic injuries.

Packets of 6 plasters; 20 packets to the box. Apply one medicated adhesive to the area for 24 hours, and repeat. Loses efficacy in bath or shower.

Prohibited to apply to abdomen of pregnant women. Do not apply to open wounds or skin lesions.

See NOTE at head of chapter.

Active ingredients:

Zinc Oxide	12.%	Musk Gland	5
Frankincense Resin	8	Borneol Crystal	5
Myrrh Resin	8	Others to	100

84 KOU PI PLASTERS
Gou Pi Gao
"Dog Skin Plaster"
Beijing Tung Jen Tang; Beijing

Relaxes muscles and tendons, promotes circulation of blood and *qi*. Use for rheumatic numbness, muscular spasm, sore lower back or legs, and contused wounds.

Boxes of 10 plasters. Use one plaster per treatment. Steam or heat so that resin may dissolve and spread along the skin. Apply directly, leaving on for 10-20 minutes. Guard against applying when too hot, so as to avoid burn. Can be resteamed for repeated use.

Prohibited in pregnancy to torso.

See NOTE at head of chapter.

Active ingredients:

Eucommia Bark	.21%	Dragon Blood Resin	.21
Ligusticum Rhizome	.21	Myrrh Resin	.21
Saussurea Root	.21	Camphor Crystal	.21
Mantis Egg-case	.21	Musk Gland	.22
Frankincense Resin	.21	Other agents to	100.00

85 MUSK RHEUMATISM-EXPELLING PLASTERS

She Xiang Zhui Feng Gao
"Musk Gland Chase-away Wind Plaster"
Guilin Fourth Pharmaceutical Factory; Guilin, Guizhou

Dispels wind in the joints, clears the channels, invigorates *qi* and blood, stops pain. Use for rheumatic pains characterized by stiff painful joints, lower back pain, or numbness in the limbs.

Small boxes of 10 plasters. Apply externally and leave on for 2-3 days, or until bath.

Caution: Do not apply to abdomen or lower back during pregnancy.

See NOTE at head of chapter.

Main ingredients:

Musk Gland	Mantis Egg-case
Gastrodia Rhizome	Centipede
Achyranthes Root	Santalum Wood
Angelica Root	Dragon Blood Resin

86 SHANG SHI ZHI TONG GAO:
PLASTER FOR RHEUMATIC PAINS
Shang Shi Zhi Gao
"Injury [from] Damp Stop Pain Plaster"
Shanghai Chinese Medicine Works; Shanghai

Plaster-adhesive for rheumatic pains due to wind-damp or trauma. Promotes circulation of *qi* and blood. Also suitable for sprains, strains and contusions.

Apply externally and leave on for 2-3 days, or until bath.

Prohibited to apply to abdomen of pregnant women.

Caution: Wintergreen Oil is considered dangerous both orally and externally by the Food and Drug Administration (USA).

Caryophyllum Flower	42.5%	Styrax Resin	10.6
Camphor Oil	17.0	Menthol Crystal	8.5
Wintergreen Oil	12.8	Borneol Crystal	8.5

ALSO APPLICABLE for wind-damp external application:

110 MAGIC PLASTER
111 PLASTER FOR BRUISE AND ANALGESIC
112 PO SUM ON MEDICATED OIL
113 SHANG SHI BAO ZHEN GAO
115 YUN XIANG JING

GROUP 5

PRODUCTS FOR BLOOD STAGNATION, BLEEDING, AND PAIN

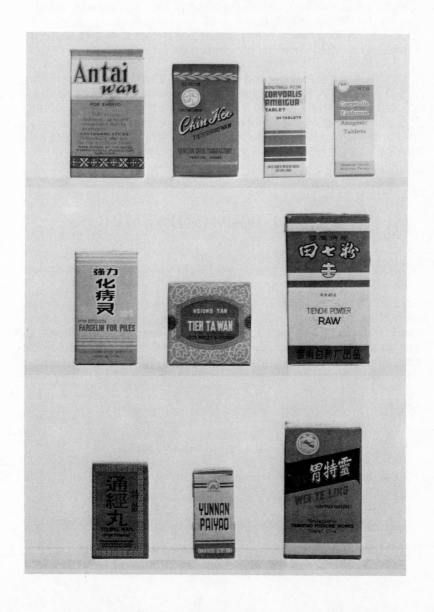

GROUP 5-A: PILLS

NOTE 1: Stagnation of blood may be the result of trauma, stagnation of *qi*, or congestion of liver *qi*. It includes various presentations of pain, abscesses and ulcers, and tumors or swollen masses.Bleeding may be due to trauma, deficiency of *yin*, arrogant *yang*, heat in the blood, or deficiency of spleen *qi*. Causative factors should be taken into consideration when choosing an appropriate patent.

NOTE 2: Synthetic substitutions similiar biochemically but not of animal origin may have been substituted for the following products: OX GALLSTONE, MUSK GLAND, and TOAD SECRETION. Common domestic animal substitutions may have been made for the following substances: RHINOCEROS HORN, TIGER BONE, and BEAR GALLBLADDER.

87 AN TAI WAN (FOR EMBRYO)
An Tai Wan
"Peaceful Fetus Pill"
United Pharmaceutical Manufactory; Guangzhou, Guangdong

Circulates blood and *qi* so as to relax tendons and muscles, calms fetus, cools blood heat, stops pain. Use for restless fetus, premature uterine contractions and threatened abortion causing lower abdominal pain and fetal agitation during pregnancy. (All use of herbal patent medicines during pregnancy should be monitered by a qualified practitioner of Traditional Chinese Medicine).

Bottles of 100 pills. Take 7 pills, 3 x day.

Angelica Dang Gui	28.2%	Atractylodes Rhizome	17.2
Paeonia Root	22.2	Ligusticum Rhizome	16.2
Scutellaria Root	16.2		

88 CHIN KOO TIEH SHANG WAN
Jin Gu Die Shang Wan
"Muscles and Bone Traumatic Injury Pill"
Tientsin Drug Manufactory; Tianjin

Stops internal bleeding, bruising and swelling, invigorates blood and fluids, breaks up blood stagnation, stops pain, strengthens tendons, promotes healing. Use for acute traumatic injuries including fractures, sprains, strains, wounds, with accompanying pain and swelling.

Bottles of 120 pills. Take 10 pills, 2-3 x day, until injury is significantly better.

Prohibited during pregnancy.

Pseudoginseng Root	20.%	Myrrh Resin	10
Dragon Blood Resin	15	Carthamus Flower	10
Angelica Dang Gui	15	Others	15
Frankincense Resin	15		

89 CORYDALIS YANHUSUS ANALGESIC TABLETS
Yan Hu Suo Zhi Tong Pian
"Corydalis Stop Pain Tablets"
Chongqing Chinese Medicine Factory; Chongqing, Sichuan

Breaks obstructions of *qi* and blood in the channels, invigorates *qi* and blood, dispels wind-damp, stops pain. Use for a wide variety of pain presentations, including stomachache, headache, menstrual cramps, toothache, and sinusitis. Particularly useful in pain aggravated by wind or wind-damp, including joint inflammation, headache and sinus headaches. Can be combined with other formulas.

Bottles of 24 pills. Take 4 pills, 3 x day.

Use with caution in weaker persons.

Corydalis Rhizome	66.%
Angelica Root	34.

Also available as CORYDALIS AMBIGUA TABLETS.

90 FARGELIN FOR PILES
Qiang Li Hua Zhi Ling
"Better Strength Dissolve Hemorrhoids Efficacious-Cure"
United Pharmaceutical Manufactury; Guangzhou, Guangdong

Invigorates blood circulation, breaks up blood stagnation, relieves swelling, dispels heat, stops pain. Use for acute and chronic hemorrhoids due to blood stagnation and heat. Reported to give immediate relief of swelling.

Bottles of 36 or 60 tablets. Take 3 tablets, 3 x day.

See NOTE 2 at the head of the chapter.

Pseudoginseng Root	20.%	Callicarpa Root	15
Succinum Resin	15	Sanguisorba Root	10
Sophora Flower	15	Corydalis Rhizome	5
Scutellaria Root	15	Bear Gallbladder	5

91 GASTROPATHY CAPSULES
707 Gastropathy Capsules
Wei Yao
"Stomach Medicine"
Zhenjiang Chinese Medicine Works; Zhenjiang, Jiangsu

Reduces heat and inflammation, disperses stagnation of blood, stops bleeding, stops pain, strengthens spleen and stomach, opens the center, This product contains calcium and other mineral-salts which neutralize excessive stomach acid. Use for gastric and duodenal bleeding ulcers accompanied by pain during or following eating. Also useful for flatulence aggravated by heat and stagnation in the stomach.

Bottles of 42 capsules. Take 2-3 capsules, 3 x day.

Caution: This product contains aluminum, a heavy metal.

Corydalis Rhizome	21.0 %	Alum Mineral-Salt	15.8
Mother-of-Pearl Shell	21.0	Cuttlefish Bone	10.5
Chicken-Egg Lining	21.0	Aristolochia Fruit	10.5

92 HSIUNG TAN TIEH TA WAN
Xiong Dan Die Da Wan
"Bear Gallbladder Traumatic Injury Pill"
United Pharmaceutical Manufactory; Guangzhou, Guangdong

Invigorates blood circulation, breaks up blood swelling and stagnation, reduces heat, promotes healing to injured blood vessels. Use for acute bruises, sprains, and swellings due to trauma. Also suitable for swelling and bruising in chronic traumatic conditions. Popular in China for injuries due to sports and martial arts training.

Boxes of 10 pills.
Internally: 1 pill at a time
Children, 1/2 pill. Chew and swallow, or cut into smaller pieces. May be dissolved in hot water. Externally: dissolve in rice wine (Sake) or alcohol and rub vigorously into affected area.

See Note 2 at head of chapter.

Prohibited during pregnancy (internally, and externally to abdomen), and during bleeding injuries.

Reduce dosage or discontinue if diarrhea develops.

Angelica Dang Gui	18.%	Amomum Fruit	15
Rhubarb Rhizome	17	Carthamus Flower	10
Inula Root	15	Pseudoginseng Root	8
Curcuma Root	15	Bear Gallbladder	2

93 PROSTATE GLAND PILLS
Qian Lie Xian Wan
"Prostate Gland Pills"
Wai Yeung District Medicine Company; Guangdong

Disperses blood stagnation, reduces inflammation, clears toxic pus, reduces damp-heat in lower burner and tonifies and invigorates blood. Use for chronic and acute prostate gland infection or swelling, with symptoms of dribbling or painful urination, and painful testicles. Also suitable for urinary tract infections with accompanying lower back or abdominal pain.

Bottles of 90 pills. Take 6 pills, 3 x day.

Main ingredients:

Vaccaria Seed	Peucedanum Root
Moutan Root	Licorice Root
Paeonia Chi Shao	Saussaurea Root
Astragalus Root	Akebia Stem
Patrinia Plant	

94 TIENCHI GINSENG TABLET
Yun Nan Te Chan Tian Qi Pian
"Yunnan Specially Produced Psuedoginseng Tablet"
Yunnan Pai Yao Factory; Yunnan

A single herb patent medicine which warms and activates blood circulation, disperses clots and deposits in blood vessels, stops bleeding, reduces swelling, and relieves pain. Modern research (PRC) demonstrates that raw Tien Qi Root reduces high blood pressure and lowers blood cholesterol. Useful for nosebleed, bloody urine, traumatic bleeding (internal and external), bruises, and menstrual cramps due to cold and blood stagnation. Useful following childbirth to prevent blood stagnation.

Boxes of 30 tablets. Take 2 tablets, 3 x day.

Prohibited during pregnancy.

Pseudoginseng Root, raw   0.5 g each tablet

95 TIENCHI POWDER RAW
Sheng Tian Qi Fen
"Raw Pseudoginseng Powder"
Yunnan Pai Yao Factory; Yunnan

The same product as #94, but as a powder. Can be taken internally, or applied externally for traumatic injury, or for bleeding gums.

Bottles of powder, total of 40 g. Take 3-5 g., 2 x day: in capsules, hot water, or soup. Externally can be mixed with alcohol or rice wine (Sake) for swelling due to traumatic injury, or can be applied directly to open wounds to stop bleeding.

Prohibited internally during pregnancy.

Pseudoginseng Root, raw   100%

96 TO JING WAN
Tong Jing Wan
"Regulate Menses Pills"
China National Chemicals Import and Export Corp;
Hangzhou, Zhejiang

Breaks blood stagnation, stimulates and invigorates blood circulation, regulates blood, relieves pain. A special patent specifically for menstrual disorders due to blood stagnation, including clots and cramps, irregular periods, difficulty in starting menses or amenorrhea, or prolonged periods. Helpful as extended treatment or as symptomatic treatment for cramps while they occur.

Bottles of 80 pills. Take 20 pills, 2 x day.

Curcuma Root	20.%	Ligusticum Rhizome	10
Sparganium Rhizome	20	Angelica Dang Gui	10
Paeonia Chi Shao	20	Salvia Root	10
Carthamus Flower	10		

97 YUNNAN PAIYAO
Yun Nan Bai Yao
"Yunnan White Medicine"
Yunnan Pai Yao Factory; Yunnan

Stops bleeding, disperses stagnant blood, tonifies and invigorates blood, stops pain. Valuable first-aid remedy for internal and external bleeding, traumatic swelling, and insect bites. Commonly used for excessive menstrual bleeding, severe menstrual cramps, ulcer bleeding, and hot skin infections (carbuncles). Can be taken internally or applied externally.

Boxes of 10 bottles, 4 grams per bottles. (Also available in packets of 20 capsules). Internally: Take 0.2-0.5 gram (1-2 capsules), 4 x day. Externally: apply directly to bleeding wound (clean first, and bandage afterwards). In deep or wide wounds, squeeze cut together, pour powder on, and keep closed for 1 to 2 minutes.

In cases of serious wounds or bleeding, take the single red pill that comes with each bottle first, with wine.

Contraindicated internally during pregnancy.

Ingredients secret, although raw Pseudoginseng Root is known to be the main ingredient.

98 WEI TE LING "204"
Wei Te Ling
"Stomach Especially Effective-Remedy"
Tsingtao Medicine Works; Qingdao, Shandong

Reduces heat and inflammation, disperses blood stagnation, stops bleeding, stops pain. Contains calcium mineral-salts which neutralize excessive stomach acid. Use for gastric or duodenal ulcers with bleeding or pain. Also useful for acute and chronic gastritis, abdominal bloating with pain, and flatulence due to heat and stagnation.

Bottles of 120 tablets. Take 4-6 tablets, 3 x day, before meals.

Cuttlefish Bone	40.%	Honey Binder	30
Corydalis Rhizome	30		

99 ZHI WAN
Zhi Wan
"Hemorrhoid Pills"
Min-Kang Drug Manufactory; Yichang, Hubei

Dispels blood stagnation, sedates inflammation, stops pain, stops bleeding, promotes tissue growth. Use for hemorrhoids, itching or pain in the anus, blood in the stool, and toxic intestine.

Bottles of 100 pills. Take 6 pills, 2-3 x day.

Main ingredients:

Hedgehog Skin	18.8%	Angelica Dang Gui	2.8
Lonicera Flower	18.8	Frankincense Resin	2.8
Sophora Flower	18.8	Anteater Scales	1.5
Areca Seed	4.7	Myrrh Resin	1.5
Carthamus Flower	3.7	Others	26.6

ALSO APPLICABLE for blood stagnation:

114   TIEH TA YAO GIN = traumatic injury

Promotes blood and *qi* circulation in *luo* channels for aches in joints and muscles:
82   XIAO HUO LUO DAN
77   TA HUO LO TAN

Menstrual cramps due to liver *qi* stagnation:
123   HSIAO YAO WAN
148   BUTIAO PILLS
153, 161, 162   PAI FENG WAN - WHITE PHOENIX PILLS

GROUP 5-B
PILLS FOR HEART CONGESTION, ANGINA AND STROKE

100 DAN SHEN TABLET CO.
Fu Fang Dan Shen Pian
"Medicinal Compound [with] Salvia Root Tablet"
Shanghai Chinese Medicine Works; Shanghai

A formula for dispersing pain in the heart and blood vessels due to blood stagnation. Treats angina pectoris with pain radiating down the left arm, heart palpitations, and chest pains. Reduces blood cholesterol and lipids.

Bottles of 50 pills. Take 3 pills, 3 x day.

Salvia Root	75.%
Borneol Crystal	25.

101 KUAN HSIN SU HO WAN STYRAX PILLS FOR CORONARY HEART DISEASE
Guan Xin Su He Wan
"Cardiovascular Styrax Pills"
Shanghai Chinese Medicine Works; Shanghai

Invigorates blood, removes blood stagnation, resolves phlegm-damp, sedates internal wind, open channels, stops pain. A recent formula for the treatment of blood stagnation in the heart and blood vessels (arteriosclerosis), leading to angina, numbness in the arms, and chronic heart disease. Useful for prevention, as well as following, acute myocardial infarctions.

Bottles of 30 pills. Take 1 pill, 3 x day.

Prohibited during pregnancy.

Santalum Wood	31.0%	Myrrh Resin	15.5
Aristolochia Root	30.6	Styrax Resin	7.4
Borneol Crystal	15.0		

Also available as GUAN XIN SU HO CAPSULES, Tianjin Drug Manufactory; Tianjin (Product #102).

Bottles of 40 capsules. Take 2 capsules, 2-3 x day.

103 MAODUNGCHING CAPSULES
Mao Dong Qing
"Ilex Root"
Kwangchow Pharmaceutical Corporation; Guangzhou, Guangdong

A single herb remedy for blood stagnation in the heart and blood vessels causing angina pain, respiratory distress, numbness in the limbs and poor blood circulation. Use as a treatment and preventative in heart disease, including atherosclerosis, stroke, and embolism.

Bottles of 30 capsules. Take 3 capsules, 3 x day. Use for courses of seven days at a time, with a rest period of three days.

| Ilex Root Extract | 100.% (500 mg.) |

104 REN SHEN ZAI ZAO WAN

Ren Shen Zai Zao Wan
"Ginseng Restorative Pills"
Shanghai Chinese Medicine Works; Shanghai

Invigorates blood and *qi*, breaks up stagnation, relieves internal wind, tonifies blood, *yin* and *qi*. Primarily used to address symptoms related to stroke, including hemiplegia, speech disturbances, contractive or flaccid muscle tone in the extremities. Also valuable in chronic wind-damp rheumatism with stagnation of *qi* in the channels, causing difficulty in movement with painful joints, or numbness and tingling of limbs. Useful in Bell's Palsy (wind induced facial paralysis).

Boxes of 10 wax eggs, each containing a large tarry pill. Take 1-2 per day. Swallow whole, or cut into smaller pieces and swallow. Can also be crushed and dissolved in hot water to drink, or chewed.

Prohibited during pregnancy.

Main ingredients:

Ginseng Root	Coptis Rhizome
Cinnamon Bark	Mantis Egg-case
Angelica Dang Gui	Tortoise Plastron
Ligusticum Rhizome	Myrrh Resin
Rehmannia Root	Frankincense Resin
Gastrodia Rhizome	Dragon Blood Resin
Agkistrodon Pit Viper	Carthamus Flower
Succinum Resin	

Note: a product with the same Chinese characters is available as YAN SHEN JAI JAO WAN (#107). This product has a significantly different prescription, yet with similiar applications.

105 SU HE XIANG PILLS: STYRAX PILLS
Se He Xiang Wan
"Styrax and Musk Pills"

A classical formula to relieve blood stagnation in the heart and blood vessels, and open heart orifices closed due to cold and phlegm. Symptoms include coma with cold hands and feet, heart pain radiating down the left arm (angina), and poor circulation due to clogging in the arteries. Also useful for stuttering due to wind-phlegm in the *luo* channels. May help to reduce blood cholesterol and lipids.

Prohibited during pregnancy.

This product lists Rhinoceros Horn, a prohibited substance in North America. See NOTE 2 at head of chapter.

Caution: Cinnabar, a natural substance, contains mercury. Caution is advised for use over prolonged periods. Limit use to three weeks.

Main ingredients:

Styrax Resin
Musk Gland
Atractylodes Rhizome
Rhinoceros Horn
Cinnabar Mineral
Aquilaria Wood
Frankincene Resin

Piper Seed
Benzoin Resin
Saussaurea Root
Cyperus Rhizome
Santalum Wood
Caryophyllum Flower

106 TSAI TSAO WAN
Zai Zao Wan
"Restorative Pills"
Tientsin Drug Manufactory; Tianjin

Removes blood stagnation, invigorates blood and *qi*, relieves wind-damp, sedates liver wind, opens heart orifices, and clears phlegm-damp in the channels. A variation of the formula REN SHEN ZAI ZAO WAN (#104), used for a variety of complaints due to obstruction of the channels, including paralysis due to internal wind (stroke) or external wind (Bell's Palsy); aches and pains due to trauma or wind-damp rheumatism; numbness in limbs due to poor blood circulation; and unclear muttering due to phlegm-damp in the channels.

Take 10 pills, once daily.

Prohibited during pregnancy.

Note: This product lists Rhinoceros Horn and Tiger Bone, both prohibited substances in North America. See NOTE 2 at the head of the chapter.

Aquilaria Wood	7.5%	Dragon Blood Resin	4.5
Tiger Bone	7.2	Gastrodia Rhizome	4.4
Ginseng Root	6.6	Carthamus Flower	4.3
Myrrh Resin	6.5	Agkistrodon Pit Viper	4.2
Musk Gland	6.1	Rehmannia Root	4.0
Angelica Dang Gui	5.5	Pogostemon Herb	3.7
Ox Gallstone	5.3	Cardamon Fruit	3.6
Rhinoceros Horn	4.8	Siler Root	3.5
Astragalus Root	4.5	Ligusticum Rhizome	2.8
Cinnamon Bark	4.5		

107 YAN SHEN JAI JAO WAN
Ren Shen Zai Zao Wan
"Ginseng Restorative Pills'
United Pharmaceutical Manufactory; Foshan, Guangdong

Dispels internal wind and wind-damp, breaks up blood stagnation, clears the channels, invigorates blood and *qi*, dissolves phlegm. Same Chinese name as REN SHEN ZAI ZAO WAN (#104) with similiar applications yet significantly different prescription. Use to open up congested *luo* channels that have been blocked by wind, blood or phlegm. Indications include stroke symptoms, such as hemiplegia, spastic paralysis, facial distortion, dysphasia (difficulty speaking), and difficulty in moving limbs. Excellent for stroke symptoms if administered immediately following the stroke. Less effective after the onset of flaccid paralysis. Also useful in wind induced facial paralysis.

Prohibited during pregnancy.

Boxes of 10 wax eggs, each containing a large tarry pill. Take 1-2 per day. Swallow whole, or cut into smaller pieces and swallow. Can also be crushed and dissolved in hot water to drink, or chewed as is.

Note: This product lists Rhinoceros Horn and Tiger Bone, both prohibited substances in North America.

See NOTE 2 at the head of the chapter.

Anteater Scales	75.3%	Tiger Bone	3.1
Agkistrodon Viper	5.9	Gastrodia Rhizome	3.1
Scorpion	3.8	Rhinoceros Horn	1.6
Ginseng Root	3.1	Ox Gallstone	.9
Succinum Resin	3.1		

ALSO APPLICABLE for heart congestion:

117 BOJENMI CHINESE TEA
222 NIU HUANG CHIANG YA WAN
264 CIR-Q

GROUP 5-C
PATENTS FOR EXTERNAL APPLICATION

108 CHING WAN HUNG
Jing *Wan Hong*
"Beijing Absolute Red"
Tientsin Drug Manufactory; Tianjin

Promotes circulation of blood and *qi*, cools heat, stops pain, promotes tissue growth. Topical ointment for 1st, 2nd, and 3rd degree burns and scalds, with reportedly excellent results. Will reduce pain, swelling and blistering. Can be used topically for hemorrhoids, bedsores, acne, as well as sunburn and heat rashes.

In small tubes or larger plastic cups. Apply topically, cover with bandage. Clean and change daily. This product can discolor clothes.

Ingredients unlisted.

109 FEL URSI HEMORRHOIDS OINTMENT
Xiong Dan Zhi Chuang Gao
"Bear Gallbladder Hemorrhoid Ointment"
Chung Lien Drug Works; Wuchang, Hubei

Invigorates blood circulation, reduces inflammation, stops pain. Use topically for hemorrhoids. Will reduce swelling and stop pain and irritation.

Tubes of 5 g. Apply topically, 1-2 x day. Do not take internally.

Calamina Mineral	13.8%	Borneol Crystal	1.6
Bear Gallbladder	2.7	Musk Gland	.2
Mother-of-Pearl Shell	2.7	Vaseline Jelly	79.0

110 MAGIC PLASTER
(NOT TO BE EXCHANGED FOR GOLD)
Shen Xian Jin Bu Huan Gao
"Miraculous Spirit Gold Not Exchanged Plaster"
Beijing Tung Jen Tang; Beijing

Invigorates blood and *qi*, opens the *luo* channels, and relieves pain due to blood stagnation or wind-damp. A topical plaster used for contused wounds, muscle strain or sprain, aching joints, numbness or weakness in the muscle. Also useful in hernia, and profuse leukorrhea.

A single cloth with the medicine hardened in the center. Steam until the resin melts and spreads along the fabric, and apply to affected area. Take care that the plaster is not so hot as to inflict a burn. Can be resteamed and used a second time.

Prohibited to lower abdomen or lower back during pregnancy.

Active ingredients:

Gastrodia Rhizome	10.%	Myrrh Resin	6
Aconite Root, prep.	10	Rhubarb Rhizome	7
Mantis Egg-case	10	Ephedra Stem	4
Dragon Blood Resin	8	Dipsacus Root	4
Notopterygium Rhizome	6	Other agents	35

111 PLASTER FOR BRUISE AND ANALGESIC
Die Da Zhi Tong Gao
"Traumatic Injury Stop Pain Plaster"
United Pharmaceutical Manufactory; Guangzhou, Guangdong

Medicated plaster-adhesive applied externally to promote circulation of blood, stimulate healing and stop pain. Use for acute bruises, sprains, fractures, and traumatic swelling. Also efficacious in muscle strain, neuralgia, and musculo-skeletal pain due to wind (rheumatism).

Do not apply to lower abdomen during pregnancy.

Boxes of 10 pieces (10 x 28 cm). Also available in a can with a single extended length of 10 x 200 cm. Cut to size and apply to clean, dry (shaven) skin; leave on for 24 hours.

Menthol Crystal	20.0%	Rhubarb Rhizome	8.3
Mylabris Beetle	10.4	Taraxacum Plant	8.3
Dragon Blood Resin	10.4	Acacia Plant-resin	6.2
Dragon Tooth	10.4	Myrrh Resin	6.2
Carthamus Flower	9.2	Drynaria Rhizome	4.2
Wintergreen Oil	8.3	Dipsacus Root	4.2

112 PO SUM ON MEDICATED OIL
Bao Xin An You
"Maintain Peaceful Heart Oil"
Po Sum On Medicine Factory No. 162; Hong Kong

Liniment for aches and pains in joints due to wind-cold or stagnation of blood, including rheumatic joint pain, and chronic and acute traumatic injury. Apply often with therapeutic Tui Na massage, or apply to gauze and bandage. Also good topically (and orally) for toothache and sore throat. For chest cough, massage externally.

Bottles of 30 ml or 100 ml. Apply liberally and often. Will stain clothes, but can be removed with rubbing alcohol. For sore throat, suck on a few drops from finger.

Caution: Do not get into eyes. Wash hands thoroughly after use. Volatile; keep away from flame. Do not rub into open wounds.

Mentha Oil	57.3%	Scutellaria Root	.6
Camellia Oil	39.4	Cinnamon Oil	.3
Dragon Blood Resin	2.1	Licorice Root	.3
Alcohol			

113 SHANG SHI BAO ZHEN GAO

Shang Shi Bao Zhen Gao
"Injury [and] Damp Treasure Precious Ointment"
Shanghai Chinese Medicine Works; Shanghai

Topical plaster-adhesive to promote *qi* and blood, reduce swelling, and stop pain. Apply for acute and chronic trauma including contusions and sprains. Also for wind-damp rheumatic pain and neuralgia of joints and lower back.

Prohibited to abdominal area during pregnancy.

See NOTE 2 at head of chapter.

Boxes of 5 packets, 10 sheets. Apply to clean, dry, shaven skin. Will last 3-5 days, or until bath.

Asarum Plant Extract	53.2%	Camphor Crystal	7.1
Styrax Resin	17.7	Menthol Crystal	7.1
Wintergreen Oil	14.2	Musk Gland	.6

114 TIEH TA YAO GIN
Die Da Yao Jing
"Traumatic Injury Medicine-Essence"
United Pharmaceutical Manufactory; Foshan, Guangdong

Dispels blood and fluid stagnation, invigorates *qi* and blood, relaxes tendons and muscles, promotes healing, stops pain. Use for a wide variety of traumatic injury, including fracture, sprain, tears to ligaments and muscles, and bruising. Very effective for injuries due to sports and martial arts. Can also be taken internally to speed healing.

Bottles in various sizes, 10 ml, 30 ml, 100 ml. External application: Injuries should be clean and dry before applying the lotion. Apply 3-4 times day, cover if desired. Will stain clothes, but can be removed with rubbing alcohol. Internal: Take 1-3 tsps with water, 2 x day.

Caution: Do not get into eyes. Wash hands thoroughly after use.

Angelica Dang Gui 16.5%	Myrrh Resin	12.5
Dragon Blood Resin 15.5	Pseudoginseng Root	12.5
Carthamus Flower 13.5	Aloe Resin	12.5
Frankincense Resin 12.5	Catechu Resin	4.5

115 YUN XIANG JING

Yun Xiang Jing
"Yunnan Aromatic Essence"
Yulin Drug Manufactory; Guangxi

Externally as a liniment for pain and stiffness from either traumatic injury or wind-damp rheumatism. Can be taken orally for sore throat due to wind-heat invasion, also, for headache, nausea due to motion sickness, abdominal pain due to indigestion.

Caution: Do not get into eyes. Wash hands thoroughly after use.

Caution: volatile; keep away from flame. Will stain clothes, but can be removed with rubbing alcohol.

Internally, place a few drops on the tongue.

Entada Root	26.%	Tinospora Root	13
Piper Shan Ju	21	Asarum Plant	10
Cinnamon Twig	13	Menthol Crystal	3
Sparganium Rhizome	14	Alcohol	

116 ZHENG GU SHUI

Zheng Gu Shui
"Rectify Bone Liquid"
Yulin Drug Manufactory, Kwangsi

Dispels blood and fluid stagnation, invigorates *qi* and blood, relaxes tendons and muscles, promotes healing, stops pain. Use for a wide variety of traumatic injury, including fracture, sprain, tears to ligaments and muscles, and bruising. Effective for injuries due to sports and martial arts. Not appropriate for vigorous Tui Na massage.

Bottles of 30 cc or 100 cc. Apply often with light massage, or apply to gauze and bandage. Will stain clothes, but can be removed with rubbing alcohol.

Caution: Do not get into eyes. Wash hands thoroughly after use.

Caution: volatile; keep away from flame. Do not rub into open wounds.

Pseudoginseng Root	25.%	Gentiana Qin Jiao	12
Croton Seed	18	Inula Flower	12
Cinnamon Bark	13	Menthol Crystal	3
Angelica Root	13	Camphor Crystal	2
Alcohol			

ALSO APPLICABLE for external use in blood stagnation:

83   ANTI-RHEUMATIC PLASTER
84   KOU PI PLASTER
86   SHANG SHI ZHI TONG GAO
92   HSIUNG TAN TIEH TA WAN
95   TIENCHI POWDER RAW
97   YUNNAN PAIYAO

GROUP 6

PILLS FOR REGULATING DIGESTION AND STAGNATION OF QI

NOTE: these formulas promote digestion and relieve digestive problems. They can be taken 30 minutes prior to meals.

117 BOJENMI CHINESE TEA (EGRET RIVER BRAND)

Bao Jian Mei Jian Fei Cha
"Maintain Vigorous and Graceful, Reduce Fat Tea"
China National Native Produce & Animal By-Products,
Import and Export Corporation; Amoy, Fujian

Reduces fats, dispels damp and phlegm, benefits stomach and spleen, invigorates *qi*, promotes urination. This is a weight-reducing herbal tea that tonifies spleen *qi* to maximize nutrient absorption, and dispels fats, phlegm, and excess water. It also removes atherosclerotic plaque in the blood vessels, reducing high blood pressure and lessening the chances for heart disease and stroke.

Cans of 100 g. of tea, or as teabags. Make the same as ordinary tea, taking 1-3 cups daily. If using teabags, each can produce 2-3 cups of tea.

Tea Leaf	50.0%	Citrus Peel	3.5
Crataegus Fruit	9.0	Fermented Leaven	3.5
Poria Fungus	4.0	Cassia Seed	3.0
Phaseolus Seed	4.0	Pharbitis Seed	3.0
Pogostemon Herb	4.0	Alisma Rhizome	2.5
Hordeum Sprout	3.5	Raphanus Seed	2.0

GROUP 6

PILLS FOR REGULATING
DIGESTION AND STAGNATION OF QI

118 CARMICHAELI TEA PILLS
Fu Zi Li Zhong Wan
"Aconite Restore Center Pills"
Lanzhou Fo Ci Pharmaceutical Factory; Lanzhou, Gansu

The classical formula to remove acute cold and cold-damp in the middle burner, tonify spleen and kidney *yang*, and nourish spleen *qi*. Symptoms include poor digestion, abdominal fullness, cold diarrhea, nausea or vomiting, and cold hands or feet.

Bottles of 200 pills. Take 8-12, 3 x day.

Codonopsis Root	23.1%	Licorice Root	23.1
Ginger Rhizome	23.1	Aconite Root	7.7

Also available as ACONITUM COMPOUND PILLS from the same factory.

119 CHI CHUNG SHUI
Ji Zhong Shui
"Benefit Many [Problems] Liquid"
United Pharmaceutical Manufactory; Guangzhou, Guangdong

Harmonizes the center, benefits stomach and spleen, dispels pathogenic cold and heat, neutralizes toxins. This is an emergency remedy recommended for travelers to treat a variety of acute stomach problems characterized by cramping, nausea, vomiting, or diarrhea.

Boxes of 12 vials. Take 1/2 - 1 vial for a one time only dose. Children: 1/4 - 1/2 bottle.

Camphor Crystal	25. g.	Fennel Seed	10
Ginger Rhizome	25	Chili Fruit	5
Rhubarb Rhizome	20	Peppermint	25. cc
Cinnamon Bark	10	Alcohol	

Also available as LIU SHEN SHUI from the same manufacturer.

120 CHINA PO CHI PILL
Zhong Guo Bao Ji Wan
"China Protect [and] Benefit Pill"
Plum Flower Brand

Dispels wind, disperses damp, resolves phlegm, regulates the spleen and stomach. Use for a wide variety of digestive complaints maked by sudden onset of nausea, vomiting, diarrhea or stomach cramps, accompanied by dizziness and feelings of abdominal distension. Use for stomach flu, food stagnation, and problems with digestion while traveling. Suitable for children.

Bottles of 100 pills. Take 3-6 pills, 2-3 x day.

Poria Fungus	15.5%	Trichosanthes Root	5.5
Coix Seed	9.0	Oryza Sprout	5.5
Atractylodes Rhizome	7.2	Gastrodia Rhizome	3.6
Pueraria Root	7.2	Chrysanthemum Flower	3.7
Saussurea Root	7.2	Citrus Xiang Yuan	3.6
Magnolia Bark	7.2	Mentha Leaf	3.2
Pogostemon Leaf	7.2	Other	7.2
Angelica Root	7.2		

121 FU TZU LI CHUNG WAN
Fu Zi Li Zhong Wan
"Aconite Restore Center Pills"
United Pharmaceutical Manufactory; Guangzhou, Guangdong

Removes acute cold and cold-damp in the middle burner, tonifies spleen and kidney *yang*, and nourishes spleen *qi*. Symptoms include poor digestion, abdominal fullness, cold diarrhea, nausea or vomiting, and cold hands or feet. This is the same prescription, with slightly different percentages as CARMICHAELI TEA (#118).

Boxes of 10 large pills. Crack wax-egg case, chew or swallow whole, or divide into smaller pieces. Take 1 per day for 3 days.

Also available in bottles of 100 pills. Take 8 pills, 3 x day.

Codonopsis Root	21.7%	Licorice Root	21.7
Ginger Rhizome	21.7	Aconite Root	13.2
Atractylodes Rhizome	21.7		

122 GINSENG STOMACHIC PILLS
Ren Shen Jian Pi Wan
"Ginseng Strengthen Spleen Pill"
Lanchow Chinese Medicine Works; Lanzhou, Gansu

Tonifies spleen and stomach, regulates *qi*, resolves stomach phlegm, promotes digestion. Use for chronically poor digestion with abdominal bloating and pain, erratic or pasty stools. Also useful for inability to gain or maintain weight

200 pills per bottle. Take 6 pills, 3 x day.

Aurantium Fruit	24.%	Hordeum Sprout	16
Ginseng Root	16	Citrus Peel	16
Atractylodes Rhizome	16	Crataegus Fruit	12

Also available as STOMACHIC PILLS, Lanzhou Fo Ci Pharmaceutical Factory; Lanzhou, Gansu.

123 HSIAO YAO WAN - BUPLEURUM SEDATIVE PILLS
Xiao Yao Wan
"Free and Relaxed Pills"
Lanchow Fo Ci Pharmaceutical Factory; Lanzhou, Gansu

Nourishes liver blood and *yin*, invigorates congested liver ·*qi*, strengthens spleen, harmonizes liver with stomach-spleen. This is a basic formula for stagnation of liver*qi* due to deficiency of liver blood. Symptoms are diverse and include digestive dysfunction (abdominal bloating and fullness, hiccups, poor appetite), menstrual and pre-menstrual disorders (cramps, irregular periods, infertility, breast distension, depression, irritability), as well as vertigo, headache, fatigue, blurred vision or red, painful eyes. Also useful in food allergies, chronic hayfever, and hypoglycemia.

[If stagnation of liver *qi* is due to deficiency of *qi*, combine· with CENTRAL QI PILLS (#140). If accompanied by liver heat, combine with JI GU CAO PILL (#57) or LUNG TAN XIE GAN PILL (#42). If blood deficiency is obvious, nourish the blood.]

Bottles of 200 pills. Take 8 pills, 3 x day.

Buplerum Root	14.3%	Atractylodes Rhizome	14.3
Paeonia Root	14.3	Ginger Rhizome	14.3
Angelica Dang Gui	14.3	Licorice Root	11.3
Poria Fungus	14.3	Mentha Leaf	2.9

124 HSIANG SHA YANG WEI PIEN
Xiang Sha Yang Wei Pian
"Saussurea, Amomum Nourish Stomach Pills"
Tientsin Drug Manufactory; Tianjin

Use in deficiency of stomach or spleen *qi*, with cold and phlegm-damp in the middle burner. This formula treats accumulation of phlegm-damp or food stagnation in the stomach, with symptoms of nausea, vomiting, flatulence, poor digestion, abdominal pain following meals, pasty or loose stools, and loss of appetite. Appropriate for morning sickness. Useful for deficiency conditions; not indicated for heat.

[This is the same Chinese name as XIANG SHA YANG WEI WAN (#138), but with a different prescription.]

20 or 60 tablets per bottle. Take 4 tablets, 3 x day.

Codonopsis Root	24.2%	Fermented Leaven	8.5
Atractylodes Rhizome	21.3	Saussurea Root	5.7
Citrus Peel	14.2	Amomum Fruit	5.7
Hordeum Sprout	8.5	Licorice Root	3.4

125 HUO HSIANG CHENG CHI PIEN (LANZHOU)

Huo Xiang Zheng Qi Pian
"Pogostemon Normalize Qi Pills"
Lanzhou Fo Ci Pharmaceutical Factory; Lanzhou, Gansu

Breaks up congestion and stagnation of *qi* at the center, dispels wind-damp and wind, resolves spleen damp, tonifies spleen *qi*. A valuable medicine for poor digestion due to deficiency of spleen with phlegm-damp or food accumulation, causing nausea, vertigo, headache, pasty or loose stools, and flatulence. Excellent for wind-damp invasion of the stomach (summer-damp-heat stomach flu). Valuable in motion-sickness and morning sickness. Traditionally used in cholera.

Bottles of 100 sugar-coated pills. Take 4-8 pills, 2 x day.

Pogostemon Herb	11.%	Platycodon Root	7
Perilla Leaf	11	Atractylodes Rhizome	7
Angelica Root	11	Magnolia Bark	7
Poria Fungus	11	Citrus Peel	7
Areca Husk	11	Other	17

Also available as LOPHANTHUS ANTIFEBRILE PILLS from the same manufacturer.

126 HUO HSIANG CHENG CHI PIEN (BEIJING)

Huo Xiang Zheng Qi Pian
"Pogostemon Normalize Qi Pills"
Beijing Tung Jen Tang, Beijing:

The same name as product #125, with a slightly different prescription. Use for the same applications.

Glass vials of 8 tablets, uncoated. Take 4-8 pills, 2 x day.

Main ingredients:

Pogostemon Herb	20.%	Perilla Leaf	5
Platycodon Root	10	Angelica Root	5
Atractylodes Rhizome	10	Poria Fungus	5
Pinellia Rhizome	10	Other	25
Licorice Root	10		

127 JENSHEN CHIEN PI WAN
Ren Shen Jian Pi Wan
"Ginseng Strengthen Spleen Pill"
Tientsin Drug Manufactory; Tianjin

The same name in Chinese as GINSENG STOMACHIC PILLS (#122), but with a different prescription. Tonifies spleen *qi*, resolves spleen-damp, opens obstructed *qi* at the center. Indicated in digestive disorders that include abdominal distension and fullness after eating, belching or passing gas, erratic or pasty stools, and poor appetite.

Bottles of 120 pills. Take 10 pills once a day.

Ginseng Root	15.%	Atractylodes Rhizome	10
Saussurea Root	10	Angelica Dang Gui	10
Crataegus Fruit	10	Coix Seed	5
Aurantium Fruit	10	Amomum Fruit	5

128 LIU JUN ZI TABLETS
Liu Jun Zi Pian
"Six Gentlemen Tablet"
Sing-kyn Drug House; Guangzhou, Guangdong

Classical foundation formula to tonify spleen *qi*, and remove damp and phlegm. For poor digestion due to phlegm-damp, with poor appetite, loose stools or diarrhea, indigestion, acid regurgitation, and nausea. Also useful for dizziness or mental disorders due to stomach phlegm accumulation.

Bottles of 96 tablets. Take 8 tablets, 3 x day.

Codonopsis Root	32.7%	Atractylodes Rhizome	16.6
Poria Fungus	16.6	Citrus Peel	8.3
Pinellia Rhizome	16.6	Licorice Root	8.3

129 MU XIANG SHUN QI WAN
APLOTAXIS CARMINATIVE PILLS
Mu Xiang Shun Qi Wan
"Saussurea Smoothe Qi Pills"
Lanchow Chinese Medicine Works; Lanzhou, Gansu

Disperses stagnant *qi* in liver, purges gallbladder heat, nourishes liver blood, tonifies spleen, disperses phlegm-damp. Use for stagnation of *qi* and food due to liver congestion, with retention of phlegm-damp in the stomach. Also useful for food stagnation due to cold food or drink, or to improper eating habits such as sleeping after a meal. Symptoms include erratic stools, belching, abdominal distension, and poor digestion.

Bottle of 200 pills. Take 8 pills, 2 x day.

Angelica Dang Gui	13.6%	Poria Fungus	5.4
Magnolia Bark	10.5	Pinellia Rhizome	5.4
Alpinia Fruit	8.4	Alisma Root	5.4
Saussurea Root	8.1	Ginger Rhizome	5.4
Amomum Fruit	8.1	Citrus Peel	5.4
Atractylodes Rhizome	8.1	Cimicifuga Rhizome	2.7
Aurantium Fruit	5.4	Bupleurum Root	2.7
Evodia Fruit	5.4		

130 PILL CURING
Kang Ning Wan
"Healthy Quiet Pill"
United Pharmaceutical Company; Guangzhou, Guangdong

Disperses wind and damp, resolves spleen damp, regulates stomach, resolves phlegm. Primarily for digestive distubances due to wind invasion of stomach channel (stomach flu). Also useful for food poisoning, as well as a variety of digestive disorders due to deficiency of spleen and stomach *qi*, or stagnation of stomach *qi*. Symptoms include sudden and violent cramping, headache, vomiting, abdominal bloating with pain, and difficulty in passing stools, or diarrhea. Useful for general nausea, motion-sickness, or morning sickness. Safe in pregnancy, and for children.

Boxes of 10 bottles or packets. Take 1-2 bottles at a time.

Coix Seed	9.0 %	Trichosanthes Root	5.5
Magnolia Bark	7.2	Oryza Sprout	5.5
Atractylodes Rhizome	7.2	Poria Fungus	5.5
Pogostemon Herb	7.2	Gastrodia Rhizome	3.6
Pueraria Root	7.2	Chrysanthemum Flower	3.2
Angelica Root	7.2	Mentha Herb	3.2
Saussurea Root	7.2	Citrus Gan Pi	2.6
Fermented Leaven	7.2	Others	11.5

131 REN DAN (YANG CHENG BRAND)
Ren Dan
"People's Powder"
United Pharmaceutical Manufactory; Guangzhou, Guangdong

Harmonizes the center, benefits spleen and stomach, relieves food stagnation, invigorates digestion, stops pain. Use for acute and emergency stomach disorders including abdominal bloating with pain, headache, nausea or vomiting, and motionsickness. Usually one or two doses are given.

Boxes of 12 plastic dispensers, each with 60 silver pellets. Take 30-60 pellets per dose. Reduce for children.

Licorice Root	45.%	Caryophyllum Flower	2
Platycodon Root	40	Camphor Crystal	2
Menthol Crystal	4	Borenol Crystal	2
Catechu Resin	4		

132 SHEN CHU CHA
Shen Chu Cha
"Fermented Leaven Tea"
China National Tea and Native Produce Import and Export Corporation; Guangdong Branch

Harmonizes stomach, dispels wind and damp, resolves phlegm, sedates stomach heat. Classical fermented product made of 14 herbs in a base of flour and bran, and molded into small blocks. Use for digestive problems due to stagnation of *qi* and food, with accumulation of phlegm. Symptoms include abdominal fullness or bloating, belching, loose stools or constipation. Helpful in facilitating nutritional absorption.

Take one package, 1-2 x day. Boil with one cup of water to make tea.

Triticum Flour	38.0 %	Magnolia Bark	4.7
Poria Fungus	5.0	Amomum Fruit	4.7
Coptis Rhizome	5.0	Scutellaria Root	4.7
Dioscorea Rhizome	5.0	Aurantium Fruit	4.7
Artemesia Qing Hao	4.7	Notopterygium Rhizome	4.7
Angelica Du Huo	4.7	Chaenomeles Fruit	4.7
Platycodon Root	4.7	Mosla Leaf	4.7

133 SHEN LING BAIZHU PIAN
Shen Ling Bai Zhu Pian
"Codonopsis, Poria, Atractylodes Formula"
Sian Chinese Drug Pharmaceutical Works; Xian, Shaanxi

Classical formula for deficiency and/or stagnation of stomach or spleen *qi*, with damp. Symptoms include belching, bloating, poor digestion, abdominal fullness, indigestion, erratic or loose stools. Excellent for children, and during pregnancy for morning sickness. Useful for prolonged periods.

Bottles of 150 pills. Take 6-12 tablets, 3 x day. Children, 3 tablets, 3 x day.

Atractylodes Rhizome	15.%	Platycodon Root	7
Codonopsis Root	1	Amomum Fruit	7
Dioscorea Root	11	Citrus Peel	4
Poria Fungus	7	Others	38

134 SHU KAN WAN (CONDENSED)
Shu Gan Wan Nong Suo
"Soothe Liver Pill, Condensed"
Tientsin Drug Manufactory; Tianjin

Invigorates *qi*, breaks up stagnation, resolves damp, stops pain. Use to break up congestion of liver *qi* affecting stomach and spleen. The principal symptoms are abdominal gas, hiccups, belching, or flatulence. Other symptoms include abdominal pain, poor digestion, loose or erratic stools, poor appetite, and cold limbs with facial flush. Useful in liver-spleen disharmonies causing symptoms common to hypoglycemia. This is a smaller formula with similiar applications as #135.

Contraindicated during pregnancy.

Bottles of 120 pills. Take 8 pills, 3 x day.

Paeonia Root	18.%	Citrus Peel	10
Amomum Fruit	15	Saussurea Root	10
Cardamon Fruit	15	Magnolia Bark	10
Corydalis Rhizome	12	Other	10

135 SHU KAN WAN:
HEPATICO-TONIC PILLS
Shu Gan Wan
"Soothe Liver Pill"
Lanchow Chinese Medicine Works; Lanzhou

This product has the same applications as SHU KAN WAN (CONDENSED), #134. This prescription is more elaborate, somewhat stronger, and more commonly used. Invigorates *qi*, breaks up stagnation, resolves damp, stops pain. Use to break up congestion of liver *qi* affecting stomach and spleen. The principal symptoms are abdominal gas, hiccups, belching, or flatulence. Other symptoms include abdominal pain, poor digestion, loose or erratic stools, poor appetite, and cold limbs with facial flush. Useful in liver-spleen disharmonies causing symptoms common to hypoglycemia.

Contraindicated during pregnancy.

Bottles of 100 pills. Take 8 pills, 3 x day.

Cyperus Rhizome	10.6%	Inula Flower	3.5
Paeonia Root	10.6	Citrus Xiang Yuan	3.5
Aurantium Fruit	7.1	Licorice Root	3.4
Amomum Fruit	7.1	Curcuma Root	2.6
Citrus Qing Pi	7.1	Aquilaria Wood	2.2
Corydalis Rhizome	7.1	Cardamon Fruit	2.6
Bupleurum Root	7.1	Santalum Wood	1.8
Citrus Peel	7.1	Other	9.5
Moutan Root-bark	7.1		

136 SIX GENTLEMEN TEA PILL
Xiang Sha Liu Jun Wan
"Saussurea, Amomum Six Gentlemen Pill"
Lanchow Chinese Medicine Works; Lanzhou, Gansu

Based on the classical formula **Xiang Sha Liu Jun Zi Tang**, this patent treats poor digestion due to deficiency of spleen *qi*, cold in the center, retention of phlegm-damp, retention of food, and stagnation of stomach *qi*. Use for poor appetite, loose stools or diarrhea, indigestion, nausea, and morning sickness. Traditionally used to build physical stamina in children.

Bottles of 100 pills. Take 8 pills, 2 x day.

Codonopsis Root	17.2 %	Citrus Peel	8.6
Pinellia Rhizome	17.2	Licorice Root	8.6
Atractylodes Rhizome	17.2	Amomum Fruit	6.9
Poria Fungus	17.2	Saussurea Root	6.9

Also available from the same manufacturer as APLOTAXIS-AMOMUM PILLS.

137 TABELLAE PING-WEI
Ping Wei Pian
"Peaceful Stomach Tablets"
Sing-kyn Drug House; Guangzhou, Guangdong

Harmonizes the center, resolves spleen damp, benefits stomach and spleen, invigorates and regulates *qi* at the center. A classical formula to soothe gastric imbalance, dyspepsia, abdominal cramping or bloating, poor appetite, diarrhea, nausea, and pain. This is a simple formula for maintaining digestive function.

Bottles of 48 tablets. Take 4 tablets, 2 x day.

Atractylodes Rhizome	33.3%	Citrus Peel	25.0
Magnolia Bark	25.0	Licorice Root	16.7

138 XIÀNG SHA YANG WEI WAN
Xiang Sha Yang Wei Wan
"Saussurea, Amomum Nourish Stomach Pill"
Lanzhou Fo Ci Pharmaceutical Factory; Lanzhou, Gansu

Tonifies spleen *qi*, resolves spleen damp, dissipates phlegm-damp, invigorates *qi* at the center. Use for poor digestion with abdominal bloating or gurgling, erratic or pasty stools, food stagnation leading to headache, nausea, and flatulence. Same Chinese name as HSIANG SHA YANG WEI WAN (#124), with a different prescription.

Bottles of 100 pills. Take 8 pills, 3 x day.

Citrus Peel	10.9%	Cyperus Rhizome	7.6
Atractylodes Rhizome	10.9	Cardamon Fruit	7.6
Poria Fungus	10.9	Amomum Fruit	7.6
Pinellia Rhizome	10.9	Magnolia Bark	7.6
Saussurea Root	7.6	Aurantium Fruit	7.6
Pogostemon Herb	7.6	Licorice Root	3.2

139 ZISHENG STOMACHIC PILLS
Zi Sheng Wan
"Provide Life Pills"
Lanchow Chinese Medicine Works; Lanzhou, Gansu

Invigorates *qi* at the center, tonifies spleen *qi*, facilitates nutrient absorption, removes spleen damp, resolves congestion of liver *qi*, removes heat in the stomach caused by stagnation of energy, dispels wind attack into the stomach channel, resolves summer-heat invasions. A broad spectrum formula for a variety of digestive disturbances with the symptoms of flatulence, abdominal bloatedness, stomach pain, nausea, poor appetite, and malnutrition.

Bottles of 200 pills. Take 8 pills, 2 x day.

Codonopsis Root	11.4%	Hordeum Sprout	5.7
Atractylodes Rhizome	11.4	Poria Fungus	5.7
Coix Seed	11.4	Lotus Seed	3.8
Fermented Leaven	7.6	Platycodon Root	1.9
Citrus Gan Pi	7.6	Pogostemon Herb	1.9
Crataegus Fruit	7.6	Licorice Root	1.3
Euryale Seed	6.4	Cardamon Fruit	1.3
Dioscorea Rhizome	5.7	Coptis Rhizome	1.3
Dolichoris Seed	5.7		

ALSO APPLICABLE for regulating digestion:

165   BA WEI DI HUANG WAN = poor digestion due to deficiency
       of *yang*

Imbalance of spleen and stomach
   20   ERH CHEN WAN
  244   PROSPEROUS FARMER
  226   YELLOW OX - SPLEEN
  252   XIAO DAO
  253   WEN ZHONG
  272   STOMACH TABS

Congestion of liver *qi* affecting digestion:
  123   HSIAO YAO WAN
  140   CENTRAL QI PILLS
  230   GREEN TIGER
  246   RELAXED WANDERER
  248   TIAO HE
  260   JIE YU
  265   EASE 1

GROUP 7-A
PILLS AND EXTRACTS TO TONIFY QI

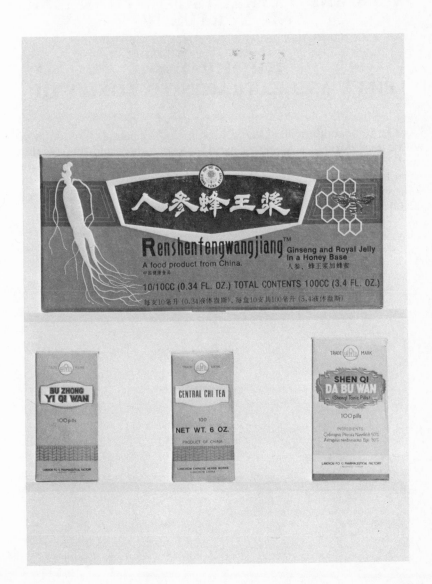

GROUP 7

PILLS AND EXTRACTS FOR TONIFYING AND NURTURING

GROUP 7-A
PILLS AND EXTRACTS TO TONIFY QI

NOTE: It is recommended that tonics, including patents that tonify *qi*, not be used during the stages of wind invasion (colds and flus), as they tend to drive wind deeper into the body. *Qi* tonics are by nature warming and slightly stagnating to energy. Caution is advised if the following symptoms develop: heat or dryness, oppressive feelings in the chest, or abdominal congestion and bloating.

140 CENTRAL QI PILLS
Bu Zhong Yi Qi Wan
"Tonify Center to Invigorate Qi Pills"
Lanzhou Fo Ci Pharmaceutical Factory; Lanzhou, Gansu

Classical formula to tonify spleen and stomach *qi*, invigorate *qi* in the liver, and raise *yang*. Treats poor digestion due to disharmony between the liver and spleen, with symptoms of abdominal bloating, pain, or gas, with erratic stools. Originally used to treat prolapse of organs due to deficiency of *qi* and *yang*, including rectum, uterus, colon, hemorrhoids, varicose veins and hernia. Useful in uterine bleeding, habitual miscarriage, and chronic diarrhea. Effective in treating hypoglycemia, especially when combined with JIAN PI SU (#144).

Bottles of 100 pills. Take 8 pills, 3 x day.

Astragalus Root	27.8%	Atractylodes Rhizome	8.3
Licorice Root	13.9	Citrus Peel	8.3
Angelica Dang Gui	8.3	Bupleurum Root	8.3
Cimicifuga Rhizome	8.3	Jujube Fruit	5.6
Codonopsis Root	8.3	Ginger Rhizome	2.8

Also available from the same manufacturer as BU ZHONG YI QI WAN. Also available as BU ZHONG YI QI WAN from Shanghai Pharmaceutical Manufactory, Shanghai. Bottles of 200 pills.

141 DEER TAIL EXTRACT

Lu Wei Ba Jing
"Deer Tail Dried Meat Extract"
Changchun Chinese Medicines and Drugs Manufactory;
Changchun, Jilin

A systemic tonic for *qi* and *yang*, treating deficiency caused by aging, illness or childbirth. Tonifies spleen *qi* to improve digestion and appetite, and tonifies kidney *qi* to nurture sexual function. Use in general fatigue, impotence, and certain cases of infertility.

Boxes of 10 glass vials, 10 cc each. Take 1-2 vials per day, alone or with water. Boxes are provided with glass-cutter, plastic safety cover, and straws.

Royal Jelly	250. mg
Deer Tail Extract	20. mg

142 EXTRACTUM ASTRAGALI

Bei Qi Jing
"Northern Astragalus Essence"
Changchun Chinese Medicines and Drugs Manufactory;
Changchun, Jilin

Nutritive tonic for spleen *qi*, *wei qi* and blood. Suitable for long-term use to regulate digestion, prevent illness, and help recovery from chronic illness and childbirth. Some benefit to strengthening immunity.

Boxes of 10 glass vials, 10 cc each. Take 1-2 vials per day, alone or with water. Boxes are provided with glass-cutter, plastic safety cover, and straws.

Astragalus Root Extract	50.%
Honey	50.

143 GINSENG ROYAL JELLY VIALS: RENSHENG FENG WANG JIANG
Ren Shen Feng Wang Jiang
"Ginseng, Royal-Jelly Syrup"
China National Import and Export Corp;
Harbin, Heilongjiang Branch

Nutritive tonic to promote spleen and lung *qi*, and aid in nutritional absorption. Promotes appetite and stimulates absorption of foods. Beneficial following illness, childbirth, or in older persons. Helpful in treatment of hypoglycemia.

Boxes of 10 glass vials, 10 cc each. Take 1-2 vials per day, alone or with water. Boxes are provided with glass-cutter, plastic safety cover, and straws.

Main ingredients:
Honey   Ginseng Root
Royal Jelly

Also available from China National Native Products, Hanzhou, with twist-off caps.

144 JIAN PI SU
Jian Pi Su
"Build Spleen Single-Ingredient"
Nei-Chiu Drug Manufactory

Tonifies spleen *qi*, strengthens stomach, builds blood. Concentrated extract of animal spleen, used for poor digestion, low appetite, abdominal bloating, loose or paty stools, and deficient blood. Can be combined with CENTRAL QI PILLS (#140) to treat hypoglycemia.

Bottles of 100 tablets. Take 4-6 tablets, 3 x day.

Main ingredient:
Spleen extract from animals   100%

145 PEKING ROYAL JELLY
Bei Jing Feng Wang Jing
"Beijing Queen Bee Essence"
Peking Dietetic Preparation Manufactory; Beijing

Tonifies *qi*, benefits digestion, nourishes blood and *yin*. Use as nutritional support as a general tonic, or following illness, surgery, trauma or childbirth.

Boxes of 10 glass vials, 10 cc each. Take 1-2 vials per day, alone or with water. Boxes are provided with glass-cutter, plastic safety cover, and straws. Also available with plastic tops.

Main ingredients:
Royal Jelly	Codonopsis Root
Schizandra Fruit	Lycium Fruit

146 SHEN QI DA BU WAN
Shen Qi Da Bu Wan
"Ginseng, Astragalus Great Tonifying Pill"
Lanzhou Fo Ci Pharmaceutical Manufactory; Lanzhou, Gansu

A general tonic for *qi*, blood, *ying* and *wei qi*. Useful for general debility, fatigue, poor digestion due to spleen and stomach deficiency, and blood deficiency. Will help strenghten immune response.

Bottles of 100 pills. Take 8 pills, 3 x day.

Codonopsis Root	50.%
Astragalus Root	50.

ALSO APPLICABLE as *qi* tonics:

Products listed in Group 7-E GENERAL TONICS all tonify *qi* in addition to other essential substances (blood, *yin* and *yang*). They should be evaluated as *qi* tonics.

Also:

239   SAGE'S GINSENG
262   ASTRA EIGHT

GROUP 7-B
PILLS AND EXTRACTS
TO NOURISH BLOOD

NOTE: It is recommended that tonics, including patents that nourish blood, not be used during the early stages of wind-invasion (colds and flus), as they tend to drive wind deeper into the body. Also, the nature of these formulas may cause indigestion, and should be monitored.

147 ANGELICA TEA
Dang Gui Pian
"Angelica Dang Gui Tablets"
Lanchow Chinese Herb Works; Lanzhou, Gansu

Nurtures and invigorates blood, fortifies spleen qi. Use for chronic blood deficiencies, or following blood loss due to surgery, childbirth, or trauma. Blood deficiency may exhibit a variety of symptoms, including amenorrhea, blood heat or stagnation causing menstrual cramps, fatigue and weakness.

Bottles of 100 pills. Take 8 pills, 2-3 x day.

Angelica Dang Gui	70.%	Atractylodes Rhizome	10
Ligusticum Rhizome	10	Jujube Fruit, red	10

148 BUTIAO TABLETS
Bu Xue Tiao Jing Pian
"Nourish Blood, Adjust Period Tablet"
United Pharmaceutical Manufacotory; Guangzhou; Guangdong

Nourishes and activates blood, inhibits bleeding, tonifies spleen qi, strenghtens kidneys, warms the uterus. Use for blood deficiency with stagnation causing menstrual disorders and fatigue. Medicine of choice for irregular periods, cramps, or excessive uterine bleeding due to deficiency and stagnation of blood. (Often combined with TABELLAE TANG KUEI or ANGELICA TEA to enchance blood-building effect.)

Bottles of 100 tablets. Take 3 pills, 3 x day.

Cyperus Rhizome	9.0%	Ficus Root	4.5
Rosa Fruit	9.0	Baipo Leaf	4.5
Millettia Root	9.0	Artemisia Ai Ye	4.5
Loranthus Twig	9.0	Capsella Leaf	3.6
Litsea Fruit	9.0	Codonopsis Root	2.7
Rhodomyrtus Plant	9.0	Atractylodes Rhizome	2.3
Moghania Root	9.0	Licorice Root	.9
Leonurus Leaf	6.3	Donkey Skin Glue	.5
Galanga Rhizome	6.3	Cinnamon Bark	.4

149 EIGHT TREASURE TEA
Nu Ke Ba Zhen Wan
"Women's Group Eight Treasure Pills"
Lanchow Chinese Herb Works; Lanzhou, Gansu

Combines the classical formulas of **Four Gentlemen** (*Si Jun Zi Tang*) and **Four Substance** (*Si Wu Tang*) to tonify *qi* and nourish the blood. Excellent women's general tonic, useful for fatigue, dizziness, heart palpitations, low appetite, irregular menstruation, deficient menses, and recovery from childbirth and illness.

Bottles of 200 pills. Take 8 pills, 3 x day.

Rehmannia Root, prep.	18.2 %	Paeonia Root	12.1
Angelica Dang Gui	18.2	Atractylodes Rhizome	12.1
Codonopsis Root	12.1	Ligusticum Rhizome	9.1
Poria Fungus	12.1	Licorice Root	6.1

Also available as *Ba Zhen Tang* WOMEN'S PRECIOUS PILLS, Lanzhou Fo Ci Pharmaceutical Factory; Lanzhou, Gansu.

Also available as NU KE BA SHEN WAN, Lanzhou Fo Ci Pharmaceutical Factory; Lanzhou, Gansu.

150 ESSENCE OF CHICKEN WITH TANG KUEI
Ji Jing Dang Gui
"Chicken Essence [with] Angelica Dang Gui Root"
United Pharmaceutical Manufactory; Guangzhou, Guangdong

Liquid-extract concentrate to nourish blood and tonify *qi*. Use as general tonic, or following sickness or childbirth. Accompanying symptoms include lassitude, dizziness, poor appetite. Long term use strengthens *wei qi* (natural resistance to disease), and promotes general health. Excellent general tonic for women.

Bottles of 70 g. (2.5 oz). Take contents of one bottle in one or two doses, on the same day (or refrigerate after opening). Mix with hot or cold water, one part tonic to two parts water.

Essence of Chicken	70.0%	Rehmannia Root	1.5
Angelica Dang Gui	18.9	Atractylodes Rhizome	1.5
Ginseng Root	2.3	Poria Fungus	1.5
Ligusticum Rhizome	2.2	Licorice Root	.7
Paeonia Root	1.5		

151 IMPERIAL HO SHOU WO JIT
Zhong Guo Shou Wu Zhi
"China Polygonum Shou Wu Juice"
United Drug Manufactory; Guangzhou, Guangdong

Tonifies blood, warms and invigorates blood, nourishes liver and kidneys, benefits eyes and tendons. A liquid concentrate useful as a strong liver tonic for men and women. Use for depletion due to sexual excess, childbirth, or illness. Strenghtens bones and tendons in back and joint aching. Suitable for long periods of time. Similiar to product #155.

Boxes of 10 vials, each 10 cc. Take 1-2 vials per day, alone or with water.

Polygonum Shou Wu	25.0%	Angelica Root	6.7
Angelica Dang Gui	25.0	Licorice Root	1.6
Polygonatum Rhizome	20.0	Caryophyllum Flower	.8
Rehmannia Root, raw	10.0	Citrus Seed	.8
Ligusticum Rhizome	10.0		

152 KANG WEI LING

Kang Wei Ling
"Excessively Limp Efficacious-Remedy"
United Pharmaceutical Manufactory; Guangzhou, Guangdong

Tonifies blood, invigorates liver *qi*, builds sperm and *jing*. A strong tonic for male impotence, premature ejaculation, and lack of sexual drive. High clinical effectiveness rate for impotence reported in China.

Bottles of 120 pills. Take 10-15 pills, 2 x day, with wine, for 15 days.

| Angelica Dang Gui | 30.% | Paeonia Root | 30 |
| Licorice Root | 30 | Centipede | 10 |

153 PAI FENG WAN
WHITE PHOENIX PILLS

Bai Feng Wan
"White Phoenix Pill"
Peking Chinese Drug Manufactory; Beijing

Nourishes blood and *qi*, alleviates congestion of liver *qi*, invigorates blood to remove stagnation. This version of the White Phoenix pills contains 30% of the valuable black-skinned white rooster (from which the formula gets its name). Use for menstrual disorders due to deficiency of blood or *yin*, including cramps, headache, amenorrhea, and prolonged periods. Also used for post-partum fatigue, to clear blood stagnation and replenish blood.

Caution in heat conditions.

Boxes of 10 large gummy pills. Take half to one pill, 2 x day. Chew, or cut and form into smaller pieces and swallow. May also be crushed and dissolved in water.

Black Rooster	30.%	Paeonia Root	6
Rehmannia Root	12	Ginseng Root	6
Angelica Dang Gui	7	Ligusticum Rhizome	3
Cyperus Rhizome	6	Honey Binder	30

154 REHMANNIA GLUTINOSA COMPOUND PILLS
Fu Ke Zhong Zi Wan
"Women's Group Ova-Seed Pill"
Lanchow Chinese Herb Works; Lanzhou, Gansu

Nourishes, invigorates the blood, warms the uterus and cools the liver. Use in blood deficiency with cold uterus causing infertility, amenorrhea, or threatened miscarriage; also, menstrual cramps due to cold, with cold feet and a warm or flushed face.

Bottles of 100. Take 8 pills, 3 x day.

Rehmannia Root	23.5%	Dipsacus Root	8.8
Eucommia Bark	11.8	Artemisia Ai Ye	8.8
Cyperus Rhizome	11.8	Donkey Skin Glue	5.9
Ligusticum Rhizome	8.8	Scutellaria Root	5.9
Angelica Dang Gui	8.8	Paeonia Root	5.9

155 SHOU WU CHIH
Shou Wu Zhi
"Polygonum Shou Wu Juice"
United Drug Manufactory; Guangzhou, Guangdong

Tonifies blood, warms and invigorates blood, nourishes liver and kidneys, benefits eyes and tendons. A liquid concentrate useful as a strong liver tonic for men and women. Use for depletion due to sexual excess, childbirth, or illness. Strenghtens bones and tendons in back and joint aching. Suitable for long periods of time. Similiar to product #151.

Bottles of liquid (14 oz). Take 2-3 tablespoons, 3 x day with tea or water, or in soup.

Polygonum Shou Wu	25.0%	Angelica Root	6.7
Angelica Dang Gui	25.0	Amomum Fruit	1.6
Polygonatum Rhizome	20.0	Caryophyllum Flower	.9
Rehmannia Root	10.0	Citrus Seed	.9
Ligusticum Rhizome	10.0		

156 SHOU WU PIAN
Shou Wu Pian
"Polygonum Shou Wu Tablet"
Shanghai Chinese Medicine Works; Shanghai

Nourishes liver blood, tonifies kidney *qi* and kidney *jing*. Useful for chronic defiencies of liver blood, affecting vitality, or menstruation. Counters liver fire due to deficiency, with accompanying symptoms of headaches, eye pain, dizziness. Benefits lower back and joint aching due to weak kidney. Commonly used in China to keep hair from greying.

Bottles of 100 pills. Take 4 pills, 3 x day.

Polygonum Shou Wu   100.%

157 SUGAR COATED PLACENTA TABLETS
Tai Pan Tang Yi Pian
"Placenta Sugar-Coated Tablet"
Central Medical Manufactory Company; Tianjin

Pure extract of human placenta. Nutritive tonic for blood, *qi* and *jing*, useful following blood loss in childbirth, surgery, or traumatic bleeding. Use for *jing* deficiency causing infertility, impotence, vertigo, tinnitus; and blood and *qi* deficiency causing fatigue, weakness, and dry cough. Suitable for both men and women.

Bottles of 100 tablets. Take 3-5 tablets, 3 x day.

Human Placenta   100.%

158 TABELLAE TANG KUEI
Dang Gui Wan
"Angelica Dang Gui Pill"
Sing-kyn Drug House; Guangzhou, Guangdong

Nourishes blood and invigorates blood circulation. General female tonic commonly used for blood deficiency, scanty or infrequent menstruation, or menorrhagia. Combine with other patent formulas for blood deficiency to enhance dosage of Angelica Dang Gui.

Bottles of 100 pills. Take 2-5 tablets, 3 x day.

Angelica Dang Gui   100.%

159 TANG KWE GIN
Dang Gui Gin Gao
"Angelica Dang Gui Syrup"
Chung Lien Drug Works; Wuchang, Hubei

Nurtures and invigorates blood, tonifies spleenqi. An excellent liquid tonic for improving the quality of blood. Recommended as a general woman's tonic, or for both men and women exhibiting blood deficiency with fatique following illness, surgery or trauma.

Bottles of 100 ml, or 200 cc. Take 1 tablespoon 2 x day. Shake well before using. Also available in boxes of 10 vials, each 10 cc. Take 1-2 vials per day.

Angelica Dang Gui	69.0%	Poria Fungus	4.5
Donkey Skin Glue	4.5	Paeonia Root	4.5
Codonopsis Root	4.5	Ligusticum Rhizome	2.0
Astragalus Root	4.5	Licorice Root	2.0
Rehmannia Root	4.5	Sugar	

160 TIENCHI POWDER PREPARED
Shu Tian Qi Fen
"Prepared Pseudoginseng Powder"
Yunnan Pai Yao Factory; Yunnan

Pseudoginseng in its prepared (steamed) state, used to build or tonify blood following loss in injury, childbirth, menorrhagia, and anemia. Retains some ability to resolve blood stagnation and stop bleeding. Useful in scanty menses with prolonged spotting, and irregular periods with cramps.

Bottles of powder, total 40 g. Take 3-5 g., 2 x day: in capsules, hot water, or soup.

Prohibited internally during pregnancy.

Pseudoginseng Root   100.%

161 WU CHI PAI FENG WAN: WHITE PHOENIX PILLS (CONDENSED)
Wu Ji Bai Feng Wan Nong Suo
"Black Cock, White Phoenix Pills - Condensed"
Tientsin Drug Manufactory; Tianjin

Tonifies blood and *qi*, warms the uterus, nurtures *yin*, resolves stagnation of liver *qi* and blood. Use for menstrual disorders due to deficiency or cold, including amenorrhea, dysmenorrhea, or infertility. Beneficial in post-partum fatigue. Effective for menstrual cramps and pre-menstrual syndrome due to blood deficiency, stagnation and congestion of liver *qi*. Also useful for habitual dry cough or dry skin.

Bottles of 120 pills; take 5 pills, 3 x day.

Black Rooster	12.%	Salvia Root	6
Deer Horn Glue	12	Rehmannia Rt, prep.	6
Ginseng Root	10	Rehmannia Root, raw	5
Cyperus Rhizome	6	Paeonia Root	5
Mantis Egg-case	6	Asparagus Root	5
Angelica Dang Gui	6	Tortoise Plastron	5
Licorice Root	6	Stellaria Root	4
Astragalus Root	6		

162 WU CHI PAI FENG WAN - TIENTSIN FORMULA
Wu Ji Bai Feng Wan - Tian Jin
"Black Cock, White Phoenix Pills - Tianjin"
Tientsin Drug Manufactory; Tianjin

Tonifies blood and *qi*, warms the uterus, nurtures *yin*, resolves stagnation of liver *qi* and blood. Use for menstrual disorders due to deficiency or cold, including amenorrhea, dysmenorrhea, or infertility. Beneficial in post-partum fatigue. Effective for menstrual cramps and pre-menstrual syndrome due to blood deficiency, stagnation and congestion of liver *qi*. Also useful for habitual dry cough or dry skin. A stronger prescription than that for #161, with significant increases in Black Rooster and Rehmannia Root.

Boxes of 10 wax "eggs". Crack off the wax, and take the contents once or twice per day. Best if chewed.

Black Rooster	33.9%	Angelica Dang Gui	6.4
Rehmannia Root, prep.	12.9	Paeonia Root	6.4
Rehmannia Root, raw	12.9	Ginseng Root	6.4
Deer Horn Glue	6.5	Batatatis Rhizome	6.4
Cyperus Rhizome	6.4	Astragalus Root	1.6

163 YUNG SHENG HE AH CHIAO (FAMOUS ASS GLUE)

Yong Sheng He E Jiao
"Eternally Vigorous Combination Donkey Skin Glue"
Peking Chinese Drug Manufactory; Beijing

Nourishes blood and *yin*, moistens lungs, stops internal bleeding. Use for deficiency of blood, with or without heat, causing fatigue, dizziness, insomnia, or emaciation. Also for dry or bloody coughs due to deficiency of *yin*. Useful in bleeding disorders due to deficiency heat, including nosebleed, uterine bleeding, and excessive menstrual bleeding.

Comes in solid blocks, usually 30 g. Dissolve 15 g. in boiling water or hot rice wine, or double-boil* into liquid; can be sucked on in mouth. Take 1-2 times per day.

Contraindicated during bleeding gastrointestinal disorders.

Donkey Skin Glue	90.0 %	Rehmannia Root	.3
Angelica Dang Gui	1.5	Rice Wine	3.0
Astragalus Root	.5	Sugar	2.2
Ophiopogon Root	.3	Sesame Oil Binder	2.0
Poria Fungus	.3		

* To double-boil: Place 15 g. into ceramic cup with one cup of water. Cover, if possible. Place into pot of water and cover. Boil until dissolved; this may require refilling the outer water.

ALSO APPLICABLE to nourish blood:

202 SHIH SAN TAI PAO WAN = first trimester of pregnancy
203 SHEN YUNG PAI FENG WAN = menstrual cramps
223 TIENMA AND SHOU WU = deficiency of liver blood
causing hypertension
246 RELAXED WANDERER = liver blood and *yin*

To tonify *qi* and blood:

150 ESSENCE OF CHICKEN WITH TANG KUEI
196 GINSENG POLYGONA ROOT EXTRACT
204 TEN FLAVOR TEA
235 WOMEN'S LONGEVITY
236 TANG KUEI
249 BU XUE

Tonifies heart blood, *yin* and/or *shen*, for treatment of insomnia, restlessness, dizziness, and vivid dreaming:

193 KWEI BI WAN
209 AN SHENG PU SHIN WAN
212 DING XIN WAN
213 EMPERORS'S TEA: TIEN WANG PU HSIN WAN
232 RED HORSE - HEART / RADIANCE
242 COMPASSIONATE SAGE
251 YANG XIN

GROUP 7-C
TONICS FOR DEFICIENCY OF YANG

NOTE: It is recommended that tonics, including patents that tonify *yang*, not be used during the early stages of wind invasions (colds and flus), as they tend to drive wind deeper into the body.

164 ANTI-LUMBAGO TABLETS
Yao Tong Pian
"Waist Pain [Lumbago] Tablets"
Hu Qing Yu Tang Medicine Factory; Hangzhou, Zhejiang

Tonifies kidney *yang* and *qi*, nourishes liver blood, strengthens tendon and bone, circulates *qi* and blood, alleviates pain. Use for lumbago, lower back pain, and sciatica due to weak kidneys or deficient kidney *yang*.

Bottles of 100 tablets. Take 6 tablets, 3 x day.

Angelica Dang Gui	17.4%	Atractylodes Rhizome	13.0
Eucommia Bark	17.4	Psoralea Fruit	13.0
Dipsacus Root	13.0	Achyranthes Root	13.0
Cibotium Rhizome	13.0		

165 BA WEI DI HUANG WAN
Ba Wei Di Huang Wan
"Eight Flavor Rehmannia Pill"
Tianjin Drug Manufactory; Tianjin

Tonifies kidney and spleen *yang*, warms the middle and lower burners. A classical variation of GOLDEN BOOK TEA (#171), further adjusted to tonify spleen *yang* by adding Evodia Fruit. Indicated for general digestive weakness due to internal cold, with symptoms of abdominal distension and undigested food in stool. Useful for kidney *yang* deficiency symptoms including cold limbs, cold hands or feet, sore back, or profuse clear urine.

Bottles of 240 pills. Take 20 pills, 2 x day.

Rehmannia Root	30.%	Poria Fungus	11
Dioscorea Rhizome	15	Alisma Rhizome	11
Evodia Fruit	15	Cinnamon Bark	4
Moutan Bark	11	Aconite Root	3

166 BOWSUN WAN
Nan Xing Bu Shen Wan
"Male Gender Tonify Kidney Pill"
Lanzhou Fo Ci Pharmaceutical Factory, Lanzhou, Gansu

Tonifies kidney *yang* and *qi*, nurtures *jing*, benefits urination. A variation of GOLDEN BOOK TEA (171) to enhance kidney function, especially if accompanied by lower back pain, urinary dribbling or incontinence, lowered sexual drive and cold limbs. Useful for deficiencies of kidney *yang* affecting the heart or lungs.

Boxes of 20 capsules. Take 1-2 capsules per day.

Rehmannia Root	23.5%	Alisma Rhizome	8.8
Dioscorea Rhizome	11.8	Schizandra Fruit	5.9
Poria Fungus	17.6	Plantago Seed	5.9
Cornus Fruit	11.8	Aconite Root	2.9
Paeonia Root	8.8	Cinnamon Root	2.9

167 CHING CHUN BAO
RECOVERY OF YOUTH TABLET
Qing Chun Bao
"Green Vitality Treasure"
Hangzhou Chinese Medicine Factory #2; Hangzhou, Zhejiang

Strengthens kidney *yang*, tonifies *qi* and blood, promotes blood circulation, benefits heart and kidney, enriches sexual function, counters fatigue. Tonic for aged and dehabilitated patients. Useful for poor memory, senility, fatigue, poor resistance to disease, and strengthening the heart.

Packets of 20 capsules. Take 2-5 capsules, 2 x day. Also available in bottles of 80 tablets. Take 3-5 tablets, 2 x day for 30 days for one course of treatment. See #175.

Main listed ingredients (it probably contains at least 20 herbs):
Ginseng Root	Rehmannia Root
Asparagus Root	

168 CHIN SO KU CHING: GOLDEN LOCK TEA

Jin Suo Gu Jing Wan
"Golden Lock Consolidate Jing Pill"
Lanchow Chinese Medicine Works; Lanzhou, Gansu

Classical prescription to tonify kidney *yang* and *qi*, and astringe seminal discharge. Specific for the male sexual dysfunctions of nocturnal emission and premature ejaculation due to weak kidneys. (Less useful in spermatorrhea due to liver fire). Useful in ejaculation control (Daoist sexual practices). Also useful as an astringent for leukorrhea (vaginal discharge), excessive sweating, and diarrhea.

Bottles of 100 pills. Take 15 pills, 3 x day.

Lotus Seed	33.%	Lotus Stamen	17
Astragalus Seed	17	Dragon Tooth	8
Euryale Seed	17	Oyster Shell	8

169 DUZHONG BU TIAN SU

Du Zhong Bu Tian Su
"Eucommia Benefit Heaven Basic Pill"
Kweiyang Chinese Medicine Factory; Guiyang, Guizhou

Tonifies kidney *yang*, qi and blood, strenghtens kidney-heart relation. Use for weak heart with difficult breathing, edema, insomnia, restlessness, and heart palpitations (congestive heart failure). Useful for backache, incontinence of urine or frequent urination, poor memory or dizziness following male sexual ejaculation, and fatigue following childbirth.

Boxes of 12 vials, 8 tablets to each vial. Take 2-4 tablets, 2 x day.

Eucommia Bark	18.8 %	Morinda Root	4.3
Lycium Fruit	16.8	Cornus Fruit	4.3
Astragalus Root	16.8	Cistanche Stem	4.3
Codonopsis Root	11.5	Lotus Seed	1.4
Angelica Dang Gui	11.6	Biota Seed	1.4
Rehmannia Root	8.6		

170 GEJIE BU SHEN WAN

Ge Jie Bu Shen Wan
"Gecko Tonify Kidney Pills"
Yulin Drugs Manufactory; Yulin, Guangxi

General tonic for kidney *yang* and *qi*. Use for deficiency of kidney *yang* causing general weakness, frequent urination, cold extremities, poor circulation, and poor digestion with undigested food in the stools. Very helpful in impotence, or fatigue and poor memory following male sexual ejaculation.

Bottles of 50 capsules. Take 3-4 capsules, 3 x day.

Gecko Lizard	20.%	Eucommia Bark	10
Poria Fungus	17	Deer Horn	5
Atractylodes Rhizome	13	Ginseng Root	5
Lycium Fruit	10	Dog Penis and Testes	5
Astragalus Root	10	Cordiceps Fungus	5

171 GOLDEN BOOK TEA

Jin Kui Shen Qi Wan
"Golden Deficient Kidney Qi Pill"
Lanchow Chinese Medicine Works; Lanzhou, Gansu

Classical foundation prescription for kidney *qi* and *yang*, also known as REHMANNIA 8 FORMULA or SEXOTAN. Use for *yang* and *qi* deficiency symptoms including cold hands or feet, lower backaches, poor digestion with gas or undigested food in stools, persistent diarrhea, poor circulation, frequent urination, edema, impotence and infertility, and sexual dysfunction.

Bottles of 120 and 200 pills. Take 8-10 pills, 3 x day.

Rehmannia Root	29.6 %	Poria Fungus	11.1
Dioscorea Root	14.8	Alisma Rhizome	11.1
Cornus Fruit	14.8	Cinnamon Bark	3.7
Moutan Bark	11.1	Aconite Root	3.7

Also available as CHIN KUEI SHEN QI WAN and SEXOTAN from the same manufacturer, Lanchow Chinese Medicine Works; Lanzhou, Gansu.

172 HAILUNG TONIC PILLS
Hai Long Bu Wan
"Sea Horse, Pipe Fish Nourishing Pills"
Tsingtao Medicine Works; Qingdao, Shandong

Warming general tonic to invigorate kidney *yang*, and tonify kidney and spleen *qi*. Good product for impotence or reduced sexual drive in men. Also appropriate for weak back, restlessness, fatigue, cold limbs, general weakness, anemia, frequent urination, and insomnia. A useful general tonic following illness or surgery.

Contraindicated in heat conditions, including *yin*-deficiency heat.

Bottles of 150 pills; take 5 pills, 3 x day.

Pipe Fish	35. %	Paeonia Root	4
Sea Horse	10	Dendrobrium Leaf	4
Sheep Penis	10	Alisma Rhizome	3
Ginseng Root	5	Rehmannia Root	2
Angelica Dang Gui	5	Ginger Rhizome	2
Cuscuta Seed	5	Schizandra Fruit	2
Cinnamon Bark	5	Asarum Plant	2
Moutan Root-bark	4	Cnidium Fruit	2

173 KANG GU ZENG SHENG PIAN
Kang Gu Zheng Sheng Pian
"Combat Bone Hyperplasia Pill"
United Pharmaceutical Manufactory; Foshan, Guangdong

Strengthens *qi* and *yang*, tonifies kidney and liver, fortifies marrow, tendon and bone, clears damp, relieves pain. A recently formulated patent specific for vertebral calcification following injury, or in spontaneous multiplicative spondylitis. Useful in chronic vertebral subluxations and other dysfunctions, and spinal inflammations. Beneficial for tendon pain and numbness accompanying back pain.

Bottles of 100 tablets. Take 6 tablets, 3 x day.

Caution: This product lists Tiger Bone, a prohibited substance in North America (substitution with a domestic animal product may have been made).

Rehmannia Root	15.0 %	Epimedium Leaf	8.5
Cistanche Stem	12.5	Dioscorea Root	8.2
Pyrola Leaf	10.0	Tiger Bone	8.0
Hedera Stem	10.0	Erodium Plant	8.0
Liquidambar Fruit	10.0	Other	9.8

174 KWEI LING CHI
Gui Ling Ji
"Tortoise Age Collection"
Shansi Drug Manufactory; Shanxi

Systemic tonic to strengthen kidney *qi* and *yang*, nourish blood, and warm the organs. Useful in infertility, cold uterus, and cold-damp vaginal discharges. Treats *yang* deficiency symptoms of poor digestion with abdominal bloating or loose stools, sexual dysfunction, fatigue, weakness after childbirth or illness, mental debility due to old age, and weakness in back or legs.

Bottles of 30 capsules. Take 1-2 capsules per day.

Contraindicated during pregnancy.

Deer Horn	25.%	Caryophyllum Flower	2
Ginseng Root	20	Eucommia Bark	2
Sea Horse	8	Anteater Scales	2
Rehmannia Root, prep.	6	Cuscuta Seed	2
Cistanche Stem	6	Psoralea Seed	2
Achyranthes Root	3	Epimedium Leaf	2
Amomum Fruit	3	Licorice Root	2
Lycium Fruit	3	Asparagus Root	1
Sparrow Brain	2	Spirifera Fossil	1
Cynomorium Stem	2		

175 NAN BAO CAPSULES: STRONG MAN BAO
Nan Bao
"Male's Treasure"
Shanxi Drug Manufactory; Shanxi

Strong male tonic for deficiency of kidney *yang*, kidney and spleen *qi*, and blood. Use for impotence, premature ejaculation, failure to obtain an erection, and lowered sexual drive. Useful in problems accompanying aging in men, including fatigue, low back pain, poor memory, and poor digestion.

20 capsules to a packet. Take 2 capsules, 2 x day.

Contraindicated during pregnancy.

Main ingredients:

Donkey Kidney	Sea Horse
Dog Kidney	Donkey-skin Glue
Ginseng Root	Astragalus Root
Angelica Dang Gui	Rehmannia Root, prep.
Eucommia Bark	Poria Fungus
Cinnamon Bark	Atractylodes Rhizome
Deer Horn	Paeonia Root
Cornus Fruit	Epimedium Leaf
Cuscuta Seed	Aconite Root
Psoralea Fruit	Lycium Fruit
Cistanche Stem	Morinda Root
Rubus Fruit	Ophiopogon Root
Trigonella Seed	Cynomorium Stem
Dipsacus Root	Curculigo Rhizome
Achyranthes Root	Scrophularia Root
Licorice Root	

176 SEA HORSE HERB TEA
Hai Ma Bu Shen Wan
"Sea Horse Tonify Kidney Pill"
Tianjin Drug Manufactory; Tianjin

General purpose tonic for *qi* and blood, kidney *qi* and *yang*; also strengthens heart. Recommended for persons whose kidney deficiency has affected the heart or digestion. Useful in aged, and those recovering from illness and childbirth. Recommended for symptoms associated with congestive heart failure, including fatigue, poor digestion with undigested food in the stool, edema, difficulty breathing, and insomnia. Also useful for lowered sexual drive or impotence, lower back pain, or cold limbs.

Caution: A little too warm to use over extended periods of time, except in significant *yang* deficiency. Evaluate and monitor usage. Contraindicated in heat or *yin* deficiency fever.

Note: This product lists Tiger Bone, a prohibited substance in North America (substitution with domestic animal products may have been made).

Bottles of 120 pills. Take 3 pills, 3 x day.

Main ingredients:

Sea Horse	Astragalus Root
Ginseng Root	Juglans Seed
Dragon Bone	Deer Horn
Lycium Fruit	Gecko Lizard
Deer Ligament	Tiger Bone
Psoralea Fruit	Cornus Fruit
Poria Fungus	Angelica Dang Gui
Caryophyllum Flower	Rehmannia Root

177 TABELLAE CHUANG YAO TONIC
Zhuang Yao Jian Shen Pian
"Strengthen Lower-back, Make-strong Kidney Tablet"
United Pharmaceutical Manufactory; Guangzhou, Guangdong

Tonifies kidney *yang* and *qi*, benefits tendons and bone. Use for various symptoms associated with deficiency of kidney *yang*, including lower back pain, weak waist and legs, pain in kidneys, dizziness, difficult breathing, and ear-ringing. Also urinary dribbling, incontinence, or weak stream. Treats problems due to excessive male sexual activity, including fatigue, poor memory and lower backache. Can be used for long periods as a general kidney *yang* tonic.

Bottles of 100 pills. Take 4 pills, 1-2 x day.

Cibotium Rhizome	26.3 %	Cordyceps Fungus	5.3
Millettia Root	15.8	Poria Fungus	7.8
Eucommia Bark	15.8	Rubus Fruit	2.6
Rosa Fruit	7.9	Others	10.5
Loranthus Twig	7.9		

178 XIONG BAO
Xiong Bao
"Male's Treasure"
Tianjin Drug Manufactory; Tianjin

Nurtures *qi* and blood, tonifies kidney *yin* and *yang*, benefits the organs, strengthens the muscles and sinews. A smaller version of NAN BAO CAPSULES (#175), this is a recommended tonic for the aging with problems of fatigue, impotence, lowered sex drive, poor memory, back pain, and restless sleep.

Bottles of 40 capsules. Take 2 capsules, 2 x day.

Dog Penis and Testes	34.%	Deer Horn	5
Horse Penis & Testes	17	Amomum Fruit	5
Epimedium Leaf	17	Seahorse	5
Lycium Fruit	12	Eucommia Bark	5

ALSO APPLICABLE for deficiencies of *yang*:

120	FU ZI LI CHUNG WAN = poor digestion due to deficiency of *yang* and preponderance of cold
152	KANG WEI LING = impotence

To tonify *yang* and *qi*:

192	ALRODEER PILLS
195	GEJIE TA BU WAN
201	SHEN KUE LU JUNG WAN
243	DYNAMIC WARRIOR
228	BLACK BOAR - KIDNEY YANG / DYNAMIC
257	JIAN GU
270	REJUVENATE 8

BA XIAN
CHANG SHOU WAN

200 PILLS

ACTIONS:
A GENERAL TONIC ALSO GOOD
FOR SECRETION OF SALIVA.

LANCHOW CHINESE MEDICINE WORKS
LANCHOW CHINA

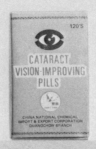

120'S

CATARACT
VISION-IMPROVING
PILLS

CHINA NATIONAL CHEMICAL
IMPORT & EXPORT CORPORATION
GUANGCHOW BRANCH

CHIH PAI
DI HUANG WAN

(CHIH PAI PA WEI WAN)

200 pills

Actions & Indications:
For the treatment of
febrile illness, lumbago,
fidgetiness and night sweat.
Also effective in relieving
internal heat.

LANZHOU FO CI PHARMACEUTICAL FACTORY
LANHOW, CHINA

潤腸丸

FRUCTUS PERSICA
COMPOUND, PILLS

200粒

中國 蘭州
蘭州佛慈製藥廠

KAI KIT PILL

INDICATIONS
ENLARGED PROSTATE

MARKLE PHARMACEUTICAL WORKS

杞菊地黃丸

LICII & CHRYSENTOMUM TEA

100

NET WT. 8 OZ.
PRODUCT OF CHINA

LANCHOW CHINESE HERBS WORKS
LANCHOW CHINA

LIU WEI
DI HUANG WAN

200 pills

Actions & Indications:
Nourishing the vital es-
sence of kidney, used
for general debility, weakness of knees, dizziness and
tinnitus, nocturnal emis-
sion and hematuria.

LANZHOU FO CI PHARMACEUTICAL FACTORY
LANHOW CHINA

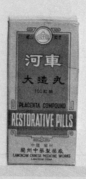

河車
大造丸
100 KE MI

PLACENTA COMPOUND
RESTORATIVE PILLS

中國 蘭州製藥廠
蘭州中藥製藥廠
LANCHOW CHINESE MEDICINE WORKS
LANCHOW CHINA

明目地黃丸
REHMANNIA TEA

WT. 1½ OZ   PRODUCT OF CHINA
LANCHOW CHINESE HERBS WORKS, LANCHOW, CHINA

GROUP 7-D
TONICS FOR DEFICIENCY OF YIN OR FLUIDS

NOTE: It is recommended that tonics, including patent medicines that nourish *yin*, not be used during the early stages of wind invasion (colds and flus), as they tend to drive wind deeper into the body.

179 BA XIAN CHANG SHOU WAN
Ba Xian Chang Shou Wan
"Eight Immortals Long Life Pills"
Lanchow Chinese Medicine Works; Lanzhou, China

Nurtures kidney *qi* and *yin*, nourishes lung *yin*, moistens and cools lung to stop cough. A variation of SIX FLAVOR TEA (#188), formulated to benefit the lungs. Use for dry cough due to chronic heat or deficiency of *yin*. Use for *yin* deficiency causing heat in palms, heart palpitation, dizziness, ringing of ears, or night sweating.

Bottles of 200 pills. Take 8 pills, 3 x day.

Rehmannia Root, prep.	26.7 %	Alisma Rhizome	10.0
Cornus Fruit	13.3	Poria Fungus	10.0
Dioscorea Rhizome	13.3	Ophiopogon Root	10.0
Moutan Root-bark	10.0	Schizandra Fruit	6.7

180 CATARACT VISION-IMPROVING PILLS
Nei Zhang Ming Yan Wan
"Inner Obstruction [to] Eyesight Pills"
China National Chemical Import and Export Corp; Wangdong Branch

Benefits clarity of vision, nourishes liver and kidney *yin* and blood, sedates heat, tonifies and circulates *qi* and blood, nourishes spleen *qi*. Use for impairment of vision due to liver *yin* deficiency with heat, with the symptoms of cataract, glaucoma, itchy painful eyes, impaired day or night vision, and recovery following eye surgery.

Bottles of 120 pills. Take 8 pills, 3 x day.

Caution: Alum is a natural mineral containing aluminum. Monitor and limit use.

Dendrobrium Leaf	15. %	Rehmannia Root, prep.	5
Chrysanthemum Flower	8	Phellodendron Bark	5
Paeonia Root	8	Schizandra Fruit	5
Lycium Fruit	8	Astragalus Root	5
Angelica Dang Gui	8	Lycium Root-bark	5
Cuscuta Seed	6	Rhubarb Rhizome	3
Achyranthes Root	6	Coptis Rhizome	2
Rehmannia Root, raw	5	Alum Mineral-salt	1

181 DA BU YIN WAN
Da Bu Yin Wan
"Great Tonify Yin *Pill"*
Lanchow Chinese Medicine Works; Lanzhou, Gansu

Tonfies kidney *yin*, sedates deficiency fire. A classical formula for severe deficiency of kidney *yin* with fire symptoms of night sweating, hot flashing, feverish palms or soles, restless insomnia, and burning sensation over the kidneys. Very good for acute menopausal hot-flashing.

Bottles of 200 pills. Take 8 pills, 3 x day.

Rehmannia Root, prep.	30.%	Anemarrhena Rhizome	20
Tortoise Plastron	30	Phellodendron Bark	20

182 DENDROBRIUM MONILFORME NIGHT SIGHT PILLS
Shi Hu Ye Guang Wan
"Dendrobrium Leaf Night Sight Pills"
Tientsin Drug Manufactory; Tianjin

Nourishes *yin* and blood, tonifies kidney and liver, tonifies *qi*, dispels liver fire and wind, benefits the eyes. Use to improve vision, especially eyesight that is beginning to diminish with blurriness or dizziness. Valuable in early stage of cataract. Also suitable for eye tearing, red or itchy eye, and hypertensive pressure behind the eyes. Also useful in dry eye.

Boxes of 10 pills, each 6 grams. Take one pill, 2 x day.

Caution: This products lists Rhinoceros Horn, a prohibited substance in North America.

Ginseng Root	16.%	Tribulus Fruit	4
Lycium Fruit	6	Siler Root	4
Chrysanthemum Flower	6	Ligusticum Rhizome	4
Ophiopogon Root	8	Cistanche Stem	4
Rehmannia Root	8	Rhinoceros Horn	4
Cassia Seed	6	Schizandra Fruit	4
Achyranthes Root	6	Aurantium Fruit	4
Dendrobrium Leaf	4	Celosia Seed	4
Antelope Horn	4	Coptis Rhizome	4

183 EIGHT FLAVOR TEA
Zhi Bai Ba Wei Wan
"Anemarrhena, Phellodendron, Eight Flavor Pill"
Lanchow Chinese Medicine Works; Lanzhou, Gansu

The classical prescription SIX FLAVOR TEA (#188) with the addition of two heat reducing herbs. Use to treat deficiency of kidney *yin* with heat in the lungs, liver, heart, or systemic heat and fever. Symptoms include tidal fever, night sweating, hot flashes, heat in soles of feet or palms, insomnia, restless sleep, or high blood pressure due to deficiency of kidney *yin*.

Rehmannia Root	28.%	Paeonia Root	10
Cornus Fruit	14	Poria Fungus	10
Dioscorea Rhizome	14	Phellodendron Bark	7
Alisma Rhizome	10	Anemarrhena Rhizome	7

Also available from the same factory as CHIH PAI DI HUANG WAN.

184 KAI KIT PILL
Jie Jie Wan
"Dispel [Prostate] Swelling Pill"
Hanyang Pharmaceutical Works; Hanyang, Hubei

Tonifies kidney *qi* and *yin*, invigorates *qi* and blood, promotes urination, resolves pain, astringes damp. A specific remedy to treat enlarged prostate gland due to deficiency, with accompanying symptoms of painful or difficult urination, and pain in the groin. Recommended for chronic condition where swelling is pronounced.

Bottles of 54 pills. Take 3-6 pills, 2-3 x day.

Rehmannia Root	20	Achyranthes Root	5
Astragalus Root	20	Salvia Root	5
Codonopsis Root	20	Alisma Rhizome	5
Ligustrum Fruit	10	Cuscuta Seed	5
Plantago Seed	5	Mantis Egg-case	5

185   LYCII AND CHRYSANTHEMUM TEA

Qi Ju Di Huang Wan
"Lycium, Chrysanthemum, Rehmannia Pills"
Lanzhou Fo Ci Pharmaceutical Factory; Lanzhou, Gansu

Nourishes kidney *yin*, replenishes liver blood and *yin*, benefits the eyes. A classical variation of SIX FLAVOR TEA (#188) modified to treat vision problems due to deficiency of kidney *yin* or *qi*. Symptoms include blurry vision, dry and painful eyes, pressure behind the eyes, and poor night vision. Also applicable for dizziness, headaches, pain behind eyes, outbursts of anger, heat in palms, restlessness and insomnia.

Bottles of 100 pills. Take 8 pills, 3 x day.

Rehmannia Root, prep.	27.7 %	Alisma Rhizome	10.3
Dioscorea Rhizome	13.8	Paeonia Root	10.3
Cornus Fruit	13.8	Lycium Fruit	6.9
Poria Fungus	10.3	Chrysanthemum Flower	6.9

Also available from the same manufacturer as LYCIUM AND CHRYSANTHEMUM TEA, and LYCIUM-REHMANNIA PILLS.

186   REHMANNIA TEA
Ming Mu Di Huang Wan
"Bright Eyes Rehmannia Pills"
Lanzhou Fo Ci Pharmaceutical Manufactory; Lanzhou, Gansu

Replenishes liver and kidney *yin*, nourishes liver blood, sedates liver fire and wind, benefits the eyes. A variation of SIX FLAVOR TEA (#188), adjusted to benefit vision problems affected by liver heat and internal wind, including dry eyes, red and itchy eyes, poor eyesight, photophobia, excessive tearing, and such eye diseases as glaucoma and cataract.

Bottles of 200 pills. Take 10 pills, 3 x day.

Rehmannia Root	18.2 %	Lycium Fruit	6.8
Dioscorea Root	9.1	Paeonia Root	6.8
Haliotis Shell	9.1	Alisma Rhizome	6.8
Cornus Fruit	9.1	Paeonia Chi Shao	6.8
Angelica Dang Gui	6.8	Tribulus Fruit	6.7
Chrysanthemum Flower	6.8	Poria Fungus	6.8

Also available from the same manufacturer as MING MU TI HUANG WAN.

187 RESTORATIVE PILLS
He Che Da Zao Wan
"Placenta Great Creation Pill"
Lanchow Chinese Medicine Works; Lanzhou, Gansu

Replenishes kidney, heart or liver *yin*, nourishes blood, tonifies *qi*, strengthens kidney, and relieves false fire due to deficiency of *yin*. This prescription is intended for significant deficiencies of *qi*, *yin* and blood, causing fatigue, fever with thirst, burning soles of feet, night sweating, hot flashes, dry cough and restless insomnia. Very good for menopausal disorders.

Bottles of 100 pills. Take 8 pills, 3 x day.

Tortoise Plastron	15.0 %	Achyranthes Root	8.0
Rehmannia Root, prep.	15.0	Asparagus Root	8.0
Codonopsis Root	15.0	Ophiopogon Root	8.0
Phellodendron Bark	11.0	Poria Fungus	3.5
Eucommia Bark	11.0	Amomum Fruit	1.5
Human Placenta	8.0		

Also available as PLACENTA COMPOUND RESTORATIVE PILLS from the same manufacturer, and as HO CHEH TA TSAO WAN, from Tianjin Drug Manufactory; Tianjin.

188 SIX FLAVOR TEA

Liu Wei Di Huang Wan
"Six Flavor Rehmannia Pill"
Lanzhou Fo Ci Pharmaceutical Manufactory; Lanzhou, Gansu

Classical foundation prescription for nourishing kidney, liver and spleen *yin*, and tonifying kidney and spleen *qi*. Accompanying symptoms include weakness or pain in lower back, restlessness, insomnia, burning in soles or palms, mild night sweats, dizziness, tinnitus, sore throat, impotence, and high blood pressure due to kidney *yin* deficiency. Foundation formula for diabetes. May be taken over long periods of time. Caution in excessively damp conditions.

Bottles of 200 pills. Take 8-16 pills, 3 x day.

Rehmannia Rt, raw	33. %	Moutan Bark	12
Cornus Fruit	16	Poria Fungus	12
Dioscoria Root	16	Alisma Rhizome	12

Also available from the same manufacturer as LIU WEI DI HUANG WAN.

189 SMOOTH TEA PILLS
Run Chang Wan
"Moisten Intestines Pill"
Lanzhou Fo Ci Pharmaceutical Factory; Lanzhou, Gansu

Moistens intestines, reduces heat in lower burner, stimulates peristalsis. Use for chronic constipation due to heat, deficiency of fluid, or deficiency of *qi*. Helpful in constipation due to weakness or older age, and constipation following childbirth.

Bottles of 200 pills. Take 4 pills, 3 x day.

Note: Cannabis Seed has been cooked and unable to germinate; thus it is not considered a controlled substance in North America.

Persica Fruit	28.6 %	Aralia Root	14.3
Cannabis Seed	28.6	Rhubarb Rhizome	14.3
Peucedanum Root	14.3		

Also available from the same manufacturer as FRUCTUS PERSICA COMPOUND PILLS.

190 TSO-TZU OTIC PILLS
Er Ming Zuo Ci Wan
"Ear-ringing Left Loving Pills"
Lanchow Chinese Medicine Works; Lanzhou, Gansu

A variation of SIX FLAVOR TEA (188), with the addition of Bupleurum Root and Magnitite Mineral. Used to treat deficiency of *yin* with liver fire, causing heat symptoms in the upper burner including ear-ringing, headache, high blood pressure, eye pressure, insomnia, thirst, and eye irritation.

Bottles of 200 pills. Take 8 pills, 3 x day.

Rehmannia Root, prep.	30.0 %	Poria Fungus	10.5
Dioscorea Rhizome	15.0	Alisma Rhizome	10.5
Cornus Fruit	15.0	Bupleurum Root	4.5
Moutan Root-bark	10.5	Magnitite Mineral	4.0

191   YEUCHUNG PILLS
Yu Quan Wan
"Jade Spring Pills"
The United Pharmaceutical Manufactory, Szechuan

Nurtures *yin*, strengthens kidney, lung and spleen, dispels phlegm-heat, relieves thirst, circulates fluid, regulates appetite, calms *shen*. A classical prescription for the treatment of diabetes "sugar urine disease", used for both juvenile and insipid diabetes in mainland China. Insulin levels should be monitored and adjusted while taking this (or any herbal) patent formula.

Bottles of 180 gr. of powder. Take 9 gr. per dose (fill inner cap), 4 x day. Also available in boxes of 20 vials of pills. Take the contents of one bottle at one time, 4 x day.

Rehmannia Root	29.8 %	Licorice Root	10.0
Pueraria Root	28.8	Schizandra Fruit	8.4
Trichosanthes Root	23.0		

ALSO APPLICABLE for deficiency of yin:

Nurture *yin*:
245   QUIET CONTEMPLATIVE
229   WHITE TURTLE - KIDNEY YIN / RECOVERY
227   WHITE MONKEY - LUNG YIN / CRYSTALLIZE
259   BU YIN

Tonifies heart *yin* or blood:
193   KWEI BE WAN
210   CEREBRAL TONIC PILLS
212   DING XIN WAN
213   EMPEROR'S TEA
215   PAI TZU YAN HSIN WAN

Other:
163   YUNG SHENG HE AH CHIAO = deficiency of blood and
        yin
223   TIENMA AND SHOU WU = deficiency of liver *yin* causing
        dizziness
225   TIENMA MIHUAN TABLETS = tonifies liver *yin*

GROUP 7-E
GENERAL AND COMBINATION TONICS

NOTE 1: It is recommended that tonics, including general and combination tonics, not be used during the early stages of wind invasion (colds and flus), as they tend to drive wind deeper into the body. Also, general and combination tonics tend to be warming. Caution is advised in heat, or deficiency-heat, complexes.

192 ALRODEER PILLS
Quan Lu Wan
"Complete Deer Pills"
Hanchow Chinese Medicine Works; Hangzhou, Zhejiang

Tonifies and invigorates *qi*, benefits *yang*, nurtures blood, strengthens lungs, spleen, kidney and heart. An excellent general tonic for *qi* and blood, *yang* and *yin*, made primarily from various parts of the Spotted Deer. Recommended for general weakness, lumbago, weakened muscles, and poor memory. Appropriate for the aging, and those recovering from surgery, trauma, sickness or difficult childbirth.

Bottles of 100 pills. Take 4 pills, 3 x day.

Spotted Stag	40.8%	Angelica Dang Gui	4.1
Rehmannia Root	8.2	Astragalus Root	4.1
Atractylodes Rhizome	4.1	Cistanche Stem	4.1
Lycium Fruit	4.1	Psoralea Seed	4.1
Eucommia Bark	4.1	Achyranthes Root	4.1
Dioscorea Rhizome	4.1	Schizandra Fruit	4.1
Morinda Root	4.1	Aquilaria Wood	2.0
Ginseng Root	4.1		

193 ANGELICAE LONGANA TEA
Gui Pi Wan
"Restore Spleen Pill"
Lanchow Chinese Medicine Works; Lanzhou, Gansu

Classical prescription to nurture heart *yin* and blood, strengthen spleen and heart qi, and calm. Use for fatigue with night sweating, palpitations, poor memory, restlessness, insomnia, or restless dreaming. Strengthens poor digestion by nurturing spleen *qi*. Useful in abnormal uterine bleeding and heavy menses. Also given to offset abdominal distension induced by other tonifying or invigorating patent medicines.

Bottles of 200 pills. Take 8 pills, 3 x day.

Codonopsis Root	13.%	Longan Fruit	13
Poria Fungus	13	Astragalus Root	10
Licorice Root	13	Polygala Root	7
Zizyphus Seed	13	Angelica Deng Gui	2
Atractylodes Rhizome	13	Saussurea Root	3

Also available from the same manufacturer as KWEI BE WAN.

194 ESSENCE OF CHICKEN WITH GINSENG
Ren Shen Ji Jing
"Ginseng Root [with] Chicken Essence"
United Pharmaceutical Manufactory; Guangzhou, Guangdong

Tonifies spleen *qi* and *wei qi*, builds heart blood, calms *shen*, warms the center. Use during or after chronic illness, loss of blood, or childbirth, with signs of fatigue, restless thirst, or poor digestion.

Bottles of 70 g. (2.5 oz). Take contents of one bottle in one or two doses, on the same day (or refrigerate after opening). Mix with hot or cold water, one part tonic to two parts water.

Chicken Liquid	95.%
Ginseng Root	5.

195 GEJIE TA BU WAN
Ge Jie Da Bu Wan
"Gecko Great Tonifying Pills"
Yulin Drug Manufactory; Yulin, Guangxi

Tonifies *qi*, *yang* and blood, strengthens kidney, lung, spleen and heart. Excellent long term general tonic, or following debilitating illness, surgery, or childbirth. Useful for kidney support. Caution in deficiencies with heat.

Bottles of 50 capsules. Take 3-5 capsules, 3 x day.

Gecko Lizard	21.5%	Morinda Root	4.3
Rehmannia Root	6.8	Atractylodes Rhizome	4.3
Polygonatum Rhizome	5.7	Codonopsis Root	4.3
Dioscorea Root	5.3	Eucommia Bark	4.3
Ligustrum Fruit	5.2	Astragalus Root	4.3
Poria Fungus	5.0	Lycium Fruit	4.1
Dipsacus Root	4.8	Drynaria Rhizome	4.0
Cibotium Rhizome	4.8	Angelica Dang Gui	3.8
Chaenomeles Fruit	4.7	Licorice Root	2.8

196 GINSENG POLYGONA ROOT EXTRACT
Ren Shen Shou Wu Jing
"Ginseng, Polygonum Shou Wu Extract"
Harbin Chinese Medicine Factory; Harbin, Heilongjiang

Tonifies *qi*, liver blood, and *jing*. Excellent liver blood tonic, useful for both men and women. Use as general health tonic, or to treat the symptoms of insomnia, dizziness, poor memory, poor appetite, fatigue, aching joints and tendons, and diminished sex drive.

Bottles of 50 cc, in liquid alcohol extract. Take 2 cc, 2 x day.

Polygonum Shou wu	60.%
Ginseng Root	40.

197 GINSENG TONIC CAPSULES
Ren Shen Bu Wan
"Ginseng Nourishing Pills"
Pine Brand; Tianjin

Tonifies *qi*, benefits kidney *yin* and *yang*, strengthens organs. A good tonic for the spleen and kidneys that can be taken on a regular basis. Beneficial in aged, following childbirth or sickness, or for general health promotion. Caution is advised if heat symptoms develops

Bottles of 30 capsules. Take 1-2 capsules, 2 x day.

Ginseng Root	69.2%	Achyranthes Root	4.6
Cistanche Stem	9.2	Poria Fungus	2.7
Adenophora Root	6.9	Seahorse	.5
Cornus Fruit	6.9		

198 JEN SHEN LU JUNG WAN
Ren Shen Lu Rong Wan
"Ginseng, Deer Horn Pill"
Great Wall Brand; Tianjin

A general tonic for kidney and spleen *qi*, heart blood, and kidney *yin* and *yang*. Excellent rehabilitive tonic following illness, surgery or childbirth. Useful in symptoms of poor appetite, anemia, weak legs and back, mental restlessness, insomnia, spermatorrhea, heart palpitations, lumbago and sciatica, and poor memory.

Boxes of 10 large gummy pills. Take one pill, 2 x day. Chew, or cut and form into smaller pieces and swallow. Can be crushed and dissolved in hot water.

Longan Fruit	9.0%	Morinda Root	9.0
Angelica Dang Gui	9.0	Ginseng Root	4.7
Astragalus Root	9.0	Deer Horn	3.8
Eucommia Bark	9.0	Honey Binder	37.5
Achyranthes Root	9.0		

199 JEN SHEN LU JUNG WAN
(Condensed)
Ren Shen Lu Rong Wan
"Ginseng, Deer Horn Pill"
Tianjin Drug Manufactory; Tianjin

Same in name as above product (#198), but with a different prescription and in small pills. Tonifies kidney and spleen *qi*, kidney *yang*, and nourishes blood and *yin*. Excellent rehabilitive tonic following illness, surgery or childbirth. Useful in symptoms of poor appetite, anemia, weak legs and back, mental restlessness, insomnia, spermatorrhea, heart palpitations, lumbago and sciatica, and poor memory.

Bottles of 100 pills. Take 5 pills, 3 x day.

Note: this product lists Tiger Bone, a prohibited substance in North America. Common domestic animal substitution may have been made.

Ginseng Root	15.%	Aquilaria Wood	10
Deer Horn	15	Cordyceps Fungus	10
Astragalus Root	15	Angelica Dang Gui	9
Lycium Fruit	10	Seahorse	8
Tiger Bone	10		

200 REN SHEN YANG YING WAN
Ren Shen Yang Ying Wan
"Ginseng Root Support [and] Nourish Pills"
Lanchow Chinese Medicine Works; Lanzhou, Gansu

Classical formula to nurture *qi* and blood, benefit heart, spleen, kidney, and liver; calm *shen*. This is a good general tonic that can be taken over long periods for chronic deficiency of heart blood or *qi*, especially in the aging. Useful in production and distribution of *qi* via lung, spleen and kidney. Recommended for those with insomnia, palpitations, restlessness, poor memory and fatigue.

Paeonia Root	18.4%	Aurantium Peel	7.7
Polygala Root	15.4	Angelica Dang Gui	7.7
Zizyphus Seed	11.5	Rehmannia Root, prep.	5.4
Codonopsis Root	7.7	Schizandra Fruit	5.4
Atractylodes Rhizome	7.7	Poria Fungus	5.4
Astragalus Root	7.7		

201 SHEN KUE LU JUNG WAN
Shen Gui Lu Rong Wan
"Ginseng, Cinnamon, Deer Horn Pill"
Min-Kang Drug Manufactory; Yichang, Hubei

Tonifies *qi*, blood and kidney *yang*, nourishes heart blood, calms *shen*, benefits spleen and liver. Use for general debility with symptoms of restlessness, dizziness, fatigue, palpitations, day sweating, and cold limbs.

Bottles of 100 pills. Take 6 pills, 3 x day.

Main ingredients:

Rehmannia Root, prep.	10.5%	Poria Fungus	3.5
Zizyphus Seed	5.3	Cistanche Stem	3.5
Lycium Fruit	5.3	Tortoise Plastron	3.5
Zizyphus Peel	5.3	Deer Horn	1.8
Dioscorea Root	5.3	Other	47.2
Ginseng Root	3.5		

202 SHEN YUNG PAI FENG WAN

Shuang Liao Shen Rong Bai Feng Wan
"Extra Quality Ginseng, Deer Horn, White Phoenix Pill"
United Pharmaceutical Manufactory; Guangzhou, Guangdong

Breaks blood stagnation, invigorates blood and *qi*, tonifies spleen *qi*, tonifies blood, warms the uterus. A formula for menstrual cramps due to stagnation of liver *qi* and blood, cold uterus, and systemic deficiency of *qi* and blood.

Boxes of 10 large pills. Take one pill per day. Chew, or cut into smaller pieces and swallow. Can also be crushed and dissolved in hot water to drink.

Rehmannia Root	19.5%	Cyperus Rhizome	7.5
Codonopsis Root	10.0	Dipsacus Root	7.5
Angelica Dang Gui	9.7	Atractylodes Rhizome	7.5
Astragalus Root	9.7	Corydalis Rhizome	7.3
Fritillaria Bulb	7.5	Deer Horn	5.3
Paeonia Root	7.5	Ginseng Root	1.0

203 SHIH SAN TAI PAO WAN

Shi San Tai Bao Wan
"Thirteen [Weeks] Great Protecting Pill"
Tianjin Drug Manufactory; Tianjin

Harmonizes spleen and stomach, nourishes and circulates blood, nurtures uterus. Use for the first trimester of pregnancy for fatigue, anemia, nausea, and threatened miscarriage.

Caution: All patent formulas administered during pregnancy should be under the guidance of experienced practitioners of traditional Chinese medicine.

Take 1 pill, 2 x day.

Ligusticum Rhizome	18.2%	Astragalus Root	6.1
Angelica Dang Gui	18.2	Magnolia Bark	5.3
Cuscuta Seed	18.2	Aurantium Fruit	4.5
Paeonia Root	13.6	Notopterygium Rhizome	3.8
Fritillaria Bulb	12.1		

204 TEN FLAVOR TEA:
SHIH CHUAN DA BU WAN
Shi Quan Da Bu Wan
"Ten Inclusive Great Tonifing Pills"
Lanchow Chinese Herb Works; Lanzhou, Gansu

Tonifies spleen and heart *qi*, kidney and spleen *yang*, and nourishes and invigorates blood. Basically the patent formula EIGHT TREASURE TEA (#149) for *qi* and blood, adding Cinnamon Root to warm and consolidate kidney *yang*, and Astragalus Root to nourish spleen and *wei qi*. Use for poor digestion or appetite, fatigue, weak back or legs, anxiety, and debility following illness, surgery or childbirth. **Caution if heat symptoms develop.**

Bottles of 200 pills. Take 8 pills, 3 x day.

Angelica Dang Gui	15.8%	Paeonia Root	10.5
Rehmannia Root	15.8	Poria Fungus	10.5
Codonopsis Root	10.5	Licorice Root	5.3
Astragalus Root	10.5	Cinnamon Bark	5.3
Atractylodes Rhizome	10.5	Ligusticum Rhizome	5.3

Also available as SHIH CHUAN TA BU WAN from the same manufacturer. (Available in bottles of 120 pills, under the same Chinese name, from Tianjin Drug Manufactory.)

205 TZEPAO SANPIEN EXTRACT
Zhi Bao San Bian Jing
"Priceless Treasure Three Whip Extract"
China National Native Produce and Animal By-Products
Import and Export Corp; Qingdao, Shantung

Tonifies *qi* and blood; strenghtens kidney, spleen and lung *qi*; tonifies *wei* and *ying qi*. A broad spectrum nutritive tonic which can be taken over long periods of time. Improves mind and spirit, strengthens lower back, empowers sexual function; counters fatigue, spontaneous sweating, poor memory, insomnia, chronic asthma, and weak extremities. Uses 42 ingredients.

Caution with cold and raw foods.

Boxes of 10 vials, each 10 cc. Take 1-2 vials per day, with water.

Astragalus Root	10.0%	Gecko Lizard	2.0
Ginseng Root	7.0	Cuscuta Seed	2.0
Angelica Dang Gui	6.0	Rehmannia Root	2.0
Deer Horn	5.0	Lycium Fruit	2.0
Deer Penis	5.0	Royal Jelly	2.0
Zanthoxylum Peel	1.5	Nardostachyas Rhizome	1.5
Fennel Fruit	1.5	Poria Fungus	1.0
Seahorse	1.0	Dioscorea Root	1.0
Actinolite Mineral	1.0	Achyranthes Root	1.0
Cinnamon Bark	1.0	Aquilaria Wood	1.0
Morinda Root	1.0	Cornus Fruit	1.0
Poria Fungus	1.0	Atractylodes Rhizome	0.5
Psoralea Fruit	1.0	Anemones Rhizome	0.5
Seahorse	1.0	Alisma Rhizome	0.5
Dog Penis	1.0	Cistanche Stem	0.5
Dragon Bone	1.0	Rubus Fruit	0.5
Epimedium Leaf	1.0	Polygonum Shou Wu	0.5
Eucommia Bark	1.0	Moutan Root-Bark	0.5
Mantis Egg-case	1.0	Phellodendron Bark	0.5
Psoralea Fruit	1.0	Paeonia Root	0.5
Morinda Root	1.0	Polygala Root	0.5
Honey	32.0		

206 WAN NIAN CHUN ZI PU ZIANG
Wan Nian Jun Zi Bu Jiang
"Thousand Year Spring Nourishing Syrup"
Wuhsi Chinese Medicine Works; Wuxi, Jiansu

General tonic for *qi* and blood which benefits the lung, liver, spleen and kidney. Recommended for health maintenance or promotion, and in general weakness in chronic illnesses including asthma and arthritis. Nourishing in malnutrition disorders. Good tonic for aging persons.

Bottles of 100 cc. Take 10 cc with water, once a day.

Royal Jelly	80.0%	Pseudostellaria Root	2.9
Codonopsis Root	4.3	Lycium Fruit	2.9
Ophiopogon Root	4.3	Angelica Dang Gui	1.4
Ginseng Root	2.9	Polygonum Shou Wu	1.4

207 YANG RONG WAN
(GINSENG TONIC PILLS)
Yang Rong Wan
"Support Luxurient Growth Pills"
Lanzhou Fo Ci Pharmaceutical Factory; Lanzhou, Gansu

Tonifies *qi*, blood and kidney *yang*, circulates *qi* in the center, and calms *shen*. Recommended for health maintainence or promotion, and in general weakness in chronic illnesses, or following childbirth or trauma. Good broad purpose tonic for longevity.

Bottles of 200 pills. Take 7 pills, 3 x day.

Codonopsis Root	8.2%	Jujube Fruit	8.2
Atractylodes Rhizome	8.2	Paeonia Root	8.2
Astragalus Root	8.2	Rehmannia Root, prep.	6.1
Licorice Root	8.2	Schizandra Fruit	6.1
Cinnamon Bark	8.2	Poria Fungus	6.1
Aurantium Peel	8.2	Ginger Rhizome	4.1
Angelica Dang Gui	8.2	Polygala Root	4.1

ALSO APPLICABLE as general tonics:

To tonify *qi*, blood, *yin* and *yang*:
238   FOUR GINSENGS
241   DRAGON'S BREW
261   SHENG MAI

To tonify *qi* and blood:
149   EIGHT TREASURE TEA
150   ESSENCE OF CHICKEN WITH TANG KUEI
155   SHOU WU CHIH
235   WOMEN'S LONGEVITY
237   DRAGON DIET

To tonify kidney *yang*, *qi* and blood:
169   DUZHONG BU TIAN SU
167   CHING CHUN BAO
172   HAILUNG TONIC PILLS
174   KWEI LING CHI
175   NAN BAO CAPSULES
176   SEAHORSE HERB TEA
178   XIONG BAO

Other:
152   KANG WEI LING = for impotence and premature ejaculation
193   ANGELICA LONGANA TEA = to tonify *qi*, *yin* and blood

GROUP 8

PILLS TO CALM SHEN
(RESTLESSNESS AND INSOMNIA)

NOTE: Products to calm *shen* may contain mineral substances such as MOTHER-OF-PEARL SHELL, DRAGON BONE, OYSTER SHELL, MAGNETITE, and CLAM SHELL. In excess, these can injure stomach and spleen *qi*, causing indigestion and poor appetite. Usage should be monitored and limited, if necessary. Certain patents may list CINNABAR MINERAL, which contains small amounts of mercury, a heavy metal. These products should be used for limited periods of time.

208 AN MIEN PIEN
An Mian Pian
"Peaceful Sleep Tablets"
China National Native Produce and Animal-by-products
Import and Export Corp; Hobei Branch

Cools liver heat, calms *shen*. Use for insomnia due to heat or congestion in liver, with agitation to the heart and mind. Symptoms include anxiety, mental exhaustion, red or irritated eyes, restless dreaming, and poor memory.

Bottles of 60 tablets. Take 4 tablets, 3 x day.

Main ingredients:

Zizyphus Seed	Poria Fungus
Polygala Root	Licorice Root
Gardenia Fruit	Others

209 AN SHENG PU SHIN WAN
An Shen Bu Xin Wan
"Peaceful Shen *Tonify Heart Pill"*
Shanghai Native Medicine Works; Shanghai

Tonifies heart blood, calms *shen*, relieves obstruction in the blood vessels, strenghtens heart and kidney connection. Indicated for weakness in kidneys and heart causing dizziness, insomnia, restlessness, excessive dreaming, or heart palpitations. Also useful for atherosclerotic plaque causing hardening of the arteries. Known for its soothing and tranquilizing effect.

Caution: See NOTE at head of chapter.

Caution: Acorus (gramineus) rhizome is a close relative of Acorus calamus, which is prohibited as a toxic herb by the U.S. Food and Drug Administration.

Bottles of 300 pills. Take 15 pills, 3 x day.

Mother-of-Pearl Shell	48.3%	Albizia Bark	6.6
Polygonum Shou Wu Stm	11.0	Cuscuta Seed	6.6
Ligustrum Fruit	8.8	Schizandra Fruit	3.3
Eclipta Leaf	6.6	Acorus Rhizome	2.2
Salvia Root	6.6		

210 CEREBRAL TONIC PILLS
Bu Nao Wan
"Nourish Brain Pill"
Sian Chinese Drug Pharmaceutical Works; Xian, Shaanxi

Nourishes heart *yin*, calms *shen*, clears heart phlegm, tonifies heart blood and *qi*. Useful in older persons with atherosclerotic plaque causing hardened arteries, and the accompanying symptoms of poor concentration and memory, restlessness, mental agitation, fatigue and insomnia. Also useful in manic episodes and seizures.

Caution: See NOTE at head of chapter.

Caution: Acorus (gramineus) rhizome is a close relative of Acorus calamus, which is prohibited as a toxic herb by the U.S. Food and Drug Administration.

Bottles of 300 pills. Take 10 pills, 3 x day.

Schizandra Fruit	20.%	Acorus Rhizome	4
Zizyphus Seed	16	Arisaema Rhizome	4
Angelica Dang Gui	10	Succinum Resin	4
Cistanche Stem	8	Gastrodia Rhizome	4
Lycium Fruit	8	Dragon Tooth	4
Juglans Seed	8	Polygala Root	4
Biota Seed	6		

211 CINNABAR SEDATIVE PILL
Zhu Sha An Shen Wan
"Cinnabar Peaceful Shen *Pill"*
Lanchow Chinese Medicine Works; Lanzhou, Gansu

Calms *shen*, nourishes heart blood, sedates excess heart yang. Use for anxiety, insomnia, palpitation, or heavy feeling in chest. Recommended for strong episodes of insomnia with nightmares and palpitations.

Caution: Cinnabar, a natural substance, contains small amounts of mercury, a heavy metal. Limit use to 2 weeks at a time.

Bottles of 100 pills. Take 5 pills, 3 x day.

Angelica Dang Gui	43.%	Coptis Rhizome	9
Rehmannia Root, raw	26	Licorice Root	4
Cinnabar Mineral	17		

212 DING XIN WAN
Ding Xin Wan
"Calm Heart Pill"
Min-Kang Drug Manufactory; Yichang, Hubei

Tonifies *qi*, nourishes blood and *yin*, calms *shen*, disperses internal heat. Use to treat restlessness, anxiety, insomnia, palpitations and poor memory.

Bottles of 100 pills. Take 6 pills, 2 x day.

Main ingredients:

Biota Seed	13.7%	Ophiopogon Root	9.1
Angelica Dang Gui	9.1	Codonopsis Root	4.6
Poria Fungus	9.1	Scutellaria Root	4.6
Polygala Root	9.1	Succinum Resin	2.3
Zizyphus Seed	9.1	Others	29.7

213 EMPEROR'S TEA
Tian Wang Bu Xin Wan
"Heavenly King Benefit Heart Pill"
Lanchow Fo Ci Pharmaceutical Factory; Lanzhou, Gansu

Nurtures heart blood and *yin*, calms *shen*, sedates deficiency-heat of the heart. Use for insomnia, restlessness, anxiety, palpitations, and vivid dreaming. Also useful in hyperactive thyroid and nocturnal emission.

Bottles of 200 pills. Take 8 pills, 3 x day.

Rehmannia Root, raw	31.%	Biota Seed	8
Scrophularia Root	8	Zizyphus Seed	8
Schizandra Fruit	8	Polygala Root	4
Asparagus Root	8	Poria Fungus	4
Angelica Dang Gui	8	Salvia Root	4
Ophiopogon Root	8	Codonopsis Root	4

Also available from the same manufacturer as TIEN WANG BU XIN WAN.

214 HEALTHY BRAIN PILLS
Jian Nao Wan
"Healthy Brain Pills"
Tsingtao Medicine Works; Qingdao, Shandong

Tonifies heart and liver blood, calms *shen*, sedates liver fire and wind. Use for the disturbed *shen* symptoms of sleeplessness, agitation, mental exhaustion, dizziness, poor memory, fatigue. Recommended for strong episodes of insomnia with nightmares, palpitations, and restlessness.

Caution: Cinnabar, a natural substance, contains small amounts of mercury, a heavy metal. Limit use to 2 weeks at a time.

Bottles of 300 Pills. Take 5 pills, 3 x day.

Zizyphus Seed	18.%	Dragon Tooth	4
Angelica Dang Gui	12	Ginseng Root	4
Dioscorea Root	10	Gastrodia Rhizome	4
Cistanche Stem	8	Bamboo Resin	4
Lycium Fruit	8	Anemone Rhizome	4
Schizandra Fruit	6	Cinnabar Mineral	4
Alpinia Fruit	6	Biota Seed	4
Succinum Resin	4		

215 PAI TZU YANG HSIN WAN
Bai Zi Yang Xin Wan
"Biota Seed Support Heart Pill"
Lanchow Chinese Medicine Works; Lanzhou, Gansu

Nourishes heart *yin* and blood, calms *shen*, resolves heart phlegm, and disperses heat in the upper burner. Use for insomnia, anxiety, mental restlessnes, palpitation and restlessness with dryness of mouth or lips.

Caution: Acorus (gramineus) rhizome is a close relative of Acorus calamus, which is prohibited as a toxic herb by the U.S. Food and Drug Administration.

Bottles of 200 Pills. Take 5 pills, 3 x day.

Biota Seed	26.%	Angelica Dang Gui	6
Lycium Fruit	19	Poria Fungus	6
Scrophularia Root	13	Acorus Rhizome	6
Rehmannia Root, raw	13	Licorice Root	3
Ophiopogon Root	6		

216 SHEN CHING SHUAI JAO WAN
Shen Jing Shuai Ruo Wan
"Nerve Weak Pill"
Beijing Tung Jen Tang; Beijing

Tonifies heart *qi*, blood and *yin*, nourishes liver *yin* and blood, calms *shen*, reduces heat. Use to relieve deficiency of heart blood causing insomnia, restless sleep, nightmares, night sweating, insomnia, vertigo, tinnitus, palpitation, and fatigue.

Caution: See NOTE at head of chapter.

Bottles of 200 pills. Take 20 pills, 2 x day.

Ginseng Root	15.%	Ophiopogon Root	6
Zizyphus Seed	12	Clam Shell	6
Human Placenta	12	Schizandra Fruit	6
Coptis Rhizome	6	Angelica Dang Gui	3
Polygonum Shou Wu	6	Poria Fungus	3
Donkey Skin Glue	6	Other	19

217 TABELLAE SUAN ZAO REN TANG
Suan Zao Ren Tang Pian
"Zizyphus Seed Soup Tablet"
Sing-kyn Drug House; Guangzhou, Guangdong

Classical prescription to calm disturbed *shen*, reduce heat, nurture the heart, break stagnation, and stop pain. Use for insomnia, dreaminess, restlessness, heart palpitations, and mental agitation.

Bottles of 48 tablets. Take 2 tablets, 3 x day.

Zizyphus Seed	78.5%	Anemarrhena Rhizome	6.1
Ligusticum Rhizome	6.1	Licorice Root	3.1
Poria Fungus	6.1		

218 TZE ZHU PILLS
Ci Zhu Wan
"Magnetite, Cinnabar Pills"
Kwangchow Pharmaceutical Industry Co; Guangzhou,
Guangdong

Calms disturbed *shen*, cools heart fire, brightens the eyes. A classical formula for heart fire disturbing *shen*, with accompanying dizziness, insomnia, palpitation, headaches, or ringing in the ears. Also useful in vision problems due to heart fire, including swollen eyes, cataract, glaucoma, poor day or night vision, and blurry vision. Useful in epilepsy and manic disorders.

Caution: Cinnabar, a natural substance, contains small amounts of mercury, a heavy metal. Limit use to 2 weeks at a time. Caution: See NOTE at head of chapter.

Bottles of 120 pills. Take 5-6 pills, 2 x day.

Magnetite Mineral	62.%	Cinnabar Mineral	10
Fermented Leaven	28		

ALSO APPLICABLE for restless *shen*:

186	ANGELICA LONGANA TEA
232	RED HORSE - HEART / RADIANCE
242	COMPASSIONATE SAGE - HEART SPIRIT
233	PEACEFUL
250	AN SHEN
251	YANG XIN
266	EASE PLUS

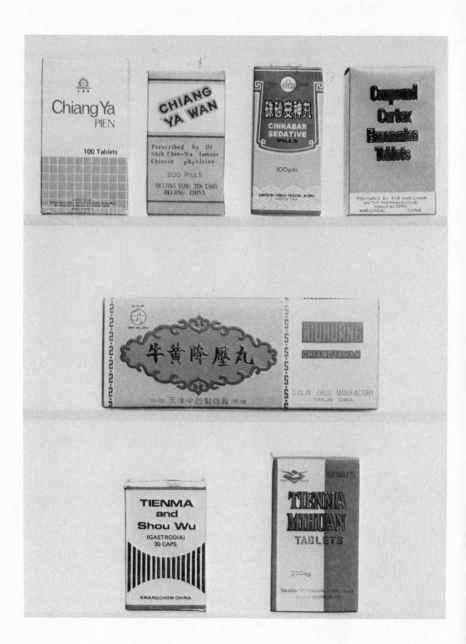

GROUP 9

PILLS TO CONTROL ENDOGENOUS LIVER WIND AND HYPERTENSION

NOTE: Products containing RHINOCEROS HORN, OX GALLSTONE or BORNEOL CRYSTAL should be used for limited time only. Do not use in coma following excessive sweating, vomitting, or hemorrhage, or if person is in shock with cold sweating and cold limbs. Also, Water Buffalo Horn may have been substituted for RHINOCEROS HORN.

219 CHIANG YA WAN
Jiang Ya Wan
"Lower [Blood] Pressure Tablets"
Beijing Tung Jen Tang; Beijing

Pacifies liver wind and fire, promotes blood circulation and removes blood stagnation, tonifies blood, benefits kidneys, stops pain. Use for symptoms of hypertension due to liver fire, including vertigo, bursting headache, stiff neck, red face, dizziness, and poor gait.

Bottles of 200 pills. Take 20 pills, 2 x day.

Prohibited during pregnancy.

Leonurus Leaf	15.%	Prunella Spike	5
Achyranthes Root	13	Moutan Bark	5
Rehmannia Root	10	Gastrodia Rhizome	4
Donkey Skin Glue	10	Rhubarb Rhizome	4
Angelica Dang Gui	8	Succinum Resin	3
Uncaria Stem	7	Coptis Rhizome	3
Aquilaria Wood	5	Antelope Horn	3
Ligusticum Rhizome	5		

220 COMPOUND CORTEX EUCOMMIA TABLETS
Fu Fang Du Zhong Pian
"Medicinal Compound with Eucommia Bark Tablet"
Kweichow United Pharmaceutical Manufactory; Guizhou

Sedates liver fire, calms liver wind, tonifies kidney *qi*. A modern formula for the relief of symptoms associated with hypertension due to deficient kidney *qi* with hyperactive liver, including flushed face, palpitations, headache, and dizziness.

Bottles of 100 tablets. Take 5 tablets, 3 x day.

Eucommia Bark	50.%	Prunella Spike	20
Uncaria Stem	20	Scutellaria Root	10

221 HYPERTENSION REPRESSING TABLETS
Jiang Ya Ping Pian
"Lower [Blood] Pressure Calming Tablet"
Liaoyuan Pharmaceutical Works; Liaoyuan, Jilin

Sedates liver fire and calms endogenous liver wind. Use to reduce symptoms associated with hypertension due to liver fire, including dizziness, ear ringing, headache, and flushed face. (May need to be combined with a blood or *yin* tonic). Effective in lowering blood cholesterol and preventing hardening of the arteries.

Boxes of 12 bottles, each with 12 tablets. Take 4 tablets, 3 x day, in three courses of 14 days each.

Prunella Spike	25.%	Chrysanthemum Flower	15
Scutellaria Root	25	Sophora Root	15
Earthworm	20		

222 NIU HUANG CHIANG YA WAN
Niu Huang Jiang Yá Wan
"Ox Gallstone Lower [Blood] Pressure Pill"
Tianjin Drug Manufactory; Tianjin

Reduces liver heat and wind, resolves heart phlegm, opens heart orifice, calms *shen*. Use for hypertension due to liver fire, causing headache, dizziness, insomnia, and restlessness. Demonstrated to lower fatty deposits in blood vessels.

Boxes of 10 gummy pills encased in a wax "egg". Take one pill per day: chew, or cut into smaller pieces and swallow. May be dissolved in water.

Caution: See NOTE at head of chapter.

Caution: Rhinoceros Horn is a controlled substance in North America.

Peonia Root	14.8%	Antelope Horn	2.5
Astragalus Root	6.2	Pearl	2.5
Ox Gallstone	4.9	Other	10.4
Borneol Crystal	4.9	Honey Binder	50.1
Rhinoceros Horn	3.7		

223 TIENMA AND SHOU WU
Tian Ma Shou Wu Wan
"Gastrodia and Polygonum Shou Wu Pill"
Luo Jiang Pharmaceutical Manufactory;
Guangzhou, Guangdong

Treats deficiency of liver blood with rising *yang* and/or internal wind. Use as a general tonic where liver blood is deficient, with symptoms of vertigo, dizziness, headache, fatigue, poor appetite, or poor memory. Reported to treat greying and thinning hair if used daily for a year.

Bottles of 30 capsules. Take three capsules, 2 x day.

Main Ingredients:

Gastrodia Rhizome	Epimedium Leaf
Polygonum Shou Wu	Ginseng Root

224 TIANMA CHU FENG PU PIEN
Tian Ma Qu Feng Bu Pian
"Gastrodia Dispel Wind Formula Tablets"
Kunming Native Drugs Factory; Kunming, Yunnan

Dispels internal wind due to hyperactive liver *yang*, disperses exogenous wind and wind-damp, nourishes liver blood, reinforces kidneys. Use for symptoms associated with hypertension, including headache, dizziness, or poor memory; for the wind symptoms of facial paralysis, and stiff or paralyzed limbs; and wind-damp in joints and muscles.

Bottles of 60 tablets. Take 5-10 tablets, 3 x day.

Gastrodia Rhizome	27.%	Achyranthes Root	10
Angelica Dang Gui	20	Eucommia Bark	10
Rehmannia Root	13	Notopterygium Rhizome	5
Cinnamon Bark	10	Typhonus Rhizome	5

225 TIENMA MIHUAN TABLETS
Tian Ma Mi Huan Pian
"Gastrodia Honey Surrounding Tablet"

Tonifies liver *yin* and blood, calms liver fire and wind, and invigorates the blood. This formula offers Gastrodia Rhizome (in a base of Armillariella Fungus) as a single herb patent. Use for symptoms of hypertension including headache and dizziness, as well as numbness or tingling in limbs, and insomnia due to liver *yang*.

Take 4-5 tablets, 3 x day.

Gastrodia Rhizome	Armillariella Fungus

ALSO APPLICABLE for liver wind:

79 TIAN MA HU GU WAN
185 LYCIUM AND CHRYSANTHEMUM TEA
190 TSO-TZU OTIC PILLS

For effects of stroke:
104 RENSHEN ZAI ZAO WAN
106 TSAI TSAO WAN
107 YAN SHEN JAI JAO WAN

Liver wind affecting eyes:
186 MING MU SHANG CHING PIEN
186 REHMANNIA TEA

APPENDIX I

EAST EARTH HERB COMPANY
Reedsport, Oregon

East Earth Herb Company is a manufacturing company based in Oregon. They produce a variety of herbal products made from imported Chinese herbs, including TURTLE MOUNTAIN PROFESSIONAL PRODUCTS, DRAGON EGGS, and JADE PHARMACY. They also are producing a line of products called JADE MEDICINE which is distributed through stores.

TURTLE MOUNTAIN PRODUCTS and DRAGON EGGS are the same herbal formulas, but with different labels, quantities, and distributors. The TURTLE MOUNTAIN line is directly marketed to health practitioners, while DRAGON EGGS are distributed to health and food stores. Both TURTLE MOUNTAIN and DRAGON EGGS are created and manufactured by Bill Brevoort, who has been making and distributing his products since 1978.

The pills are formed out of dried powdered Chinese herbs and are further processed by extraction in both alcohol and water. This process makes them more concentrated and stronger than the patents from China, allowing for smaller dosages.

The TURTLE MOUNTAIN line comes in packets of 10 tablets, bottles of 75 tablets, or boxes of 150 or 300 tablets individually sealed in plastic strips. It is also available in 1/4 oz. and 1 oz. concentrated liquid extract. DRAGON EGGS are offered in bottles of either 24 or 30 tablets.

JADE PHARMACY are formulas created by Ted Kaptchuk, author of *The Web That Has No Weaver*, and manufactured by East Earth Herb. They are based on classical prescriptions which have been expanded by Dr. Kaptchuk.

Currently, six formulas are being produced, and the line will soon be expanded to twenty products. Dr. Kaptchuk has written a small book describing these formulas, which is available from the distributor, K'AN HERB COMPANY.

JADE PHARMACY is available in packets of 10 tablets, bottles of 75 tablets, or boxes of 150 or 300 tablets individually sealed in plastic strips. It is also available in 1/4 oz. and 1 oz. concentrated liquid extract.

DOSAGES FOR EAST EARTH HERB PRODUCTS:

In general, it is recommended that persons take two tablets per day, one in the morning and one in the early evening. JADE PHARMACY is recommending 2-6 tablets per day, on instruction of the practitioner.

The formulas are better absorbed if chewed or sucked before swallowing. Dosage should be adjusted according to the person and the condition. If using the extract, four drops equal one tablet. This may be taken in a small glass of water.

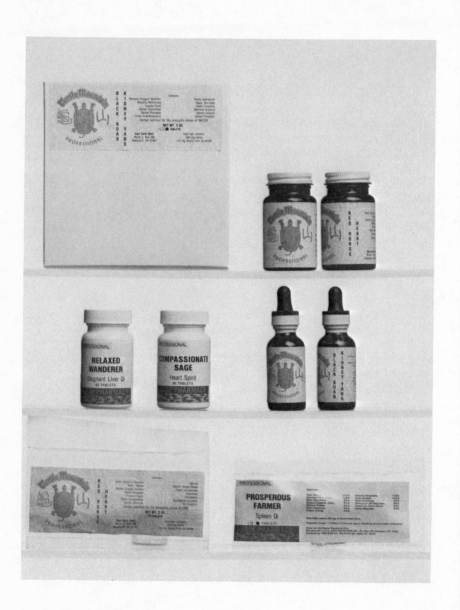

TURTLE MOUNTAIN PROFESSIONAL PRODUCTS / DRAGON EGGS

Herbal products developed by Bill Brevoort
Manufactured by East Earth Herb Company; Reedsport, Oregon

PACKAGING:

TURTLE MOUNTAIN (TM) comes in packets of 10 tablets, bottles of 75 tablets, or boxes of 150 or 300 tablets individually sealed in plastic strips; also available in 1/4 oz. and 1 oz. concentrated liquid extract.

DRAGON EGGS (DE) are offered in bottles of 24 tablets.

GROUP I
FIVE ELEMENT FORMULAS

226 BLACK BOAR - KIDNEY YANG (TM) DYNAMIC (DE)

Tonifies kidney *yang* and *qi*, nourishes *jing*. Useful in systemic cold, cold extremities, decreased sex drive, and backache. Balance with WHITE TURTLE-KIDNEY YIN formula to tonify or regulate kidney *qi*. Combine with YELLOW OX-SPLEEN for deficency of spleen and kidney *yang* leading to poor digestion with undigested food in the stool.

Epimedium Leaf	14.6%	Cistanche Root	7.3
Rehmannia Rhizome	14.6	Eucommia Bark	7.3
Polygonum Shou Wu	7.3	Psoralea Seed	7.3
Achyranthes Root	7.3	Cuscuta Seed	7.3
Morinda Root	7.3	Cinnamon Bark	7.3
Cornus Fruit	7.3	Acanthopanax Root-Bark	4.9

227 GREEN TIGER - LIVER (TM) HARMONY (DE)

Sedates liver fire, calms liver wind, breaks up *qi* stagnation to smooth and harmonize the liver, nourishes liver *yin* and blood, and dispels blood stagnation. Use for upward flaring of liver fire causing headache, dizziness, red or painful eyes, or insomnia. Suitable for congested liver affecting digestion, menstruation, and pre-menstrual syndrome. Useful in smoking and drug withdrawl.

Chrysanthemum Flower	20.7%	Bupleurum Root	10.3
Lycium Fruit	10.3	Ligusticum Rhizome	10.3
Cyperus Rhizome	10.3	Prunus Seed	8.6
Paeonia Root	10.3	Polygonum Rhizome	5.2
Moutan Root-bark	10.3	Gastrodia Rhizome	3.4

228 LUNG DISPERSING WATER (TM)

Disperses wind, damp and phlegm from lungs, stops cough, tonifies lung *qi*. Use for acute or chronic cough due to wind-invasion (including bronchitis), as well as chronic breathing difficulties related to asthma or emphysema.

Platycodon Root	20.%	Inula Flower	10
Morus Root-Bark	20	Perilla Seed	10
Citrus Peel	10	Pinellia Rhizome	5
Cynanchum Root	10	Asarum Leaf	5
Magnolia Flower	10		

229 RED HORSE - HEART (TM) RADIANCE (DE)

Nurtures heart blood and *yin*, resolves stagnation and invigorates blood, resolves heart-phlegm, roots restless *shen*. Use for symptoms of insomnia, mental restlessness, poor memory or inability to concentrate. Useful in opening up congested or hardened heart blood vessels, and in chronic seizures. May help to reduce blood cholesterol and lipids.

Longan Fruit	10.9%	Succinum Resin	8.7
Salvia Root	10.9	Leonurus Leaf	4.3
Angelica Dang Gui	8.7	Polygala Root	4.3
Albizzia Bark	8.7	Arisaema Rhizome	4.3
Biota Seed	8.7	Pseudoginseng Root	4.3
Zizyphus Seed	8.7	Dragon Bone	4.3
Ganoderma Fungus	8.7		

230 WHITE MONKEY - LUNGS (TM) CRYSTALLIZE (DE)

Nourishes lung *yin* and *qi*, resolves phlegm-heat. Use for deficiency of *qi* and *yin* with heat in the lungs, causing difficult breathing, dry cough, and sticky, unproductive phlegm. Caution in excessively damp conditions.

Adenophora Root	24.5%	Lily Bulb	9.8
Schizandra Fruit	22.0	Ophiopogon Root	9.8
Poria Fungus	9.8	Asparagus Root	9.8
Polygonatum Rhizome	9.8	American Ginseng Root	4.6

231 WHITE TURTLE - KIDNEY YIN (TM) RECOVERY (DE)

Nourishes kidney *yin*; nurtures *qi*, blood and *jing*. Useful in restlessness, deficiency fevers, heat in palms or soles, and night sweating. Balance with BLACK BOAR-KIDNEY YANG to regulate or tonify kidney *qi*. Combine with RED HORSE-HEART for deficiency of heart *yin* due to deficiency of kidney *yin*.

Rehmannia Root	23.8%	Euryale Seed	9.5
Poria Fungus	9.5	Morus Fruit	4.8
Dioscorea Root	9.5	Desmodium Leaf	4.8
Alisma Rhizome	9.5	Smilax Rhizome	4.8
Poria Skin	9.5	Rosa Fruit	4.8
Scrophularia Root	9.5		

232 YELLOW OX - SPLEEN (TM) COMBUSTION (DE)

Invigorates stagnation of *qi* in the middle burner, tonifies and warms spleen *qi* to promote digestion. Use for symptoms of abdominal distension, bloating, poor digestion, poor appetite, flatulence, hiccups, erratic or pasty stools, and fatigue.

Astragalus Root	11.5%	Fennel Seed	5.8
Atractylodes Rhizome	11.5	Magnolia Bark	5.8
Codonopsis Root	11.5	Ginger Rhizome	5.8
Crataegus Fruit	11.5	Licorice Root	5.8
Dioscorea Root	11.5	Evodia Fruit	1.9
Ginseng Root	5.8		

GROUP II
BASIC FORMULAS

Both TURTLE MOUNTAIN and DRAGON EGGS use the same names for the following products.

PACKAGING:
TURTLE MOUNTAIN products come in packets of 10 tablets, bottles of 75 tablets, or boxes of 150 or 300 tablets individually sealed in plastic strips; also available in 1/4 oz. and 1 oz. concentrated liquid extract.

DRAGON EGGS are offered in bottles of 30 tablets.

233 DETOX

Sedates liver fire, heat and inflammation, dispels wind. Use for fevers and inflammations, whether systemic or isolated in the liver, stomach or lungs. Useful in allergenic reaction including hives; also, boils and carbuncles, constipation, dysentery, acute hepatitis, red irritated eyes, sore throat, toothache, and tonsillitis. Not indicated for fevers due to colds or flus.

CAUTION: Limit use to period of heat or inflammation, usually within 5 days.

CAUTION in weak patients. If diarrhea occurs, reduce dosage or discontinue.

Gardenia Fruit	8.3%	Coptis Rhizome	8.3
Phellodendron Bark	8.3	Plantago seed	8.3
Scutellaria Root	8.3	Benincasa Seed	8.3
Rhubarb Rhizome	8.3	Arctium Fruit	8.3
Lonicera Flower	8.3	Cimicifuga Rhizome	8.3
Forsythia Fuit	8.3	Licorice Root	8.3

234 DRAGON DIET

Tonifies kidney and spleen *qi*, nurtures blood, disperses spleen damp, regulates liver, benefits digestion. A general tonic to help digestive function, and counter abdominal bloating, gurgling, pasty stools, and poor appetite. Recommended as an herbal supplement while dieting, to provide nutrition and aid in discharging water and wastes.

Main ingredients:

Angelica Root
Soja Seed
Crataegus Fruit
Zizyphus Seed
Epimedium Leaf
Pseudoginseng Root
Stephania Root
Rehmannia Root
Astragalus Root
Codonopsis Root
Angelica Dang Gui
Polygonum Shou Wu

Peonia Root
Moutan Root-Bark
Ginseng Root
Adenophorea Root
Cinnamon Bark
Licorice Root
Poria Fungus
Lycium Fruit
Schizandra Fruit
Tremella Fungus
Pseudoginseng Root

235 EXPRESS

Invigorates and stimulates *qi* and blood circulation in the channels and collaterals, tonifies *qi*, nourishes blood and *yin*, clears the mind. Formulated as an an herbal stimulant for energy and clarity. Useful in quitting coffee.

Contraindicated in patients with deficient heart *qi*.

CAUTION: Ephedra Leaf may cause sleeplessness or heart palpitations. Reduce dosage or discontinue if these symptoms develop.

Main ingredients:

Ephedra Leaf	Pseudoginseng Root
Ginseng Root	Adenophorea Root
Astragalus Root	Angelica Dang Gui
Jujube Fruit	Lycium Fruit
Ginger Rhizome	Cinnamon Bark
Licorice Root	Polygonum Shou Wu
Polygonatum Root	Tremella Fungus
Bee Pollen	

236 FOUR GINSENGS

Tonifies spleen and lung *qi*, nurtures and invigorates blood, benefits kidneys, nourishes liver *yin* and blood, promotes digestion. This is a broad spectrum general tonic for *qi* and blood, *yin* and *yang*, strengthening the function of all the *zang-fu* organs. It can be taken over long periods of time.

Ginseng Root	9.4%	Peonia Root	3.1
Angelica Dang Gui	6.3	Cyperus Rhizome	3.1
Scutellaria Root	6.3	Poria Fungus	3.1
Polygonum Shou Wu	6.3	Adenophorea Root	3.1
Ginger Rhizome	4.7	Atractylodes Rhizome	3.1
Schizandra Fruit	4.7	Eucommia Bark	3.1
Lycium Fruit	3.1	Licorice Root	3.1
Ligusticum Rhizome	3.1	Dioscorea Rhizome	3.1
Jujube Fruit	3.1	Cistanche Stem	3.1
Biota Seed	3.1	Cornus Fruit	3.1
Longan Fruit	3.1	Scrophularia Root	3.1
Salvia Root	3.1	Aconite Root	1.6
Polygala Root	3.1	Bupleurum Root	1.6
Moutan Root-Bark	3.1		

237 PEACEFUL

Tonifies and harmonizes heart *qi*, nourishes heart *yin*, disperses stagnant *qi* and blood, pacifies upward *yang* and liver heat, and calms *shen*. Use for high blood pressure with reddening of face, insomnia, mental agitation or restlessness, and poor memory. Recommended by the manufacturer for periods of emotional stress. Helpful in nicotine withdrawal and hardening of the arteries. May help to reduce blood cholesterol and lipids.

Morus Fruit	10.3%	Longan Fruit	3.1
Schizandra Fruit	10.3	Polygala Root	3.1
Albizzia Bark	8.2	Eucommia Bark	3.1
Polygonum Shou Wu	8.2	Prunella Spike	3.1
Angelica Dang Gui	6.2	Arisaema Rhizome	3.1
Zizyphus Seed	6.2	Cistanche Stem	3.1
Ligusticum Rhizome	5.2	Dragon Bone	2.1
Cuscuta Seed	5.2	Salvia Root	2.1
Succinum Resin	4.1	Gastrodia Rhizome	1.0
Scutellaria Root	4.1	Cinnabar Mineral	0.1

238 SAGE'S GINSENG

Tonifies spleen and lung *qi*, benefits heart and kidneys, nourishes *jing*, calms *shen*, invigorates the blood. Combines high quality ginseng roots with harmonizing herbs. Valuable tonic for health and longevity.

Bottles of 10 tablets.

Pseudoginseng Root	19.66%
Poria Fungus	19.66
Ganoderma Fungus	19.66
Schizandra Fruit	19.66
Lycium Fruit	14.75
American Ginseng Rt (wild)	5.90
Ginseng Root (semi-wild Yi-Sun)	.49
Ginseng (wild Tung Pei)	.22

239 TANG KUEI

Tonifies and invigorates blood, benefits liver, heart and uterus. Use for fatigue, anemia, amenorrhea, pre-menstrual depression or irritability, and to regulate the period. May be combined with other patents to reinforce effect of nourishing and invigorating blood.

Angelica Dang Gui   100.%

240 TURTLE MOUNTAIN TONIC (TM) DRAGON'S BREW (DE)

General tonic for *qi* and blood, *yin* and *yang*. Tonifies *qi* of lungs, spleen, kidneys and liver; nourishes *yin* of liver, lungs and kidney; tonifies and invigorates blood, aids digestion and harmonzies middle burner. Recommended as a daily tonic and invigorater. This product is an herbal concentrate with a live fermented enzyme component.

Bottles of 6.3 oz, or 25.6 oz. Take one teaspoon daily with tea or hot water. Refrigerate before first opening to avoid bubbling.

Main ingredients:

Citrus Peel	Moutan Bark
Pseudoginseng Root	Lotus Seed
Codonopsis Root	Bupleurum Root
Ginseng Root	Schizandra Fruit
Adenophora Root	Polygala Root
Scrophularia Root	Jujube Fruit
Salvia Root	Cinnamon Bark
Licorice Root	Polygonum Shou Wu
Atractylodes Rhizome	Astragalus Root
Ginger Rhizome	Ligusticum Rhizome
Eucommia Bark	Peonia Root
Royal Jelly	Tremella Fungus
Ganoderma Fungus	Poria Fungus
Angelica Dang Gui	Alisma Rhizome
Rehmannia Roott	Aconite Root
Cornus Fruit	Psoralea Fruit
Lycium Fruit	Polygonatum Root
Fennel Seed	

241 WOMEN'S LONGEVITY

Tonifies blood and *qi*, invigorates blood circulation in middle and lower burners, invigorates liver *qi*, benefits menstruation and the uterus. Tonifies and regulates heart, spleen, liver, kidneys and lungs. A very rich and complex general tonic for women, or for both genders following long-term illness, or loss of blood due to trauma, childbirth or surgery. Useful for fatigue, amenorrhea, excessive bleeding during menses, and pre-menstrual symptoms.

CAUTION: discontinue or adjust usage if signs of heat develop.

Angelica Dang Gui	6.2 %	Cimicifucga Rhizome	2.0
Rehmannia Root	5.0	Rosa Fruit	2.0
Peonia Root	5.0	Euryale Seed	2.0
Schizandra Fruit	5.0	Lotus Seed	2.0
Ligusticum Rhizome	5.0	Polygonatum Rhizome	2.0
Polygonum Shou Wu	4.0	Lycium Fruit	2.0
Achyranthes Root	3.0	Adenophora Root	1.9
Crataegus Fruit	3.0	Succinum Resin	1.9
Poria Fungus	2.5	Cistanche Stem	1.5
Cinnamon Bark	2.5	Succinum Resin	1.9
Cyperus Rhizome	2.5	Biota Seed	2.0
Eucommia Bark	2.4	Euryale Seed	2.0
Albizia Bark	2.2	Ginseng Root	2.0
Scrophularia Root	2.1	Lotus Seed	2.0
Atractylodes Rhizome	2.0	Ginger Rhizome	2.0
Jujube Fruit	2.0	Polygonatum Rhizome	2.0
Codonopsis Root	2.0	Cuscuta Seed	2.0
Cimicifucga Rhizome	2.0	Tremella Fungus	2.0
Licorice Root	2.0	Alisma Root	2.0
Rosa Fruit	2.0	Psoralea Fruit	2.0
Adenophora Root	1.9	Astragalus Root	1.5
Salvia Root	1.5	Cistanche Stem	1.5
Polygala Root	1.5	Platycodon Root	1.1
Cornus Fruit	1.5	Bupleurum Root	1.0
Moutan Root-Bark	1.5	Aconite Root	1.0

JADE PHARMACY

Herbal products developed by Ted Kaptchuk, O.M.D.
Manufactured by East Earth Herb Company
Reedsport, Oregon

242 COMPASSIONATE SAGE - HEART SPIRIT

Calms disturbed *shen*, nurtures heart blood and *yin*, invigorates blood to break stagnation, tonifies heart *qi*, reduces heart fire. An important formula for regulating the heart in a variety of complaints, including deficiency and congestion. Calms restlessness, insomnia, poor memory, palpitations, and anxiety. Useful for resolving fatty deposits in the heart and blood vessels.

Take 2-6 tablets per day, or 8-24 drops of the extract.

Dragon Bone	12.8%	Albizzia Bark	6.4
Zizyphus Seed	9.5	Salvia Root	6.4
Polygala Root	9.5	Succinum Resin	4.8
Biota Seed	9.5	Coptis Rhizome	3.2
Poria Fungus	9.5	Angelica Dang Gui	3.2
Codonopsis Root	6.4	Ganoderma Fungus	3.2
Acorus Rhizome	6.4	Licorice Root	3.2
Longan Fruit	6.4		

243 DYNAMIC WARRIOR - KIDNEY YANG

Tonifies kidney *yang* and *qi*. Using the classic *Jin Kui Shen Qi Wan* (#171) as its foundation, this formula treats sore back and legs, cold hands or feet, difficulty in mobility, poor circulation, edema, urinary dysfunction, sexual dysfunction, and infertility due to cold. Also useful for asthma due to a weak kidney-lung dynamic.

Take 2-6 tablets per day, or 8-24 drops of the extract.

Eucommia Bark	10.3%	Dioscorea Root	5.1
Morinda Root	10.3	Cornus Fruit	5.1
Cistanche Stem	10.3	Lycium Fruit	5.1
Psoralea Fruit	10.3	Ginseng Root	5.1
Rehmannia Root	10.3	Aconite Root	2.6
Cuscuta Seed	10.3	Angelica Dang Gui	1.7
Achyranthes Root	6.8	Cinnamon Bark	1.7
Schizandra Fruit	5.1		

244 PROSPEROUS FARMER - SPLEEN QI

Tonifies spleen *qi*, invigorates stomach *qi*, resolves spleen damp, regulates stomach and spleen. Using the classical *Liu Jun Zi Tang* (#128) as its foundation, this formula is a tonic for the spleen, invigorating its energy and dispelling damp. Symptoms include abdominal bloating, loose, pasty or erratic stools, sluggish digestion with poor appetite, chronic fatigue, and poor or chaotic nutrient absorption.

Take 2-6 tablets per day, or 8-24 drops of the extract.

Ginseng Root	11.8%	Amomum Fruit	5.9
Atractylodes Rhizome	11.8	Saussurea Root	5.9
Poria Fungus	11.8	Magnolia Bark	5.9
Astragalus Root	11.8	Crataegus Fruit	3.9
Pinellia Rhizome	9.8	Ginger Rhizome	3.9
Dioscorea Root	7.8	Licorice Root	3.9
Citrus Peel	5.9		

245 QUIET CONTEMPLATIVE - KIDNEY YIN

Nurtures kidney *yin*, and *qi*, nourishes liver *yin* and blood, tonifies *jing*. A variation of the classical *Liu Wei Di Huang Wan* (#188). Use for kidney yin deficiency leading to lower back pain, dry skin or mouth, dizziness, dry eyes, ringing in ears, sexual dysfunction, night sweats, and hot flashes.

Take 2-6 tablets per day, or 8-24 drops of the extract.

Rehmannia Root	18.0%	Cuscuta Seed	6.0
Cornus Fruit	12.0	Lycium Fruit	6.0
Dioscorea Rhizome	12.0	Polygonum Shou Wu	6.0
Poria Fungus	9.0	Morus Fruit	4.5
Alisma Rhizome	9.0	Ligustrum Fruit	4.5
Moutan Root-bark	9.0	Eclipta Leaf	4.5

246 RELAXED WANDERER - STAGNANT LIVER QI

Relieves congestion of liver *qi*, reduces heat in the liver, invigorates the blood to dispel stagnation, nourishes liver blood, strengthens stomach and spleen. Building upon the classical *Xiao Yao Wan* (#123) as its foundation, this formula is intended for liver congestion affecting digestion, menstruation, or the upper burner. Symptoms include loose stools, flatulence, abdominal distension, stomachache, and belching. Gynecological symptoms include premenstrual syndrome (headache, irritability, water retention, breast tenderness), and menstrual problems including irregular or painful periods.

Take 2-6 tablets per day, or 8-24 drops of the extract.

Angelica Dang Gui	13.3%	Cyperus Rhizome	4.4
Paeonia Root	13.3	Moutan Root-Bark	4.4
Atractylodes Rhizome	13.3	Gardenia Fruit	4.4
Poria Fungus	13.3	Gastrodia Rhizome	4.4
Buplerum Root	8.9	Licorice Root	4.4
Ligusticum Rhizome	6.7	Ginger Rhizome	4.4
Mentha Herb	4.4		

247 WISE JUDGE - LUNG YIN AND QI

Tonifies lung *qi*, nurtures and moistens lung *yin*, resolves phlegm-heat. Use for lung deficiency marked by dryness and heat, or sticky phlegm. Symptoms include chronic dry cough, dry throat with thirst, hoarseness, or dry nostrils. Useful following fever with thirst, or after quitting smoking.

Take 2-6 tablets per day, or 8-24 drops of the extract.

Glehnia Root	9.0%	Fritillaria Zhe Bei	6.0
Ophiopogon Root	9.0	Tremella Fungus	6.0
Polygonatum Rhizome	9.0	Angelica Dang Gui	4.5
Lily Bulb	9.0	Rehmannia Root, prep	4.5
American Ginseng Root	9.0	Licorice Root	4.5
Pseudostellaria Root	9.0	Poria Fungus	4.5
Asparagus Root	6.0	Schizandra Fruit	3.0
Platycodon Root	6.0		

APPENDIX II

CONSTITUTIONAL THERAPIES

Herbal Products developed by
Subhuti Dharmananda, Ph.D.
Manufactured by Nature's Sunshine Products
Spanish Fork, Utah

Nature's Sunshine Products has produced a line of fourteen herb formulas called CONSTITUTIONAL THERAPIES, devised by Subhuti Dharmananda and based on his book *Your Nature, Your Health*. Each formula is representative of the traditional and patent formulas that treat well-defined constitutions, conformations, conditions and symptom-complexes.

The products were developed as seven pairs. The first member of each pair is defined as an "anti-stress" formula, used to treat the excess conditions for those of stronger constitution requiring purging and dispersing formulas. The second member is defined as a "strengthening" formula, used for deficiency conditions affecting those of weaker constitution, and requiring tonifying and consolidating therapies.

The seven pairs include five based on Five Phase (Five Element) Theory, and the remaining two pairs relate to specific energetic problems.

The products are made of dried herbs ground into a powder and put into capsules, each with an average of 500 mg. Eight to nine capsules are recommended per day.

The formulas have two names: the Chinese name is based on the therapeutic strategy, and the English name is based on the principal herbs of the formula.

WOOD CONSTITUTION

248 TIAO HE
BUPLEURUM AND PEONY TWELVE COMBINATION
"Mediate Harmony"

Invigorates liver *qi* to remove stagnation, nourishes liver blood, strengthens spleen *qi*, relieves the surface. Classified as the anti-stress formula for persons of the wood excess constitution or condition. Use for liver congestion affecting stomach and spleen digestion with symptoms of abdominal distension, erratic stools, flatulence or belching, and problems involving sugar metabolism. Also, for liver congestion affecting menstruation with dysmenorrhea, cramps and clots. Related to the classical prescription *Xiao Yao Wan* (#123) and *Chai Hu Gui Zhi Tang*.

Bottles of 100 capsules. Take 4 capsules, 2 x day, or 3 capsules, 3 x day.

Bupleurum Root	Aurantium Peel
Peonia Root	Ginseng Root
Scutellaria Root	Licorice Root
Angelica Dang Gui	Pinellia Rhizome
Atractylodes Rhizome	Cinnamon Twig
Poria-Spirit Fungus	Ginger Rhizome

249 BU XUE
DANGGUI AND PEONY SIXTEEN FORMULA
"Tonify Blood"

Nourishes blood and *yin*, invigorates blood, resolves stagnation of blood and *qi*, tonifies *qi*. Classified as the strengthening formula for persons of the wood deficiency constitution or condition, this formula is a general tonic for *qi* and blood with direct affect on the liver. Use for chronic hepatitis or cirrhosis, pre-menstrual syndrome, menstrual disorders including amenorrhea, general fatigue, chronic food allergies, and impaired immune system. Related to the classical formula *Shi Chuan Da Bu Tang* (#204).

Bottles of 100 capsules. Take 4 capsules, 2 x day, or 3 capsules, 3 x day.

Angelica Dang Gui	Salvia Root
Peonia Root	Ganoderma Fungus
Rehmannia Root	Curcuma Root
Ligusticum Rhizome	Ginseng Root
Bupleurum Root	Ligustrum Fruit
Astragalus Root	Achyranthes Root
Alisma Rhizome	Atractylodes Rhizome
Lycium Fruit	Polygonum Shou Wu
Cornus Fruit	Cyperus Rhizome

FIRE CONSTITUTION

250 AN SHEN

FUSHEN AND DRAGON BONE SIXTEEN COMBINATION
"Pacify the Spirit"

Calms disturbed *shen*, nourishes heart blood and *yin*, connects kidney and heart, opens the orifices (senses). Classified as the anti-stress formula for the fire excess constitution or condition. Use for anxiety, insomnia, paranoia, heart palpitations, chest pain, restlessness, and dream-disturbed sleep. Also useful in mania, and epilepsy.

Caution: this product uses minerals and shells which can inhibit spleen and stomach function. Use only for duration of symptoms.

Bottles of 100 capsules. Take 4 capsules, 2 x day, or 3 capsules, 3 x day.

Poria-Spirit Fungus	Acorus Rhizome
Dragon Bone	Saussurea Root
Oyster Shell	Ginseng Root
Haliotis Shell	Polygonum Shou Wu
Albizia Bark	Zizyphus Seed
Coptis Rhizome	Licorice Root
Cinnamon Bark	Ginger Rhizome
Polygala Root	Curcuma Root

251 YANG XIN
BIOTA AND ZIZYPHUS EIGHTEEN FORMULA
"Support the Heart"

Nurtures heart *yin* and blood, tonifies heart *qi* and *yang* , calms *shen*. Classified as the strengthening formula for the fire deficiency constitution or condition. Use for insomnia, vivid dreaming, anxiety, frightfulness, heart palpitation, and irregular heart beat. Also useful for weak digestion, nightsweating, impotence, and premature ejaculation.

Bottles of 100 capsules. Take 4 capsules, 2 x day, or 3 capsules, 3 x day.

Biota Seed	Angelica Dang Gui
Zizyphus Seed	Lycium Fruit
Cistanche Stem	Polygala Root
Schizandra Fruit	Lotus Seed
Succinum Resin	Ginseng Root
Cuscuta Seed	Astragalus Root
Acorus Rhizome	Dioscorea Rhizome
Ophiopogon Root	Poria Fungus
Rehmannia Root, prep.	Polygonatum Rhizome

EARTH CONSTITUTION

252 XIAO DAO

AGASTACHE AND SHENQU SIXTEEN COMBINATION
"Clear Congestion"

Clears congestion and phlegm, disperses stagnation of stomach *qi* and damp, tonifies *qi*. Classified as the anti-stress formula for the earth excess constitution or condition. Use for poor digestion with symptoms of indigestion, flatulence, abdominal bloating or pain, stomachache, overnight accumulation of undigested food, headache, and diarrhea.

Bottles of 100 capsules. Take 4 capsules, 2 x day, or 3 capsules, 3 x day.

Pogostemon Herb	Citrus Peel
Fermented Leaven	Pinellia Rhizome
Magnolia Bark	Cardamon Fruit
Atractylodes Rhizome	Ginger Rhizome
Saussurea Root	Licorice Root
Oryza Sprout	Crataegus Fruit
Poria Fungus	Ginseng Root
Gastrodia Rhizome	Platycodon Root

253 WEN ZHONG
GINSENG AND LICORICE EIGHTEEN FORMULA
"Warm the Center"

Tonifies *qi*, strengthens spleen and kidney, disperses stagnant *qi* and damp, warms the interior. Classified as the strengthening formula for the earth deficiency constitution or condition. Use for poor digestion, chronic diarrhea, loss of appetite, weight loss, gastroenteritis, and abdominal cramps or pain. Also useful for hernia. Related to the classical formulas *Shen Ling Bai Zhu San* (#133) and also *Qian Jin Dang Gui Tang*.

Bottles of 100 capsules. Take 4 capsules, 2 x day, or 3 capsules, 3 x day.

Ginseng Root	Citrus Peel
Licorice Root	Angelica Dang Gui
Atractylodes Rhizome	Saussurea Root
Poria Fungus	Magnolia Bark
Ginger Rhizome	Chaenomeles Fruit
Dioscorea Rhizome	Zanthoxyulum Husk
Lotus Seed	Pinellia Rhizome
Dolichos Seed	Alpinia Rhizome
Astragalus Root	Cardamon Fruit

METAL CONSTITUTION

254 XUAN FEI
PINELLIA AND CITRUS SIXTEEN COMBINATION
"Ventilate the Lungs"

Resolves phlegm, relieves cough, regulates the breath, benefits the lungs. Classified as the anti-stress formula for excess of the metal constitution or condition. Use for difficult breathing with or without cough, including acute and chronic bronchitis, asthma, and emphysema. Relieves congestion in chest, and is useful for numbness in the arms. Based on the classical prescription *Qing Fei Tang*.

Bottles of 100 capsules. Take 4 capsules, 2 x day, or 3 capsules, 3 x day.

Pinellia Rhizome	Poria Fungus
Citrus Peel	Ginger Rhizome
Fritillaria Zhe Bei	Licorice Root
Bamboo Resin	Bupleurum Root
Platycodon Root	Magnolia Bark
Ophiopogon Root	Armeniaca Seed
Schizandra Fruit	Ephedra Leaf
Tussilago Flower	Morus Root Bark

255 FU LEI
ASTRAGALUS AND ANEMARRHENA SIXTEEN FORMULA
"Support the Weak and Thin"

Tonifies lung and spleen *qi*, nurtures lung *yin*, sedates deficiency fire, resolves phlegm-heat, benefits the lung. This is the strengthening formula for the metal deficiency constitution or condition. Use to treat difficult breathing with cough or phlegm, aggravated by chronic deficiency of *qi* and *yin*. Use for chronic bronchitis, emphysema, dry throat with thirst, dry cough, and sticky phlegm. Other symptoms might include night sweating, spontaneous sweating, loss of weight, frequent infections (deficient *wei qi*). Related to the classical prescription *Qing Shu Yi Qi Tang*.

Bottles of 100 capsules. Take 4 capsules, 2 x day, or 3 capsules, 3 x day.

Astragalus Root	Ginseng Root
Anemarrhena Rhizome	Citrus Qing Pi
Aster Root	Platycodon Root
Bupleurum Root	Angelica Dang Gui
Gentiana Qin Jiao	Schizandra Fruit
Lycium Root-bark	Ophiopogon Root
Pinellia Rhizome	Citrus Peel
Licorice Root	Atractylodes Rhizome

WATER CONSTITUTION

256 QU SHI
ALISMA AND HOELEN SIXTEEN FORMULA
"Remove Dampness"

Promotes the flow of water, resolves edema, dispels spleen-damp, benefits kidneys. Classified as the anti-stress formula for the water excess constitution or condition. Use for edema of the limbs, poor digestion with loose stools, abdominal gurgling, ascites, and joint swelling. Also useful for related symptoms of headaches and rapid breathing. Based on the classical prescription *Wei Ling Tang*.

Bottles of 100 capsules. Take 4 capsules, 2 x day, or 3 capsules, 3 x day.

Alisma Rhizome	Atractylodes Rhizome
Poria Fungus	Pinellia Rhizome
Stephania Root	Areca Husk
Astragalus Root	Magnolia Bark
Morus Root Bark	Chaenomeles Fruit
Citrus Peel	Cinnamon Twig
Ginger Rhizome	Akebia Stem
Polyporous Fungus	Licorice Root

257 JIAN GU

EUCOMMIA AND ACHYRANTHES EIGHTEEN FORMULA
"Strengthen Bones"

Tonifies kidney *yang*, *yin* and *qi*, nurtures *jing*, strengthens bones and ligaments, benefits the lower back. Classified as the strengthening formula of the water deficiency constitution or condition. Use for weak and sore back and legs, urinary disfunction, impotence, spermatorrhea, recovery from broken bones, osteoporosis, diminished hearing and weakness of work and over stress. Also useful for difficult breathing due to kidney deficiency. Related to the patent formula *Ge Jie Ta Bu Wan* (#195).

Bottles of 100 capsules. Take 4 capsules, 2 x day, or 3 capsules, 3 x day.

Eucommia Bark	Poria Fungus
Achyranthes Root	Dipsacus Root
Lycium Fruit	Cistanche Stem
Rehmannia Root	Angelica Dang Gui
Morinda Root	Ginseng Root
Dioscorea Rhizome	Atractylodes Rhizome
Drynaria Rhizome	Astragalus Root
Ligustrum Fruit	Epimedium Leaf
Cornus Fruit	Liquidambar Fruit

ENERGETIC FORMULAS

258 QING RE
FORSYTHIA AND SCHIZONEPETA EIGHTEEN FORMULA
"Clear Heat"

Clears heat, relieves toxic inflammation, dispels wind and wind-heat, invigorates the blood. Classified as an anti-stress formula for the Heat excess constitution or condition. Use for acute or chronic inflammation of throat, skin, lymph glands, or eyes. Helpful for headaches, sore throats, carbuncles and fever; also acute wind-heat invasions. Useful in obesity and arthritis with heat signs. Related to the classical formula *Chai Hu Qin Gan Tang*.

Bottles of 100 capsules. Take 4 capsules, 2 x day, or 3 capsules, 3 x day.

Forsythia Fruit	Bupleurum Root
Schizonepeta Herb	Licorice Root
Phellodendron Bark	Coptis Rhizome
Lonicera Flower	Angelica Dang Gui
Carthamus Flower	Peonia Root
Platycodon Root	Chrysanthemum Flower
Scutellaria Root	Vitex Fruit
Siler Root	Arctium Fruit
Ligusticum Rhizome	Gardenia Fruit

259 BU YIN

REHMANNIA AND OPHIOPOGON SIXTEEN FORMULA
"Tonify Yin"

Nourishes *yin*, relieves thirst, clears deficiency-heat. Classified as a moistening formula for the deficiency-dryness constitution or condition. Use for deficiency of *yin* causing thirst, constipation, low grade fever, heat in palms or soles, sore throat, and dry cough. Also useful in tinnitus and backache due to *yin* deficiency, and diabetes. Related to the classical formula *Mai Men Dong Yin Zi*.

Bottles of 100 capsules. Take 4 capsules, 2 x day, or 3 capsules, 3 x day.

Rehmannia Root	Poria Fungus
Ophiopogon Root	Eucommia Bark
Dendrobrium Leaf	Asparagus Root
Trichosanthes Root	Cornus Fruit
Schizandra Fruit	Moutan Root-bark
Pueraria Root	Anemarrhena Rhizome
Phellodendron Bark	Alisma Rhizome
Achyranthes Root	Licorice Root

260 JIE YU
BUPLEURUM AND CYPERUS EIGHTEEN COMBINATION
"Relieve Depression"

Disperses constrained liver *qi*, clears liver and heart fire, invigorates blood, clears phlegm. Classified as an anti-stress formula for the constrained *qi* excess constitution or condition. Use for congestion of liver *qi* causing discomfort in the hypochondric region, depression, premenstrual symptoms, breast lumps, general aches and pain, irritability. and headache. Also useful for heart fire symptoms including insomnia, palpitation, and nightmares. Useful in digestive problems due to liver invasion, including abdominal distension, and stagnation of food. Related to the classical formula *Zhu Ru Wen Dan Tang*.

Bottles of 100 capsules. Take 4 capsules, 2 x day, or 3 capsules, 3 x day.

Bupleurum Root	Pinellia Rhizome
Cyperus Rhizome	Aurantium Fruit
Bamboo Resin	Aurantium Zhi-ke
Coptis Rhizome	Ophiopogon Root
Poria Fungus	Angelica Dang Gui
Uncaria Stem	Saussurea Root
Licorice Root	Perilla Leaf
Ginger Rhizome	Ligusticum Rhizome
Ginseng Root	Platycodon Root

261 SHENG MAI
ASTRAGALUS AND GANODERMA EIGHTEEN FORMULA
"Generate the Pulse"

General tonic for *qi* and blood, *yin* and *yang*, and all *zang-fu* organs. Classified as the strengthening formula for the *qi* deficiency constitution or condition. Use for recovery from debilitating illness, injury or childbirth; also anemia, impaired organ function, weak digestion, extreme fatigue, and problems associated with aging. Useful for strengthening the immune system.\\Related to the classical formula *Ren Shen Yang Ying Wan* (#200).

Bottles of 100 capsules. Take 4 capsules, 2 x day, or 3 capsules, 3 x day.

Astragalus Root	Schizandra Fruit
Ganoderma Fungus	Atractylodes Rhizome
Ginseng Root	Poria Fungus
Angelica Dang Gui	Eucommia Bark
Peonia Root	Achyranthes Root
Rehmannia Root	Lycium Fruit
Polygala Root	Ophiopogon Root
Epimedium Leaf	Licorice Root
Ligustrum Fruit	Citrus Peel

APPENDIX III

CHINESE TRADITIONAL FORMULAS

Herbal Products developed by
Subhuti Dharmananda, Ph.D.
Manufactured by Health Concerns; Seattle, Washington

Chinese Traditional Formulas is a recently introduced line of products manufactured by Health Concerns, Seattle Washington. The products are either designed or selected from classical formulas by Subhuti Dharmananda, Ph.D. The newly designed products are prepared as powdered herbs compressed into tablets.

262 ASTRA EIGHT
Astragalus Eight Combination

Tonifies *qi* and *wei qi*, strenthens natural immunity. Using the classical prescription *Si Jun Zi Tang* (Four Gentlemen Tea) as its foundation, the formula has been designed for tonifying and reinforcing the body's natural immune defense system. Use as a preventative to keep *wei qi* and the immune system strong, or as a tonic in chronic deficiencies of *qi*. Can be taken over long periods.

Bottles of 90 tablets. Take 3 tablets, 2 x day.

Astragalus Root	Ganoderma Fungus
Ligustrum Fruit	Licorice Root
Codonopsis Root	Schizandra Fruit
Atractylodes Rhizome	Eleutheroginseng Root

263   ASTRA-GARLIC

Invigorates and detoxifies blood, nourishes blood production, breaks blood stagnation, kills parasites. Use to clean and purify blood, and break up atherosclerotic plaque. Also valuable for treating chronic bacterial, fungal and protozoan (amoebic) infections, with an accompanying deficiency of *qi*, *wei qi*, or blood. The garlic used in this product is odorless.

Bottles of 60 tablets. Take 2 tablets, 2 x day.

Garlic Bulb	Crataegus Fruit
Astragalus Root	Angelica Dang gui
Polygonum Shou Wu	Salvia Root
Ganoderma Fungus	Atractylodes Rhizome

264   CIR-Q

Clears the senses, activates blood circulation to break blood stagnation, resolves phlegm, regulates *qi*, reduces hypertension. Based on the classical prescription *Yen Ling Tang* , this is an aromatic formula designed to open congested blood vessels, reduce fatty deposits, or treat the immediate effects of stroke. Use for angina pain, pain in the extremities due to arterial occlusion, and unclear thinking. Also useful for abdominal pain and lung congestion due to stagnation of *qi*, blood or phlegm.

Bottles of 30 tablets. Take 1 tablet, 2 x day.

Amomum Fruit	Aquilaria Wood
Saussurea Root	Acorus Rhizome
Borneol Crystal	Aristolochia Root
Frankincense Resin	Aurantium Fruit
Prunella Spike	Melia Fruit
Eucommia Bark	Caryophylum Flower
Licorice Root	Santalum Wood
Ginger Rhizome	Terminalia Fruit

265   EASE PLUS
Bupleurum Plus Combination

Invigorates liver *qi*, tonifies spleen *qi*, calms *shen*. This fomula is based on the classical prescription *Chai Hu Mu Li Long Gu Tang* (Bupleurum, Oyster Shell, Dragon Bone Decoction), used for disturbed *shen* affected by rising liver *yang* or wind. Symptoms include insomnia, restless nervousness, muscular uncoordination, or seizures. Very effective for withdrawal from tobacco, medications and drugs.

Bottles of 30 or 90 tablets. Take 2-4 tablets, 3 x day.

Bupleurum Root	Rhubarb Rhizome
Scutellaria Root	Oyster Shell
Ginseng Root	Dragon Bone
Ginger Rhizome	Cinnamon Bark
Jujube Fruit	Poria Fungus
Pinellia Rhizome	

266   EASE 2

Invigorates liver *qi*, harmonizes liver and spleen, relieves the surface, tonifies spleen *qi*. This formula is based on the classic prescription *Chai Hu Gui Zhi Tang* (Bupleurum and Cinnamon Combination), used to treat constrained liver *qi* causing digestive disturbances. Symptoms include loose or constipated stools, food allergies, abdominal tenderness or bloating, or belching. Other symptoms might include muscle tension, irritability, back ache, and cold extremities. Useful for lingering colds and flus in the Shaoyang stage; also hypoglycemia.

Bottles of 30 or 90 tablets. Take 2-4 tablets, 3 x day.

Bupleurum Root	Licorice Root
Scutellaria Root	Cinnamon Twig
Ginseng Root	Pueraria Root
Ginger Rhizome	Peonia Root
Pinellia Rhizome	Jujube Fruit

267 MOBILITY 1
Coix Combination

Dispels wind-damp, invigorates and tonifies blood, relieves pain. Use for chronic and acute wind-damp joint pain and immobility causing arthritis, rheumatism, and general muscle or joint aching. Useful in early stage of rheumatoid arthritis.

Bottles of 30 or 90 tablets. Take 2-4 tablets, 3 x day.

Caution: Ephedra leaf may cause sleeplessness or heart palpitations. Reduce dosage or discontinue if these symptoms develop.

Ephedra Leaf
Coix Seed
Angelica Dang Gui
Peonia Root

Atractylodes Rhizome
Cinnamon Twig
Licorice Root

268 MOBILITY 2
Clematis Combination

Invigorates blood, dispels wind-damp, promotes water circulation, relieves the surface, stops pain. Based on the classical prescription *Shu Qing Huo Xie Tang*, it is used for wind-damp joint dysfunction found in arthritis and rheumatism. Also useful in sciatic pain, numbness in extremities, gout, edema, and abdominal pain due to blood stagnation.

Bottles of 30 or 90 tablets. Take 2-4 tablets, 3 x day.

Angelica Dang Gui
Ligusticum Rhizome
Peonia Root
Achyranthes Root
Persica Seed
Gentiana Qin Jiao
Siler Root
Angelica Root
Notopterygium Rhizome

Atractylodes Rhizome
Clematis Root
Ginger Rhizome
Citrus Peel
Stephania Root
Poria Fungus
Licorice Root
Rehmannia Root

269   NASAL TABS
Pueraria Combination

Sedates heat, clears phlegm-heat, dispels wind. This is the classical prescription *Qing Bi Tang*, and is used for acute and chronic sinus congestion, rhinitis and hayfever, headache or snoring. Effective for facial congestion due to recent wind invasion (colds and flus).

Bottles of 30 or 90 tablets. Take 2-4 tablets, 3 x day.

Caution: Ephedra leaf may cause sleeplessness or heart palpitations. Reduce dosage or discontinue if these symptoms develop.

Ephedra Leaf	Peonia Root
Magnolia Flower	Ginger Rhizome
Pueraria Root	Licorice Root
Rhubarb Rhizome	Jujube Fruit
Coix Seed	Ligusticum Rhizome
Gypsum Mineral	Platycodon Root
Cinnamon Twig	

270   REJUVENATE 8
Rehmannia Eight Formula

Tonifies kidney *qi* and *yang*, warms the center, benefits the back. This is the classical prescription *Jin Kui Shen Qi Wan* (#171). Use for backache, numbness or cold in the legs, impotence or premature ejaculation, ringing in the ears, general fatigue, and poor digestion with undigested food in the stools. Also useful in constipation due to deficiency, glaucoma, amnesia, and atherosclerosis. Helpful in problems associated with aging.

Bottles of 30 or 90 tablets. Take 2-4 tablets, 3 x day.

Rehmannia Root	Moutan Root-bark
Cornus Fruit	Alisma Rhizome
Aconite Root	Dioscorea Rhizome
Cinnamon Bark	Poria Fungus

271 RESP
Blue Dragon Combination

Clears phlegm-damp, dispels wind, benefits the lungs. This is the classical formula *Xiao Qing Long Tang*, used for lung congestion, asthma, cough with thin or thick sputum, and sinus congestion. Also useful for colds with chills, wind-damp pain in the arms and shoulders, and chronic conjunctivitis.

Bottles of 30 or 90 tablets. Take 2-4 tablets, 3 x day.

Caution: Ephedra leaf may cause sleeplessness or heart palpitations. Reduce dosage or discontinue if these symptoms develop.

Ephedra Leaf	Cinnamon Twig
Schizandra Fruit	Licorice Root
Pinellia Rhizome	Ginger Rhizome
Peonia Root	Asarum Plant

272 STOMACH TABS
Magnolia and Ginger Combination

Disperses stagnant *qi* in the center, resolves spleen-damp, dispels food stagnation, resolves stomach phlegm. Based on the classical prescription *Ping Wei San* (#137), for the improvement of digestion. Use for the symptoms of abdominal bloating, acute and chronic gastritis, flatulence, and headache and malaise from overeating. Also useful for obesity, and stomach ulcer.

Bottles of 30 or 90 tablets. Take 2-4 tablets, 3 x day, 30 minutes before meal.

Bupleurum Root	Licorice Root
Pinellia Rhizome	Oryza Sprout
Magnolia Bark	Ginger Rhizome
Citrus Peel	

273 ASTRA 18 - DIET FUEL

Regulates the center, tonifies spleen *qi*, removes damp, disperses stagnant *qi*, clears phlegm, softens hard masses. This product combines the traditional formula, *Fang Feng Tong Shen San*, a popular remedy for obesity, with *Wei Ling Tang*, used for abdominal bloating and disturbed digestion. Use for eating disorders, abdominal bloating, ascites, congestion of stomach phlegm, and loose or erratic stools. Also useful for accompanying fatigue, headaches, and joint swelling. The seaweeds, Laminaria and Sargassum, regulate the thyroid, clear damp and phlegm, and dissolve masses.

Combine with ASTRA DIET TEA (#274).

Bottles of 60 or 90 tablets, each 500 mg. Take 3-4 tablets 30 minutes before meals.

Angelica Dang Gui	Gardenia Fruit
Peonia Root	Alisma Rhizome
Atractylodes Rhizome	Ginger Rhizome
Platycodon Root	Laminaria Plant
Sargassum Plant	Licorice Root
Siler Root	Stephania Root
Ephedra Leaf	Magnolia Bark
Astragalus Root	Pinellia Rhizome
Scutellaria Root	Citrus Peel

274 ASTRA DIET TEA

Circulates *qi*, regulates stomach and spleen, suppresses appetite, clears stomach phlegm. This is a beverage tea useful in reducing appetite and invigorating energy. Take with ASTRA 18 HERBAL SUPPLEMENT (#273) thirty minutes before meals.

Boxes of 16 tea bags.

Perilla Leaf	Lophatherum Leaf
Ginger Rhizome	Eriobotrya Leaf
Mentha Leaf	Eleutheroginseng Leaf

CROSS REFERENCE OF HERBAL NAMES

HERB: leaf and stem
LEAF: leaf only
PLANT: whole plant, including leaf and root
STEM: stem only

ENGLISH	PHARMACEUTICAL	PINYIN	WADE-GILES	DR. HSU
ABRUS LEAF	Herba Abrus	Ji Gu Cao	Chi-ku-ts'ao	
ACANTHOPANAX ROOT-BARK	Cortex Acanthopanacis Radicis	Wu Jia Pi	Wu-chia-pi	Acanthopanax
ACHYRANTHES ROOT	Radix Achyranthis	Niu Xi	Niu-hsi	Achyranthes
ACONITE ROOT	Radix Aconiti Carmichaeli Preparata	Fu Zi	Fu-tzu	Aconite
ACONITE BEI WU TOU	Radix Aconiti Kusnezoffii	Bei Wu Tou	Bei-wu-t'ou	Wu-Tou
ACORUS RHIZOME	Rhizoma Acori Graminei	Shi Chang Pu	Shih-chang-pu	Acorus
ACTINOLITE MINERAL	Actinolitum	Yang Qi Shi	Yang-chi-shih	Actinolite
ADENOPHORA ROOT	Radix Adenophorae	Nan Sha Shen	Nan-sha-sheng	Adenophora
AGKISTRODON PIT VIPER	Agkistrodon Acutus	Bai Hua She	Pai-hua-sheh	Agkistrodon
AGRIMONY LEAF	Herba Agrimoniae	Xian He Cao	Hsien-ho-tsao	Agrimony
AILANTHUS BARK	Cortex Ailanthi	Chun Pi	Ch'un-p'i	
AKEBIA STEM	Caulis Akebiae	Mu Tong	Mu-tung	Akebia
ALBIZIA BARK	Cortex Albiziae	He Huan Pi	Ho-huan-p'i	
ALISMA RHIZOME	Rhizoma Alismatis	Ze Xie	Tse-hsieh	Alisma
ALOE RESIN	Herba Aloe	Lu Hui	Lu-huei	Aloe
ALPINIA FRUIT	Fructus Alpiniae Oxyphyllae	Yi Zhi Ren	I-chih-jen	
ALPINIA RHIZOME	Rhizoma Alpiniae Officinalis	Gao Liang Jiang	Kao-liang-chiang	
ALUM MINERAL-SALT	Alumen	Bai Fan	Pai-fen	Alum

English Name	Latin Name	Pinyin	Wade-Giles	English
AMERICAN GINSENG ROOT	Radix Panacis Quinquefolii	Xi Yang Shen	Hsi-yang-sheng	
AMOMUM FRUIT	Fructus Amomi	Sha Ren	Sha-jen	Cardamon
ANDROGRAPHIS PLANT	Herba Andrographis	Chuan Xin Lian	Ch'uan-hsin-lien	
ANEMARRHENA RHIZOME	Rhizoma Anemarrhenae	Zhi Mu	Chih-mu	Anemarrhena
ANEMONES RHIZOME	Rhizoma Anemonis Altaicae	Jiu Jie Chang Bu	Chiu-chieh-chang-pu	Altaica
ANGELICA ROOT	Radix Angelicae	Bai Zhi	Pai-chih	Angelica
ANGELICA DANG GUI	Radix Angelicae Sinensis	Dang Gui	Tang-kuei	Tang-Kuei
ANGELICA DU HUO	Radix Angelicae Tuhuo	Du Huo	Tu-huo	Tuhuo
ANTEATER SCALES	Squama Manitis	Chuan Shan Jia	Chuan-shan-chia	Anteater Scales
ANTELOPE HORN	Cornu Antelopis	Ling Yang Jiao	Ling-yang-chiao	Antelope Horn
AQUILARIA WOOD	Lignum Aquilaria Resinatum	Chen Xiang	Shen-hsiang	Aquilaria
ARALIA ROOT	Radix Araliae Cordatae	Tu Dang Gui	Tu-tang-kuei	
ARCTIUM FRUIT	Fructus Arctii	Niu Bang Zi	Niu-pang-tzu	Arctium
ARECA HUSK	Pericarpium Arecae	Da Fu Pi	Ta-fu-pi	Areca
ARISAEMA RHIZOME	Rhizoma Arisaematis	Tian Nan Xing	T'ien-nan-hsing	Arisaema
ARISTOLOCHIA FRUIT	Fructus Aristolochiae	Ma Dou Ling	Ma-tou-ling	Aristolochia
ARISTOLOCHIA ROOT	Radix Aristolochiae	Qing Mu Xiang	Ching-mu-hsiang	Birthwort
ARMENIACA SEED	Semen Armeniacae Amarae	Xing Ren	Hsing-jen	Apricot Seed
ARTEMESIA AI YE	Folium Artemesiae Argyi	Ai Ye	Ai-yeh	Artemesia
ARTEMEMSIA QING HAO	Herba Artemisia Apiaceae	Qing Hao	Ching-hao	
ASARUM PLANT	Herba Asari cum Radice	Xi Xin	Hsi-hsin	Asarum
ASPARAGUS ROOT	Radix Asparagi	Tian Men Dong	T'ien-men-tong	Asparagus
ASTER ROOT	Radix Asteris	Zi Wan	Tzu-wan	Aster
ASTRAGALUS ROOT	Radix Astragali	Huang Qi	Huang-chi	Astragalus
ATRACTYLODES RHIZOME	Rhizoma Atractylodes Macro.	Bai Zhu	Pai-chu	White Atractyl
ATRACTYLODES CANG ZHU	Rhizoma Atractylodis Chinen.	Cang Zhu	Ts'ang-chu	Atractylodes
AURANTIUM FRUIT	Fructus Aurantii Immat.	Zhi Shi	Chih-shih	Chih-shih
AURANTIUM ZHI KE	Fructus Citri Immaturus	Zhi Ke	Chih-ko	Chih-ko
BAMBOO RESIN	Saccus Bambusae	Zhu Li	Chu-li	Bamboo Sap
BAMBOO SHAVINGS	Caulis Bambusae in Taenia	Zhu Ru	Chu-ju	Bamboo
BEAR GALLBLADDER	Fel Ursi	Xiong Dan	Hsiung-tan	Bear Gall

ENGLISH	PHARMACEUTICAL	PINYIN	WADE-GILES	DR. HSU
BENINCASA SEED	Semen Benincasae	Dong Gua Zi	Tung-kua-tzu	Benincasa
BENZOIN RESIN	Benzoinum	An Xi Xiang	An-hsi-hsiang	Benzoin
BIOTA SEED	Semen Biotae	Bai Zi Ren	Pai-tzu-jen	Biota
BIOTA TWIG	Ramulus Biotae	Ce Bai Ye	Tse-pai-yeh	
BLACK ROOSTER	Gaiius Nigrosceus	Wu Ji	Wu-chi	
BLACK-STRIPED SNAKE	Zaocys Dhumnades	Wu Shao She	Wu-shao-sheh	Zaocys
BLETILLA RHIZOME	Rhizoma Bletillae	Bai Ji	Pai-chi	Bletilla
BORAX MINERAL-SALT	Hydra. Sodium Tetraborate	Peng Sha	P'eng-sha	
BORNEOL CRYSTAL	Borneolum	Bing Pian	Ping-pien	Borneol
BUPLEURUM ROOT	Radix Bupleuri	Chai Hu	Chai-hu	Bupleurum
CALAMINA MINERAL	Calamina	Lu Gan Shi	Lu-kan-shih	
CALLICARPA ROOT	Radix Callicarpae Macro.	Da Ye Zi Ju	Ta-yeh-tzu-chu	
CALCITE MINERAL	Calcitum	Han Shui Shi	Han-sui-shih	Calcite
CAMELLIA OIL	Fructus Camelliae Oleifera	Cha Zi Bing	Cha-tzu-ping	
CAMPHOR CRYSTAL	Camphora	Zhang Nao	Chang-nao	
CANNABIS SEED	Semen Cannabis	Huo Ma Ren	Huo-ma-jen	Cannabis Seed
CAPILLARIS LEAF	Herba Artem. Capillaris	Yin Chen	Yin-chen	Capillaris
CAPSELLA LEAF	Herba Capsellae	Ji Cai	Chi-tsao	
CARDAMON FRUIT	Fructus Amomi Cardamomi	Dou Kou	Tou-kou	Cluster
CARTHAMUS FLOWER	Flos Carthami	Hong Hua	Hung-hua	Carthamus
CARYOPHYLLUM FLOWER	Flos Caryophylli	Ding Xiang	Ting-hsiang	Clove
CASSIA SEED	Semen Cassiae Torae	Jue Ming Zi	Chueh-ming-tsu	Cassia Seed
CATECHU RESIN	Catechu (Acacia; Uncaria gambier)	Er Cha	Erh-cha	Catechu
CELOSIA SEED	Semen Celosiae	Qing Xiang Zi	Ching-hsiang-tzu	Celosia
CENTIPEDE	Scolopendra	Wu Gong	Wu-kung	
CHAENOMELES FRUIT	Fructus Chaenomelis	Mu Gua	Mu-kua	Chaenomeles
CHICKEN-EGG LINING	Membrana Folliculatis Ova	Feng Huang Yi	Feng-huang-i	
CHICKEN-GIZZARD SKIN	Endothelium Corneum Gigeriae Galli	Ji Nei Jin	Chi-nei-chin	

English	Latin	Pinyin	Wade-Giles	Common
CHRYSANTHEMUM FLOWER	Flos Chrysanthemi Morifolii	Ju Hua	Chu-hua	Chrysanthemum
CIBOTIUM RHIZOME	Rhizoma Cibotii	Gou Ji	Kou-chi	
CICADA SKIN	Periostracum Cicadae	Chan Tui	Chan-shui	Cicada
CIMICIFUGA RHIZOME	Rhizoma Cimicifugae	Sheng Ma	Sheng-ma	Cimicifuga
CINNABAR MINERAL	Cinnibaris	Zhu Sha	Chu-sha	Cinnabar
CINNAMON BARK	Cortex Cinnamomi	Rou Gui	Jou-gui	Cinnamon Bark
CINNAMON TWIG	Ramulus Cinnamomi	Gui Zhi	Kuei-chih	Cinnamon Twig
CISTANCHE STEM	Caulis Cistanchis	Rou Cong Rong	Jou-tsung-jung	Cistanche
CITRUS GAN PI	Pericarpium Citri Nobilis	Gan Pi	Kan-p'i	
CITRUS PEEL	Pericarpium Citri Reticulatae	Chen Pi	Ch'en-p'i	Citrus
CITRUS QING PI	Pericarpium Citri Reticulata Viride	Qing Pi	Ching-p'i	Blue Citrus
CITRUS SEED	Semen Citri Reticulatae	Ju He	Ju-he	Chu-ho
CITRUS XIANG YUAN	Fructus Citri Medici	Xiang Yuan	Hsiang-yuan	
CLAM SHELL	Concha Cyclinae	Ge Ke	Ke-keh	
CLEMATIS ROOT	Radix Clematidis	Wei Ling Xian	Wei-ling-hsien	Clematis
CLERODENDRUM LEAF	Herba Clerodendri Serrati	San Tai Hong Hua	San-tai-hung-hua	
CNIDIUM FRUIT	Fructus Cnidii	She Chuang Zi	She-ch'uang-tzu	
COCKLE SHELL	Concha Arcae	Wa Leng Zi	Wa-leng-tzu	
CODONOPSIS ROOT	Radix Codonopsis Pilosulae	Dang Shen	Tang-sheng	
COIX SEED	Semen Coicis Lachryma Jobi	Yi Yi Ren	I-yi-jen	Coix
COPTIS ROOT	Rhizoma Coptides	Huang Lian	Huang-lien	Coptis
CORDYCEPS FUNGUS	Sclerotium Cordyciptis Sinensis	Dong Chong Xia Cao	Tung-ch'ung-hsia-tsao	
CORNUS FRUIT	Fructus Corni	Shan Zhu Yu	Shan-shu-yu	Cornus
CORYDALIS RHIZOME	Rhizoma Corydalis	Yan Hu Suo	Yen-hu-suo	Corydalis
CRATAEGUS FRUIT	Fructus Crataegi	Shan Zha	Shan-cha	Crataegus
CROTON SEED	Semen Crotonis	Ba Dou	Pa-tou	Croton
CURCULIGO RHIZOME	Rhizoma Curculiginis	Xian Mao	Hsian-mao	
CURCUMA RHIZOME	Rhizoma Curcumae	Yu Jin	Yu-chin	Curcuma
CUSCUTA SEED	Semen Cuscutae	Tu Si Zi	Tu-szu-tzu	Cuscuta
CUTTLEFISH BONE	Os Sepiae	Hai Piao Xiao	Hai-piao-chiao	Cuttlebone
CYATHULA ROOT	Radix Cyathulae	Chuan Niu Xi	Ch'uan-niu-hsi	

ENGLISH	PHARMACEUTICAL	PINYIN	WADE-GILES	DR. HSU
CYNANCHUM RHIZOME	Rhizoma Cynanchi Stauntonii	Bai Wei	Pai-wei	Pai-wei
CYNOMORIUM STEM	Herba Cynomorii	Suo Yang	Suo-yang	Cynomorium
CYPERUS RHIZOME	Rhizoma Cyperi	Xiang Fu	Hsiang-fu	Cyperus
DEER HORN	Cornu Cervi	Lu Jiao	Lu-chiao	Cervus Horn
DEER HORN GLUE	Colla Cornus Cervi	Lu Jiao Jiao	Lu-chiao-chiao	Cervus Colloid
DEER LIGAMENT	Ligamentum Cervi	Lu Jin	Lu-chin	
DEER TAIL	Cauda Cervi	Lu Wei	Lu-wei	
DENDROBIUM LEAF	Herba Dendrobii	Shi Hu	Shih-hu	Dendrobium
DESMODIUM LEAF	Herba Desmodii Styracifolii	Jin Qian Cao	Chin-qian-ts'ao	
DIANTHUS LEAF	Herba Dianthi	Qu Mai	Chu-mai	Dianthus
DICTAMNUS ROOT-BARK	Cortex Dictamni Radicis	Bai Xian Pi	Pai-hsien-p'i	Fraxinella
DIOSCOREA ROOT	Radix Dioscoreae Oppositae	Shan Yao	Shan-yao	Dioscorea
DIPSACUS ROOT	Radix Dipsaci	Xu Duan	Hsu-tuan	Dipsacus
DOG PENIS AND TESTES	Penis et Testes Canis	Huang Gou Shen	Huang-kou-shen	
DOLICHOS SEED	Semen Dolichoris	Bai Bian Dou	Pai-pien-tou	Dolichos
DONKEY SKIN GLUE	Gelatinum Asini	E Jiao	Ah-chiao	Gelatin
DRAGON BLOOD RESIN	Sanguis Draconis	Xue Jie	Hsueh-chieh	
DRAGON BONE	Os Draconis	Long Gu	Lung-ku	Dragon Bone
DRAGON TOOTH	Dens Draconis	Long Chi	Lung-ch'i	
DRYNARIA RHIZOME	Rhizoma Drynariae	Gu Sui Bu	Ku-sui-pu	Drynaria
EARTHWORM	Lumbricus	Di Long	Ti-lung	Earthworm
ECLIPTA LEAF	Herba Ecliptae	Han Lian Cao	Han-lien-tsao	Eclipta
ELAEAGNUS FRUIT	Ramulus et Fructus Elaegni	Man Hu Tui Zi	Man-hu-t'ui-tzu	
ELEUTHEROGINSENG ROOT	Radix Eleutherococcus Sent.	Ci Wu Jia	Tse-wu-jia	

ELSHOLTZIA LEAF	Herba Elsholtziae	Xiang Ju	Hsiang-ju	Elshlotzia
ENTADA ROOT	Radix et Semen Entadae	Guo Jiang Long	Kuo-chiang-lung	
EPIMEDIUM LEAF	Herba Epimedii	Yin Y ang Huo	Yin-yang-huo	Epimedium
EPHEDRA ROOT	Radix Ephedrae	Ma Huang Gen	Ma-huang-ken	
EPHEDRA LEAF	Herba Ephedrae	Ma Huang	Ma-huang	Ma-huang
ERIOBOTRYA LEAF	Folium Eriobotyae	Pi Pa Ye	P'i-p'a-yeh	Eriobotrya
ERODIUM PLANT	Herba Erodii seu Geranii	Lao Guan Cao	Lao-kuan-tsao	
ERYTHRINA BARK	Cortex Erythriniae	Hai Tong Pi	Hai-t'ung-p'i	
EUCOMMIA BARK	Cortex Eucommiae	Du Zhong	Tu-chung	Eucommia
EUPHORBIA LEAF	Herba Euphorbiae Pekensis	Jing Da Qi	Ching-ta-chi	Euphorbia
EURALYE SEED	Semen Euryales	Qian Shi	Chien-shih	Euryale
EVODIA FRUIT	Fructus Evodiae	Wu Zhu Yu	Wu-shu-yu	Evodia
FENNEL FRUIT	Fructus Foeniculi	Xiao Hui Xiang	Hsiao-hui-hsiang	Fennel
FERMENTED LEAVEN	Mass Fermentata Medicinalis	Shen Qu	Shen-chu	Shen-Chu
FICUS LEAF	Folium Fici	Yong Shu Ye	Yung-shu-yeh	
FICUS ROOT	Radix Fici	Wu Hua Guo Gen	Wu-hua-kuo-ken	
FORSYTHIA FRUIT	Fructus Forsythiae	Lian Qiao	Lien-chiao	Forsythia
FRANKINCENSE RESIN	Gumni Olibani	Ru Xiang	Ju-hsiang	Mastic
FRITILLARIA BULB	Bulbus Fritil. Cirrhosae	Chuan Bei Mu	Ch'uan-pei-mu	Fritillaria
FRITILLARIA ZHE BEI	Bulbus Fritil. Thunbergii	Zhe Bei Mu	Chih-bei-mu	
GANODERMA FUNGUS	Ganoderma Lucidum	Ling Zhi	Ling-chih	
GARDENIA FRUIT	Fructus Gardeniae	Zhi Zi	Chih-tzu	Gardenia
GARLIC BULB	Bulbus Alli Sativi	Da Suan	Ta-suan	
GASTRODIA RHIZOME	Rhizoma Gastrodiae	Tian Ma	T'ien-ma	Tian-ma
GECKO LIZARD	Gecko	Ge Jie	Ke-chieh	
GENTIANA QIN JIAO	Radix Gentianae Macrophyllae	Qin Jiao	Chin-chiao	Chin-chiu
GENTIANA ROOT	Radix Gentianae Seabrae	Long Dan Cao	Lung-tan-tsao	Gentiana
GINGER RHIZOME, prep.	Rhizoma Zingiberis	Gan Jiang	Kan-chiang	Ginger
GINSENG ROOT	Radix Panax Ginseng	Ren Shen	Jen-sheng	Ginseng
GLAUBER'S SALT	Sal Glauberis	Pi Xiao	P'i-hsiao	
GLEDITSIA FRUIT	Fructus Gleditsiae	Zao Jia	Tsao-chia	Gleditsea

ENGLISH	PHARMACEUTICAL	PINYIN	WADE-GILES	DR. HSU
GLEHNIA ROOT	Radix Glehniae	Bei Sha Shen	Pei-sha-sheng	Glehnia
GOAT HORN	Cornu Naemorhedis	Shan Yang Jiao		
GOLDEN COIN TORTOISE	Cuora Trifasciata	Jin Qian Gui	Chin-chien-kui	
GYPSUM MINERAL	Gypsum Fibrosum	Shi Gao	Shih-kao	Gypsum
HALIOTIS SHELL	Concha Haliotidis	Shi Jue Ming	Shih-chueh-ming	Haliotis
HEDERA STEM	Caulis Hederae	Cheng Qun Teng	Ch'eng-chun-t'eng	
HEDGEHOG SKIN	Corium Erinacei	Ci Wei Pi	Tse-wei-p'i	
HONEY	Mel	Feng Mi	Feng-mi	Mel
HORDEUM SPROUT	Fructus Hordie Germinatus	Mai Ya	Mai-ya	Malt
HUMAN PLACENTA	Placenta Hominis	Zhi He Che	Tzu-ho-che	Placenta
HYDNOCARPUS SEED	Semen Hydnocarpi	Da Feng Zi	Ta-feng-tzu	
ILEX ROOT	Radix Ilicis Pubescentis	Mao Dong Qing	Mao-tung-ching	
INDIGO POWDER	Indigo Pulverata Levis	Qing Dai	Ching-tai	Indigo
INULA FLOWER	Flos Inulae	Xuan Fu Hua	Suan-fu-hua	Inula
ISATIS LEAF	Folium Isatidis	Da Qing Ye	Ta-ching-yeh	
ISATIS ROOT	Radix Isatidis	Ban Lang Gen	Pan-lang-ken	
JUJUBE FRUIT	Fructus Zizyphus	Da Zao	Ta-tsao	Jujube
JUGLANS SEED	Semen Juglandis	Hu Tao Ren	Hu-t'ao-jen	
JUNCUS PITH	Medula Junci	Deng Xin Cao	Teng-hsin-tsao	Juncus
KADSURA ROOT	Radix Kadsurae	Feng Sha Teng	Feng-sha-t'ung	
KAKI CALYX	Calyx Kaki	Shi Di	Shih-ti	Kaki
	Calyx Diospyros Kaki			
LAMINARIA PLANT	Thallus Laminariae	Kun Bu	Laminaria	
LEONURUS LEAF	Herba Leonuri	Yi Mu Cao	I-mu-tsao	Leonurus
LICORICE ROOT	Radix Glycyrrhizae	Gan Cao	Kan-tsao	Licorice

English	Latin	Pinyin	Wade-Giles	Common
LIGUSTICUM GAO BEN	Rhizoma Ligustici Sinensis	Gao Ben	Kao-pen	
LIGUSTICUM RHIZOME	Rhizoma Ligustici Wallachii	Chuan Xiong	Ch'uan-chiung	Cnidium
LIGUSTRUM FRUIT	Fructus Ligustri Lucici	Nu Zhen Zi	Nu-chen-tzu	Ligustrum
LILY BULB	Bulbus Lilii	Bai He	Pai-ho	Lily
LINDERA ROOT	Radix Linderae	Wu Yao	Wu-yao	Lindera
LITCHEE SEED	Semen Litchi	Li Zhi He	Li-chih-ho	
LITSEA FRUIT	Fructus Litseae	Shang Cang Zi	Shang-tsang-tzu	
LIQUIDAMBAR FRUIT	Fructus Liquidambaris	Lu Lu Tong	Lu-lu-t'ung	
LONGAN FRUIT	Fructus Arillus Longanae	Long Yan Rou	Lung-yan-jou	Longan
LONICERA FLOWER	Flos Lonicerae	Jin Yin Hua	Chin-yin-hua	Lonicera
LOPHATHERUM LEAF	Herba Lophatheri	Dan Zhu Ye	Tan-chu-yeh	Lophatherum
LORANTHUS TWIG	Ramulus Loranthi	Sang Ji Sheng	Sang-chi-sheng	Loranthus
LOTUS PLUMULE	Plumula Nelumbinis	Lian Zi Xian	Lien-tzu-hsien	
LOTUS SEED	Semen Nelumbinis	Lian Zi	Lien-tzu	Lotus Seed
LOTUS STAMEN	Stamen Nelumbinis	Lian Xu	Lien-hsu	Lotus Stamen
LYCIUM FRUIT	Fructus Lycii	Gou Qi Zi	Kou-ch'i-tzu	Lycium Fruit
LYCIUM ROOT-BARK	Cortex Lycii Radicis	Di Gu Pi	Ti-ku-p'i	Lycium Bark
LYGODIUM FUNGUS	Herba et Spora Lygodii Japon.	Hai Jin Sha	Hai-chin-sha	Lygodium
LYSIMACHIA LEAF	Herba Desmodii Styracifolii	Jin Qian Cao	Chin-ch'ien-ts'ao	
MAGNETITE MINERAL	Magnetitum	Ci Shi	Tz'u-shih	
MAGNOLIA BARK	Cortex Magnoliae	Hou Po	Hou-p'u	Magnolia Bark
MAGNOLIA FLOWER	Flos Magnoliae Liliflorae	Xin Yi	Hsin-i	Magnolia Flower
MAHONIA ROOT	Radix Mahoniae	Shi Da Gung Lao	Shi-ta-kung-lao	
MANTIS EGG-CASE	Ootheca Mantidis	Sang Piao Xiao	Sang-p'iao-chiao	Mantis
MARGARITA PEARL	Margarita	Zhen Zhu	Chen-chu	Pearl
MELIA FRUIT	Fructus Toosendam	Chuan Lian Zi	Chuan-lien-tzu	Melia
MENTHA HERB	Herba Menthae	Bo He	Po-ho	Mentha
MILLETTIA NIU DA LI	Radix Millettiae Speciosa	Niu Da Li	Niu-ta-li	
MILLETTIA ROOT	Radix Millettiae Reticulata	Ji Xue Tang	Chi-hsueh-t'eng	Millettia
MIRABILITUM MINERAL	Natrium Sulfuricum	Mang Xiao	Mang-hsiao	Mirabilitum
MOGHANIA ROOT	Radix Moghaniae	Qian Jin Ba	Ch'ien-chin-ba	

ENGLISH	PHARMACEUTICAL	PINYIN	WADE-GILES	DR. HSU
MOMORDICA FRUIT	Fructus Momordicae Grosvenori	Lo Han Guo	Lu-han-kuo	
MONKEY GALLSTONE	Calculus Macacae	Hou Zao	Hou-tsao	
MORINDA ROOT	Radix Morindae	Ba Ji Tian	Pa-chi-t'ien	Morinda
MORUS ROOT-BARK	Cortex Mori Radicis	Sang Bai Pi	Sang-pai-p'i	Morus
MORUS FRUIT	Fructus Mori	Sang Ren	Sang-chen	Morus Fruit
MORUS LEAF	Herba Mori	Sang Ye	Sang-yeh	Morus Leaves
MOSLA LEAF	Herba Moslae Chinensis	Shi Xiang Rou	Shih-hsiang-jou	
MOTHER-OF-PEARL SHELL	Concha Margaritae	Zhen Zhu Mu	Chen-chu-mu	
MOUTAN ROOT BARK	Cortex Moutan Radicis	Mu Dan Pi	Mu-tan-pi	Moutan
MUME FRUIT	Fructus Mume	Wu Mei	Wu-mei	Mume
MUSK GLAND	Secretio Moschus Moschiferi	She Xiang	She-hsiang	Musk
MYLABRIS BEETLE	Mylabris	Ban Mao	Pan-mao	
MYRRH RESIN	Myrrhae	Mo Yao	Mo-yao	Myrrh
NARDOSTACHYS RHIZOME	Rhizoma Nardostachydis	Kan Song	K'an-sung	
NOTOPTERYGIUM RHIZOME	Rhizoma et Radix Notopterygii	Qiang Huo	Chiang-huo	Qianghuo
OPHIOPOGON ROOT	Radix Ophiopogonis	Mai Men Dong	Mai-men-tong	Ophiopogon
ORYZA SPROUT	Fructus Oryzae Geramulus	Gu Ya	Ku-ya	
OYSTER SHELL	Concha Ostreae	Mu Li	Mu-liu	Oyster Shell
OX GALLSTONE	Calculus Bovis	Niu Huang	Niu-huang	Bos
PAEONIA CHI SHAO	Radix Paeonia Rubra	Chi Shao	Chih-shao	Paeonia
PAEONIA ROOT	Radix Peoniae Alba	Bai Shao	Pai-shao	
PATRINIA PLANT	Herba Patriniae seu Thlaspi	Bai Jiang	Pai-chiang	
PERILLA LEAF	Folium Perillae	Zi Su Ye	Tzu-su-yeh	Perilla
PERSICA SEED	Semen Persicae	Tao Ren	T'ao-jen	Persica
PEUCEDANUM ROOT	Radix Peucedani	Qian Hu	Chien-hu	Peucedanum
PHARBITIS SEED	Semen Pharbitides	Qian Niu Zi	Chien-niu-tzu	Pharbitis

PHASEOLUS MUNG SEED	Semen Phaseoli Munginis	Lu Dou	Phaseolus
PHELLODENDRON BARK	Cortex Phellodendri	Huang Bo	Phellodendron
PHRAGMITES RHIZOME	Rhizoma Phragmites	Lu Gen	Phragmites
PHRYNIUM LEAF	Herba Phrynii	Dong Ye	
PIG BILE	Fel Verris	Shan Ju Dan	
PINELLIA RHIZOME	Rhizoma Pinelliae	Ban Xia	Pinellia
PIPE FISH	Syngnathus	Hai Long	
PIPER SEED	Fructus Piperis Longi	Bi Ba	Piper
PIPER SHAN JU	Herba Piperis Hancei	Shan Ju	
PISTACIA ROOT	Radix Pistaciae	Wu Ming	
PLANTAGO SEED	Semen Plantaginis	Che Qian Zi	Plantago
PLATYCODON ROOT	Radix Platycodi	Jie Geng	Platycodon
POGOSTEMON HERB	Herba Agastaches seu Pogostemi	Huo Xiang	Agastache
POLYGALA ROOT	Radix Polygalae	Yuan Zhi	Polygala
POLYGONATUM RHIZOME	Rhizoma Polygonati	Huang Jing	
POLYGONUM HU ZHANG	Rhizoma Polygoni Cuspidati	Hu Zhang	
POLYGONUM LEAF	Herba Polygoni Avicularis	Bian Xu	
POLYGONUM SHOU WU	Radix Polygoni Multiflori	He Shou Wu	Polygonum
POLYPODIUM RHIZOME	Rhizoma Polypodii	Shui Long Gu	Ho-Sou-Wu
POLYPOROUS FUNGUS	Polyporus Umbellatus	Zhu Ling	Polyporus
	Grifolia Umbellata		
PORIA FUNGUS	Poria Cocus; Pachyma	Fu Ling	Hoelen
PORIA SKIN	Cortex Poria Cocus	Fu Ling Pi	
PORIA-SPIRIT FUNGUS	Poria Cocos	Fu Shen	
PRUNELLA SPIKE	Spica Prunellae	Xia Ku Cao	Prunella
PRUNUS SEED	Semen Pruni	Yu Li Ren	
PSEUDOGINSENG ROOT	Radix Pseudoginseng	San Qi	Pseudoginseng
PSEUDOSTELLARIA ROOT	Radix Pseudostellariae	Tai Zi Shen	
PSORALEA FRUIT	Fructus Psoraleae	Bu Gu Zhi	T'ai-tzu-sheng
PUERARIA ROOT	Radix Puerariae	Ge Gen	Psoralea
PULSATILLA ROOT	Radix Pulsatillae	Bai Tou Weng	Pueraria
PYROLA LEAF	Herba Pyrolae	Lu Xian Cao	

ENGLISH	PHARMACEUTICAL	PINYIN	WADE-GILES	DR. HSU
RAPHANUS SEED	Semen Raphani Sativi	Lai Fu Zi	Lai-fu-tzu	Raphanus
REHMANNIA ROOT, Prep.	Radix Rehmanniae	Shu Di (Huang)	Hsu-ti-huang	Rehmannia-
REHMANNIA ROOT, Raw	Radix Rehmanniae	Sheng Di Huang	Sheng-ti-huang	Rehmannia
RHINOCEROS HORN	Cornu Rhinoceri	Xi Jiao	Hsi-chiao	Rhinoceros
RHODODENDRON ROOT	Radix et Ramulus Rhododendri Daurici			
RHODOMYRTUS PLANT	Herba Rhodomyrti	Man Shan Hong	Man-shan-hung	
		Gang Nian	Kang-nien	
RHUBARB RHIZOME	Rhizoma Rhei	Da Huang	Ta-huang	Rhubarb
ROSA FRUIT	Fructus Rosa Laevigatae	Jin Ying Zi	Chin-ying-tzu	Rosa Fruit
ROYAL JELLY		Feng Wang Jiang	Feng-wang-chiang	
RUBUS FRUIT	Fructus Rubi	Fu Pen Zi	Fu-p'en-tzu	Rubus
SALVIA ROOT	Radix Salviae Miltiorrhizae	Dan Shen	Tan-sheng	Salvia
SAND CLAM SHELL	Concha Meretricis	Sha Ge	Sha-ke	
SANGUISORBA ROOT	Radix Sanguisorbae	Di Yu	Ti-yu	
SANTALUM WOOD	Lignum Santali Albi	Tan Xiang	T'an-hsiang	Santalum
SARGASSUM PLANT	Sargassum	Hai Zao	Hai-ts'ao	
SAUSSUREA ROOT	Radix Saussureae	Mu Xiang	Mu-hsiang	Saussurea
SCHIZANDRA FRUIT	Fructus Schizandrae	Wu Wei Zi	Wu-wei-tzu	Schizandra
SCHIZONEPETA HERB	Herba Schizonepetae	Jing Jie	Ching-chieh	Schizonepeta
SCORPION	Scorpio	Quan Xie	Chuan-hsieh	Scorpion
SCROPHULARIA ROOT	Radix Scrophulariae	Xuan Shen	Hsuan-tsan	Scrophularia
SCUTELLARIA ROOT	Radix Scutellariae	Huang Qin	Huang-chin	Scute
SEA HORSE	Hippocampus	Hai Ma	Hai-ma	
SENNA LEAF	Herba Sennae	Fan Xie Ye	Fan-hsieh-yeh	
SHEEP PENIS	Penis Ovis vel Caprae	Yang Pian	Yang-pien	
SIEGESBECKIA LEAF	Herba Siegesbeckiae	Xi Xian Cao		
SILER ROOT	Radix Sileris	Fang Feng	Fang-feng	Siler

	Latin	Pinyin	Wade-Giles	Common
SILKWORM	Bombyx	Jiang Can	Chiang-tsan	Silkworm
SILKWORM DROPPINGS	Excrementum Bombycis	Can Sha	Tsan-sha	
SMILAX RHIZOME	Rhizoma Smilacis Glabrae	Tu Fu Ling	Tu-fu-ling	Smilax
SNAKE GALLBLADDER		She Dan	She-tan	
SNAKE GALL TRIO	San She Dan			
SOJA SEED	Semen Sojae Praeparatum	Dan Dou Chi	Tan-tou-shih	Soja
SOPHORA ROOT	Radix Sophorae	Ku Shen	Ku-sheng	Sophora
SPARGANIUM RHIZOME	Rhizoma Sparganii	San Leng	San-leng	
SPIRIFERA FOSSIL	Fossilia Spirifera	Shi Yen	Shih-yen	
SPOTTED DEER		Mei Hua Zhuang Lu	Mei-hua-chuang-lu	
STALACTITE MINERAL	Stalacitum	Zhong Ju	Chung-chu	
STELLARIA ROOT	Radix Stellariae	Yin Chai Hu	Yin-chai-hu	
STEMONA ROOT	Radix Stemonae	Bai Bu	Pai-pu	Stemona
STEPHANIA ROOT	Radix Stephaniae	Fang Ji	Fang-chi	Stephania
STERCULIA SEED	Semen Sterculiae	Pang Da Hai	P'ang-ta-hai	
STOVE ASH	Terra Flava Usta	Fu Long Gan	Fu-lung-kan	Fu-lung-kan
STRYCHNOS SEED	Semen Strychnosis Ignatii	Ku Guo	K'u-kuo	
STYRAX RESIN	Styrax Liquidis	Su He Xiang	Su-ho-hsiang	Styrax
SUCCINUM RESIN	Succinum	Hu Po	Hu-po	Succinum
TALCUM MINERAL	Talcum	Hua Shi	Hua-shih	Talc
TARAXACUM HERB	Herba Taraxaci cum Radice	Pu Gong Ying	P'u-kung-ying	Dandelion
TEA LEAF	Folium Camelliae	Cha Ye	Cha-yeh	
TERMINALIA FRUIT	Fructus Terminaliae Chebulae	He Zi	Ho-tzu	Terminalia
TIGER BONE	Os Tigris	Hu Gu	Hu-ku	Tiger's Shinbone
TINOSPERA ROOT	Radix Tinosporae	Jin Guo Lan	Chin-kuo-lan	
TOAD SECRETION	Secretio Bufonis	Chan Su	Tsan-shu	Toad Secretion
TORTOISE PLASTRON	Plastrum Testudinis	Gui Ban	Kuei-pan	Turtle Shell
TREMELLA FUNGUS	Fructificatio Tremellae	Yin Er	Yin-erh	
TRIBULUS FRUIT	Fructus Tribuli	Ji Li	Chi-li	Tribulus
TRICHOSANTHES SEED	Semen Tricosanthis	Gua Lou Ren	Kua-lou-tzu	Trichosan. Seed
TRICHOSANTHES ROOT	Radix Tricosanthis	Tian Hua Fen	Tien-hua-fen	Trichosan. Root

ENGLISH	PHARMACEUTICAL	PINYIN	WADE-GILES	DR. HSU
TRIGONELLA SEED	Semen Trigonellae	Hu Lu Ba	Hu-lu-pa	
TRITICUM GRAIN	Fructus Tritici	Fu Xiao Mai	Fu-hsiao-mai	Wheat
TURTLE SHELL	Carapax Amydae	Bie Jia	Pieh-chia	Tortoise Shell
TUSSILAGO FLOWER	Flos Farfara	Kuan Dong Hua	Kuan-tong-hua	Tussilago
	Flos Tussilago Farfara			
TYPHONUS RHIZOME	Rhizoma Typhonii	Bai Fu Zi	Pai-fu-tzu	
UNCARIA STEM	Ram. Uncariae cum Uncis	Gou Teng	Kou-teng	Gambi
VACARRIA SEED	Semen Vacarriae	Wang Bu Liu Xing	Wang-pu-liu-hsing	Vacarria
VERBANA HERB	Herba Verbanae	Ma Bian Cao	Ma-bien-tsao	
VITEX FRUIT	Fructus Viticis	Man Jing Zi	Mian-ching-tzu	Vitex
WATER-BUFFALO HORN	Cornu Bubali	Shui Niu Jiu	Shui-niu-chiu	
WINTERGREEN OIL	Radix et Ramulus Gaultheriae	Da Tou Gu Xiao	Ta-t'ou-ku-hsiao	
XANTHIUM FRUIT	Fructus Xanthii	Cang Er Zi	Tsang-erh-tzu	Xanthium
ZANTHOXYLUM HUSK	Pericarpium Zanthoxylum	Hua Jiao	Hua-chiao	Zanthoxylum
ZIZYPHUS PEEL	Pericarpium Zizyphi Jujubae	Zao Pi	Tsao-p'i	
ZIZYPHUS SEED	Semen Zizyphi	Suan Zao Ren	Suan-tsao-jen	Zizyphus

CHINESE CHARACTERS
FOR THE PRODUCTS

ALPHABETICAL BY PINYIN
with Product number

An Gong Niu Huang Wan		
An Kung Niu Huang Wan	35	安宮牛黃丸
An Mian Pian		
Mien Pien	208	安眠片
An Shen Bu Xin Wan		
An Sheng Pu Shin Wan	209	安神補心丸
An Tai Wan		
An Tai Wan (For Embryo)	87	安胎丸
Ba Wei Di Huang Wan		
Ba Wei Di Huang Wan	165	八味地黃丸
Ba Xian Chang Shou Wan		
Ba Xian Chang Shou Wan	179	八仙長壽丸
Ba Zhen Tang		
Ba Zhen Tang	149	八珍湯
Bai Feng Wan		
White Phoenix Pills	153	白鳳丸
Bai Zi Yang Xin Wan		
Pai Tzu Yang Hsin Wan	215	柏子養心丸
Bao Ji Wan		
Po Chi Pills	120	保濟丸
Bao Jian Mei Jian Fei Cha		
Bojenmi Chinese Tea	117	保健美減肥茶
Bao Xin An You		
Po Sum On Medicated Oil	112	保心安油
Bao Ying Dan		
Bo Ying Pills	63	保嬰丹
Po Ying Tan	67	
Bei Jing Feng Wang Jing		
Peking Royal Jelly	145	北京蜂王精
Bei Qi Jing		
Extractum Astragali	142	北芪精
Bi Tong Pian		
Tablet Bi-Tong	9	鼻通片

Du Huo Ji Sheng Wan
Du Huo Jisheng Wan   70   獨活寄生丸
Du Zhong Bu Tian Su
Duzhong Bu Tian Su   169   杜仲補天素
Du Zhong Feng Shi Wan
Tu Zhung Feng Shi Wan   81   杜仲風濕丸

Er Chen Wan
Erh Chen Wan   20   二陳丸
Er Ming Zuo Ci Wan
Tso-Tzu Otic Pills   190   耳鳴左慈丸

Feng Shi Pian
Hong She Pills   73   風濕片
Feng Shi Xiao Tong Wan
Feng Shih Hsiao Tung Wan   71   風濕消痛丸
Fu Fang Dan Shen Pian
Dan Shen Tablet Co.   100   復方丹參片
Fu Fang Du Zhong Pian
Compound Cortex Eucommia Tablets   220   復方杜仲片
Fu Fang Qi Guan Yan Wan
Bronchitis Pills (Compound)   14   復方氣管炎片
Fu Ke Zhong Zi Wan
Rehmannia Glutinosa Compound Pills   154   婦科種子丸
Fu Zi Li Zhong Wan
Carmichaeli Tea Pill   118   附子理中丸
Fu Tzu Li Chung Wan   120

Gan Mao Ling Pian
Ganmaoling Tablets   4   感冒靈片
Ge Jie Bu Shen Wan
Gejie Bu Shen Wan   170   蛤蚧補腎片
Ge Jie Da Bu Wan
Gejie Ta Bu Wan   195   蛤蚧大補丸
Gou Pi Gao
Kou Pi Plasters   84   狗皮膏
Guan Jie Yan Wan
Guan Jie Yan Wan   72   關節炎丸
Guan Xin Su He Wan
Guan Xin Su Ho Capsules   102   冠心蘇合丸
Kuan Hsin Su Ho Wan   101

CHINESE CHARACTERS FOR THE PRODUCTS

ALPHABETICAL BY ENGLISH NAME
with Product number

120 Aconitum Compound Pills
  Fǔ Zǐ Lǐ Zhōng Wǎn　　　　附子理中丸

192 Alrodeer Pills
  Quán Lù Wǎn　　　　全鹿丸

147 Angelica Tea
  Dāng Gūi Piàn　　　　當歸片

193 Angelicae Longana Tea
  Gūi Pí Wǎn　　　　歸脾丸

 35 An Kung Niu Huang Wan
  Ān Gōng Niú Huáng Wǎn　　　　安宮牛黃丸

208 An Mien Pien
  Ān Mián Piàn　　　　安眠片

209 An Sheng Pu Shin Wan
  Ān Shén Bǔ Xīn Wǎn　　　　安神補心丸

 87 An Tai Wan
  Ān Tāi Wǎn　　　　安胎丸

  1 Antelope Horn And
  Fructus Forsythiae Febrifrugal Tablets　　　　羚翹解毒片
  Líng Qiáo Jiě Dú Piàn

164 Anti-Lumbago Tablets
  Yāo Tòng Piàn　　　　腰痛片

 83 Anti-Rheumatic Plaster
  Jīng Zhì Gǒu Pí Gāo　　　　精制狗皮膏

136 Aplotaxis-Amomum Pills
  Xiāng Shā Liù Jūn Wǎn　　　　香沙六君丸

 55 Armadillo Counter Poison Pill
  Chuān Shān Jiǎ Qù Shī Qīng Dú Wǎn　　　　穿山甲去濕清毒丸

165 Ba Wei Di Huang Wan
  Bā Wèi Dì Huáng Wǎn　　　　八味地黃丸

179 Ba Xian Chang Shou Wan
  Bā Xiān Cháng Shòu Wǎn　　　　八仙長壽丸

149 Ba Zhen Tang
  Bā Zhēn Táng　　　　八珍湯

213	Emperor's Tea *Tian Wang Bu Xin Wan*	天王補心丸
20	Erh Chen Wan *Er Chen Wan*	二陳丸
194	Essence Of Chicken With Ginseng *Ren Shen Ji Jing*	人參雞精
150	Essence Of Chicken With Tang Kuei *Ji Jing Dang Gui*	雞精當歸
142	Extractum Astragali *Bei Qi Jing*	北芪精
90	Fargelin For Piles *Qiang Li Hua Zhi Ling*	强力化痔靈
109	Fel Ursi Hemorrhoids Ointment *Xiong Dan Zhi Chuang Gao*	熊胆痔瘡膏
71	Feng Shih Hsiao Tung Wan *Feng Shi Xiao Tong Wan*	風濕消痛丸
27	Fritillaria And Loquat Cough Mixture *Zhi Ke Chuan Bei Pi Ba Lu*	治咳川貝枇杷露
21	Fritillaria Extract Sugar-Coated Tablets *Chuan Bei Jing Tang Yi Pian*	川貝精糖衣片
120	Fu Tzu Li Chung Wan *Fu Zi Li Zhong Wan*	附子理中丸
4	Ganmaoling Tablets *Gan Mao Ling Pian*	感冒靈片
41	Gastropathy Capsules *Wei Yao*	胃藥
170	Gejie Bu Shen Wan *Ge Jie Bu Shen Wan*	蛤蚧補腎丸
195	Gejie Ta Bu Wan *Ge Jie Da Bu Wan*	蛤蚧大補丸
196	Ginseng Polygona Root Extract *Ren Shen Shou Wu Jing*	人參首烏精
143	Ginseng Royal Jelly Vials *Ren Shen Feng Wang Jiang*	人參蜂王漿
122	Ginseng Stomachic Pills *Ren Shen Jian Pi Wan*	人參健脾丸
197	Ginseng Tonic Capsules *Ren Shen Bu Wan*	人參補丸
207	Ginseng Tonic Pills *Yang Rong Wan*	養榮丸

171	Golden Book Tea *Jīn Kuì Shèn Qì Wǎn*	金匱腎氣丸
168	Golden Lock Tea *Jīn Suǒ Gù Jīng Wǎn*	金鎖固精丸
72	Guan Jie Yan Wan *Guān Jié Yán Wán*	關節炎丸
102	Guan Xin Su Ho Capsules *Guàn Xīn Sū Ho Wán*	冠心蘇合丸
172	Hailung Tonic Pills *Hǎi Lóng Bǔ Wán*	海龍補丸
214	Healthy Brain Pills *Jiàn Nǎo Wán*	健腦丸
38	Herbal Tortoise Jelly *Yào Zhì Gūi Líng Gāo*	藥制龜苓膏
187	Ho Cheh Ta Tsao Wan *Hé Chē Dà Zào Wán*	河車大造丸
73	Hong She Pills *Fēng Shī Piàn*	風濕片
64	Hou Tsao San *Hóu Zǎo Sǎn*	猴棗散
124	Hsiang Sha Yang Wei Pien *Xiāng Shā Yǎng Wèi Piàn*	香沙養胃片
28	Hsiao Keh Chuan *Xiāo Ké Chuǎn Zhuān Zhì Qì Guǎn Yán*	消咳喘專治氣管炎
123	Hsiao Yao Wan *Xiāo Yáo Wán*	消遙丸
92	Hsiung Tan Tieh Ta Wan *Xióng Dǎn Diē Dǎ Wán*	熊胆跌打丸
5	Huang Lien Shang Ching Pien *Huáng Lián Shǎng Qīng Piàn*	黃蓮上清片
65	Hui Chun Tan *Húi Chun Dān*	回春丹
125 126	Huo Hsiang Cheng Chi Pien *Hùo Xiāng Zhèng Qì Piàn*	藿香正氣片
221	Hypertension Repressing Tablets *Jiàng Yā Píng Piàn*	降壓平片
151	Imperial Ho Shou Wu Jit *Zhōng Gúo Shǒu Wū Zhī*	中國首烏汁
127	Jenshen Chien Pi Wan *Rén Shēn Jiàn Pí Wán*	人參健脾丸

198	Jen Shen Lu Jung Wan	
199	*Rén Shēn Lù Róng Wán*	人參鹿茸丸
144	Jian Pi Su	
	Jiàn Pí Sù	健脾素
57	Ji Gu Cao Pill	
	Jī Gǔ Cǎo Wán	雞骨草丸
184	Kai Kit Pill	
	Jiě Jié Wán	解結丸
74	Kai Yeung Pill	
	Huā Shé Jiě Yǎng Wán	花蛇解癢丸
173	Kang Gu Zeng Sheng Pian	
	Kàng Gǔ Zhēng Shēng Piàn	抗骨增生片
152	Kang Wei Ling	
	Kàng Wěi Líng	亢痿靈
84	Kou Pi Plasters	
	Gǒu Pí Gāo	狗皮膏
101	Kuan Hsin Su Ho Wan	
	Guàn Xīn Sū Hé Wán	冠心蘇合丸
193	Kwei Be Wan	
	Guī Pí Wán	歸脾丸
174	Kwei Ling Chi	
	Guī Líng Jí	龜齡集
39	Laryngitis Pills	
	Hóu Yán Wán	喉炎丸
58	Lidan Tablets	
	Lì Dǎn Piàn	利胆片
59	Lidian Paishi Tablets	
	Lì Dǎn Pái Shí Piàn	利胆排石片
40	Lien Chiao Pai Tu Pien	
	Lián Qiáo Bài Dú Piàn	蓮翹敗毒片
60	Li Gan Pian	
	Lì Gān Piàn	利肝片
6	Ling Yang Shang Feng Ling	
	Líng Yáng Shāng Fēng Líng	羚羊傷風靈
128	Liu Jun Zi Tablets	
	Liù Jūn Zǐ Piàn	六君子片
41	Liu Shen Wan	
	Liù Shén Wán	六神丸
119	Liu Shen Shui	
	Liù Shén Shuǐ	六神水
188	Liu Wei Di Huang Wan	
	Liù Wei Dì Huáng Wán	六味地黃丸

48	Niu Huang Qin Xin Wan *Niú Huáng Qīng Xīn Wán*	牛黃清心片
49	Niu Huang Shang Ching Wan *Niú Huáng Shàng Qīng Wán*	牛黃上清丸
50	Niu Huang Xiao Yan Wan *Niú Huáng Xiāo Yán Wán*	牛黃清炎丸
153	Pai Feng Wan *Bái Fēng Wán*	白鳳丸
215	Pai Tzu Yang Hsin Wan *Bái Zǐ Yǎng Xīn Wán*	柏子養心丸
66	Pao Ying Tan *Zhū Pò Bǎo Yīng Dān*	珠珀保嬰丹
51	Peaceful Tea *Niú Huáng Qīng Xīn Wán*	牛黃清心丸
145	Peking Royal Jelly *Běi Jīng Fēng Wáng Jīng*	北京蜂王精
130	Pill Curing *Kāng Níng Wán*	康寧丸
19	Pinellia Expectorant Pills *Qīng Qì Huā Tán Wán*	清氣化痰丸
23	Ping Chuan Pill *Píng Chuǎn Wán*	平喘丸
187	Placenta Compound Restorative Pills *Hé Chē Dà Zào Wán*	河車大造丸
111	Plaster For Bruise And Analgesic *Diē Dá Zhǐ Tòng Gāo*	跌打止痛膏
112	Po Sum On Medicated Oil *Bǎo Xīn Ān Yóu*	保心安油
67	Po Ying Tan (pills) Babies Protector *Bǎo Yīng Dān*	八寶珠珀保嬰丹
93	Prostate Gland Pills *Qián Liè Xiàn Wán*	前列腺丸
24	Pulmonary Tonic Pills *Lì Fèi Táng Yī Piàn*	利肺糖衣片
167	Recovery Of Youth Tablet *Qīng Chūn Bǎo*	靑春寶
7	Refined Sang Chu Gan Mao *Sāng Jú Gǎn Mào Piàn*	桑菊感冒片
154	Rehmannia Glutinosa Compound Pills *Fù Kē Zhong Zǐ Wán*	婦科種子丸

155	Shou Wu Chih *Shŏu Wŭ Zhī*	首烏汁
156	Shou Wu Pian *Shŏu Wŭ Piàn*	首烏片
135	Shu Kan Wan *Shū Gān Wán*	舒肝丸
134	Shu Kan Wan (Condensed) *Shū Gān Wán [Nóng Suō]*	舒肝丸（濃縮）
188	Six Flavor Tea *Liù Wèi Dì Huáng Wán*	六味地黄丸
136	Six Gentlemen Tea Pill *Xiāng Shā Liù Jūn Zĭ Wán*	香沙六君子丸
34	Snake Gall And Loquat Extract *Sān Shé Dăn Chuān Bèi Pí Pá Gāo*	三蛇胆川貝枇杷膏
61	Specific Drug Passwan *Tè Xiào Pái Shí Wán*	特效排石丸
76	Specific Lumbagin *Tè Xiào Yāo Tòng Líng*	特效腰痛靈
122	Stomachic Pills *Rén Shēn Jiàn Pí Wán*	人參健脾丸
157	Sugar Coated Placenta Tablets *Tāi Pán Táng Yī Piàn*	胎盤糖衣片
105	Su He Xiang Pills *Sè Hé Xiāng Wán*	蘇合香丸
53	Superior Sore Throat Powder Spray *Shuāng Liào Hóu Fēng Sàn*	雙料喉風散
177	Tabellae Chuang Yao Tonic *Zhuàng Yāo Jiàn Shèn Piàn*	壯腰健腎片
137	Tabellae Ping-Wei *Píng Wèi Piàn*	平胃片
217	Tabellae Suan Zao Ren Tang *Suān Zăo Rén Tāng Piàn*	酸棗仁湯片
158	Tabellae Tang Kuei *Dāng Guī Wán*	當歸丸
9	Tablet Bi-Tong *Bí Tōng Piàn*	鼻通片
77 78	Ta Huo Lo Tan *Dà Húo Lòu Dān*	大活絡丹
159	Tang Kwe Gin *Dāng Guī Jīng Gāo*	當歸精膏

68	Tao Chih Pien *Dăo Chì Piàn*	導赤片
204	Ten Flavor Tea *Shí Quán Dà Bŭ Wán*	十全大補丸
224	Tianma Chu Feng Pu Pien *Tiān Má Qŭ Fēng Bŭ Piàn*	天麻祛風補片
79	Tienma Hu Gu Wan *Tiān Má Hŭ Gu Wán*	天麻虎骨丸
114	Tieh Ta Yao Gin *Diē Dă Yào Jīng*	跌打藥精
94	Tienchi Ginseng Tablet *Yún Nán Te Chăn Tián Qì Piàn*	雲南特產田七片
160	Tienchi Powder Prepared *Shú Tián Qì Fĕn*	熟田七粉
95	Tienchi Powder Raw *Shēng Tián Qì Fĕn*	生田七粉
223	Tienma And Shou Wu *Tiān Má Shŏu Wu Wán*	天麻首烏丸
225	Tienma Mihuan Tablets *Tiān Má Mì Húan Piàn*	天麻蜜環片
213	Tien Wang Bu Xin Wan *Tiān Wáng Bŭ Xīn Wán*	天王補心丸
96	To Jing Wan *Tòng Jīng Wán*	痛經丸
80	Trisnake Itch-Removing Pill *Sān Shé Jiĕ Yăng Wán*	三蛇解癢丸
106	Tsai Tsao Wan *Zài Zào Wán*	再造丸
190	Tso-Tzu Otic Pills *Ĕr Míng Zuŏ Cí Wan*	耳鳴左慈丸
25	Tung Hsuan Li Fei Pien *Tōng Xuān Lĭ Fèi Piàn*	通宣理肺片
81	Tu Zhung Feng Shi Wan *Dù Zhòng Fēng Shī Wán*	杜仲風濕丸
205	Tzepao Sanpien Extract *Zhì Băo Sān Biān Jīng*	至寶三鞭精
218	Tze Zhu Pills *Cí Zhū Wán*	磁硃丸
54	Tzu-Hsueh-Tan *Zĭ Xuē Dan*	紫雪丹

206	Wan Nian Chun Zi Pu Ziang *Wàn Nián Jūn Zǐ Bǔ Jiang*	萬年春子補醬
98	Wei Te Ling "204" *Wèi Tè Líng*	胃特靈 "204"
161	White Phoenix Pills (Condensed) *Wú Jī Bái Fēng Wán (Nóng Sūo)*	烏雞白鳳丸
149	Women's Precious Pills *Nǔ Ke Ba Zhén Wán*	女科八珍丸
161 162	Wu Chi Pai Feng Wan *Wú Jī Bái Fēng Wán*	烏雞白鳳丸
128	Xiang Sha Yang Wei Wan *Xiāng Shā Yǎng Wèi Wán*	香砂養胃丸
82	Xiao Huo Luo Dan *Xiǎo Húo Lùo Dān*	小活絡丹
178	Xiong Bao *Xióng Bǎo*	雄寶
207	Yang Rong Wan *Yǎng Róng Wán*	養榮丸
107	Yan Shen Jai Jao Wan *Rén Shēn Zài Zǎo Wán*	人參再造丸
191	Yeuchung Pills *Yù Quán Wán*	玉泉丸
10 11	Yinchiao Chieh Tu Pien *Yín Qiào Jiě Dú Piàn*	銀翹解毒丸
62	Yudai Wan *Yù Dài Wán*	愈帶丸
163	Yung Sheng He Ah Chiao *Yǒng Shēng Hé Ē Jiāo*	永盛合阿膠
97	Yunnan Paiyao *Yún Nán Bái Yào*	雲南白藥
115	Yun Xiang Jing *Yún Xiāng Jīng*	雲南精
116	Zheng Gu Shui *Zhēng Gu Shuǐ*	珍珠水
26	Zhi Sou Ding Chuan Wan *Zhǐ Sòu Dìng Chuǎn Wán*	止嗽定喘丸
99	Zhi Wan *Zhì Wán*	痔丸
13	Zhong Gan Ling *Zhòng Gǎn Líng*	重感靈
139	Zisheng Stomachic Pills *Zi Shēng Wáng*	資生丸

A Practitioner's Pharmacy
Recommended Patents

GROUP 1
PILLS FOR PROBLEMS DUE
TO EXOGENOUS WIND-INVASION

2 BI YAN PIAN: nasal congestion, hayfever, sneezing
3 CHUAN QIONG CHA TIAO WAN: wind-cold; wind-cold headache
4 GANMAOLING TABLETS: wind-heat or cold, flu
5 HUANG LIEN SHANG CHING PIEN: heat in upper burner
8 SANG CHU YIN PIEN: wind-heat with cough, sneezing, runny nose
11 YINCHIAO CHIEH TU PIEN: TIANJIN: non-sugar coated, for first 24 hours of wind-heat invasion

GROUP 2
PATENTS FOR COUGH, PHLEGM,
AND DIFFICULT BREATHING

GROUP 2-A: PILLS

16 CHI KUAN YEN WAN: dry cough with sticky phlegm
17 CHING FEI YI HUO PIEN: heat in lungs, sore throat, phlegm-heat
18 CHUAN KE LING: chronic asthma or lung weakness
19 CLEAN AIR TEA: phlegm-heat, phlegm-damp, nasal congestion
21 FRITILLARIA EXTRACT SUGAR-COATED TABLETS: acute and chronic phlegm-heat in lungs
24 PULMONARY TONIC PILLS: deficiency of lung *qi* with heat
25 SAN SHE DAN CHUAN BEI YE: chronic phlegm in lungs
26 TUNG HSUAN LI FEI PIEN: wind-invasion with cough and nasal discharge

GROUP 2-B: SYRUPS

27 FRITILLARIA AND LOQUAT COUGH MIXTURE: syrup for cough and phlegm
31 NATURAL HERB LOQUAT FLAVORED SYRUP: acute and chronic phlegm-heat cough
34 SNAKE GALL AND LOQUAT EXTRACT: phlegm-heat with cough

GROUP 3
PILLS TO REMOVE INTERNAL, TOXIC, AND DAMP HEAT

GROUP 3-A
PILLS TO REMOVE INTERNAL AND TOXIC HEAT

36 CHUAN XIN LIAN: fever with sore throat, toxic inflammations
38 HERBAL TORTOISE JELLY: infected skin lesions
40 LIEN CHIAO PAI TU PIEN: toxic skin infections with fever
41 LIU SHEN WAN: laryngitis, tonsillitis, sore throat due to internal heat
42 LUNG TAN XIE GAN PILL: liver and gallbladder fire or damp-heat
43 MARGARITE ACNE PILLS: acne due to blood heat
44 MING MU SHANG CHING PIEN: liver fire affecting eyes
44 NIU HUANG CHIEH TU PIEN (BEZOAR ANTIPYRETIC PILLS): acute fever or infection including throat, teeth or eyes
45 NIU HUANG CHIEH TU PIEN (or #46): acute fever or infection including throat, teeth, or eyes
50 NIU HUANG XIAO YAN WAN: fever and infections
52 SAI MEI AN: Stomach ulcers without bleeding; hyperacidity

GROUP 3-B
PILLS TO REMOVE DAMP-HEAT

55 ARMADILLO COUNTER POISON PILL: skin itching
56 CHIEN CHIN CHIH TAI WAN: damp-heat leukorrhea
58 LIDAN TABLETS: gallstones and gallbladder inflammation
58 LIDIAN PAISHI TABLETS: gallstones and gallbladder inflammtion
60 LI GAN PIAN: jaundice, hepatitis, gallstones
61 SPECIFIC DRUG PASSWAN: kidney and bladder stones
62 YUDAI WAN: damp-heat leukorrhea

GROUP 3-C
FEVERS IN INFANTS AND YOUNG CHILDREN

63   BO YING PILLS (or #66, 67): colds, flu, fever, phlegm
64   HOU TSAO SAN: fever with phlegm, fits, cough, night-crying
65   HUI CHUN TAN: digestive disturbances

GROUP 4
PILLS, LINIMENTS, AND PLASTERS
FOR REMOVING WIND-DAMP

GROUP 4-A: PILLS

70   DU HUO JISHENG WAN: wind-damp sciatic and joint pain
71   FENG SHIH HSIAO TUNG WAN: wind-damp sciatic and
      joint pain
72   GUAN JIE YAN WAN: acute and chronic wind-damp joint
      rheumatism
73   HONG SHE PILLS: acute and chronic wind-damp
      rheumatism, and pain due to chronic injury
74   KAI YEUNG PILL (or #80): skin itching
76   SPECIFIC LUMBAGLIN: lower back pain or sciatica
77   TA HUO LO TAN: strongest (and most expensive) for acute
      wind-damp rheumatism
81   TU ZHUNG FENG SHI WAN: chronic lower back and joint
      pain
82   XIAO HUO LUO DAN: chronic back and joint pain aggrevated
      by cold

GROUP 4-B
PLASTERS FOR EXTERNAL APPLICATION

85   MUSK RHEUMATISM-EXPELLING PLASTERS: stick-on
      medicated bandage for stiff joints
86   SHANG SHI ZHI TONG GAO: medicated bandage for chronic
      joint pain or trauma

GROUP 5
PRODUCTS FOR BLOOD STAGNATION, BLEEDING, AND PAIN

GROUP 5-A: PILLS

88 CHIN KOO TIEH SHANG WAN: acute traumatic injuries
84 CORYDALIS YANHUSUS ANALGESIC TABLETS: general or local pain
90 FARGELIN FOR PILES: hemorrhoids
92 HSIUNG TAN TIEH TA WAN: acute and chronic traumatic injury
93 PROSTATE GLAND PILLS: prostate inflammation
96 TO JING WAN: menstrual cramps and clots
97 YUNNAN PAIYAO: traumatic bleeding and swelling, menorrhagia; can be applied topically

GROUP 5-B
PILLS FOR HEART CONGESTION, ANGINA, AND STROKE

100 DAN SHEN TABLET CO.: angina pain
101 KUAN HSIN SU HO WAN (or #102): angina, arteriosclerosis, embolisms
104 REN SHEN ZAI ZAO WAN (or #106, 107): sequelae of stroke

GROUP 5-C
PATENTS FOR EXTERNAL APPLICATION

105 CHING WAN HUNG: burns
108 PLASTER FOR BRUISE AND ANALGESIC: medicated stick-on bandage for acute and chronic trauma
109 PO SUM ON MEDICATED OIL: excellent liniment for joint and muscle stiffness
110 SHANG SHI BAO ZHEN GAO: medicated stick-on bandage for acute and chronic trauma
111 TIEH TA YAO GIN: excellent liniment for traumatic swelling, sprains
113 ZHENG GU SHUI: excellent liniment for traumatic sprains and breaks

GROUP 6
PILLS FOR PROMOTING DIGESTION AND RELIEVING STAGNATION

117   BOJENMI CHINESE TEA: weight reduction, (fats and water)
118   CARMICHAELI TEA PILLS: stagnation and phlegm-damp in stomach
120   CHINA PO CHI PILLS: acute cramping, nausea, diarrhea
123   HSIAO YAO WAN: liver stagnation with deficiency of blood
124   HSIANG SHA YANG WEI PIEN (or #138): food stagnation with phlegm; morning sickness
125   HUO HSIANG CHENG CHI PIEN (or #126): stomach-flu; food-stagnation
127   JENSHEN CHIEN PI WAN: poor digestion due to spleen deficiency with damp
129   MU XIANG SHUN QI WAN: liver heat causing stagnation and phlegm
130   PILL CURING: stomach flu; acute digestive disturbances, food stagnation
133   SHEN LING BAIZHU PIAN: spleen *qi* deficiency with stagnation
136   SIX GENTLEMEN TEA PILL: poor digestion due to spleen*qi* deficiency
139   ZISHENG STOMACHIC PILLS: broad spectrum of digestive disturbances

GROUP 7
PILLS AND EXTRACTS FOR
TONIFYING AND NURTURING

GROUP 7-A
PILLS AND EXTRACTS TO TONIFY QI

140   CENTRAL QI PILLS (BU ZHONG YI QI WAN): liver-spleen disharmonies; prolapses of lower organs; hypoglycemia
143   GINSENG ROYAL JELLY VIALS (RENSHENG FENG WANG JIANG): spleen *qi* tonic
144   JIAN PI SU: animal spleen extract to nurture spleen*qi*
145   PEKING ROYAL JELLY: nutritive tonic
146   SHEN QI DA BU WAN: codonopsis and astragalus to tonify spleen and *wei qi*

GROUP 7-B
PILLS AND EXTRACTS TO NOURISH BLOOD

147 ANGELICA TEA: tonifies and invigorates blood
148 BUTIAO TABLETS: blood deficiency and stagnation causing menstrual cramps or irregular periods
149 EIGHT TREASURE TEA: general *qi* and blood tonic for women
151 IMPERIAL SHOU WU JIT (or #155): liquid tonic for blood
154 REHMANNIA GLUTINOSA COMPOUND PILLS: cold uterus causing infertility and amenorrhea
161 WU CHI PAI FENG WAN (TIENTSIN FORMULA): menstrual cramps due to deficiency of blood and cold
162 WU CHI PAI FENG WAN (CONDENSED): menstrual cramps due to deficiency of blood and cold

GROUP 7-C
TONICS FOR DEFICIENCY OF YANG

164 ANTI-LUMBAGO TABLETS: lower back pain
165 BA WEI DI HUANG WAN: poor digestion due to *yang* deficiency
168 GOLDEN LOCK TEA: nocturnal emission; premature ejaculation
170 GEJIE BU SHEN WAN: warms kidney *yang*
171 GOLDEN BOOK TEA: tonifies kidney *qi* and *yang*
175 NAN BAO CAPSULES (or #167, 168): strong male sexual tonic for *qi*, blood, *yang*, and *jing*
176 SEA HORSE HERB TEA: strong *yang* tonic

GROUP 7-D
TONICS FOR DEFICIENCY OF YIN OR FLUIDS

179 BA XIAN CHANG SHOU WAN: deficiency of kidney and lung *yin*
181 DA BU YIN WAN: deficiency fire, night-sweats
183 EIGHT FLAVOR TEA: tonifies *yin*, sedates fire
185 LYCIUM AND CHRYSANTHEMUM TEA (LYCIUM-REHMANNIA PILLS): vision problems
186 REHMANNIA TEA: vision problems
187 RESTORATIVE PILLS: deficiency of *yin* with fire

188   SIX FLAVOR TEA (LIU WEI DI HUANG WAN): tonifyies
      kidney *qi* and *yin*
189   SMOOTH TEA (FRUCTUS PERSICA PILLS): constipation
190   TSO-TZU OTIC PILLS: deficiency of *yin* fire affecting ears,
      eyes; high blood pressure

GROUP 7-E
GENERAL, AND COMBINATION, TONICS

193   ANGELICA LONGANA TEA: heart *yin*, blood; heart and
      spleen *qi*
195   GEJIE TA BU WAN: tonifies kidney *qi* and *yang*
196   GINSENG POLYGONA ROOT EXTRACT: *qi* and blood
197   GINSENG TONIC CAPSULES: kidney *qi* and *yang*
198   JEN SHEN LU JUNG WAN: Ginseng and Deer Horn for
      kidney *qi* ; large pill
200   REN SHEN YANG YING WAN: spleen and heart *qi* and blood
201   SHIH SAN TAI PAO WAN: general tonic for first trimester of
      pregnancy
204   TEN FLAVOR TEA (SHIH CHUAN DA BU WAN): popular
      qi and blood tonic
205   TZEPAO SANPIEN EXTRACT: large formula to tonify *qi*,
      blood, *yin*, and *yang*
207   YANG RONG WAN (GINSENG TONIC PILLS): general *qi*
      and blood tonic

GROUP 8
PILLS TO CALM SHEN
(PACIFY THE SPIRIT)

208   AN MIEN PIEN: insomnia due to liver heat
209   AN SHENG PU SHIN WAN: tonifies heart blood causing
      dizziness and insomnia
213   EMPEROR'S TEA (TIEN WANG BU XIN WAN): insomnia
      due to deficient heart blood and *yin*
214   HEALTHY BRAIN PILLS: stubborn insomnia with nightmares
216   SHEN CHING SHUAI JAO WAN: restless *shen* due to
      deficiency of *qi*, blood and *yin*

GROUP 9
PILLS TO CONTROL ENDOGENOUS LIVER WIND AND HYPERTENSION

219 CHIANG YA WAN: hypertension due to liver fire
220 COMPOUND CORTEX EUCOMMIA TABLETS: similiar to #219
222 NIU HUANG CHIANG YA WAN: hypertension; arteriosclerosis
224 TIANMA CHU FENG PU PIEN: hypertension due to weak kidneys and liver wind

APPENDIX 1
EAST EARTH HERB COMPANY

A. TURTLE MOUNTAIN / DRAGON EGGS

226 BLACK BOAR - KIDNEY YANG: tonifies kidney *qi* and *yang*
227 GREEN TIGER - LIVER: invigorates liver *qi*
229 RED HORSE - HEART: nutures heart blood and *yin,* calms *shen*
230 WHITE MONKEY - LUNGS: tonifies lung *qi* and *yin*; resolves phlegm-heat
231 WHITE TURTLE - KIDNEY YIN: nourishes kidney *qi* and *yin*
232 YELLOW OX - SPLEEN: tonifies spleen *qi*; regulates the center
233 DETOX: sedates liver fire; dispels toxic heat
236 FOUR GINSENGS: tonifies *qi* ands blood, *yin* and *yang*
240 TURTLE MOUNTAIN TONIC (DRAGON'S BREW): general tonic for *qi*, blood, *yin*, *yang*, and *jing*
241 WOMEN'S LONGEVITY: tonifies *qi* and blood

B. JADE PHARMACY

242 COMPASSIONATE SAGE - HEART SPIRIT: calms *shen,* tonifies heart blood and *yin*
243 DYNAMIC WARRIOR - KIDNEY YANG: tonifies kidney *qi* and *yang*
244 PROSPEROUS FARMER - SPLEEN QI: tonifies spleen, resolves spleen-damp
245 QUIET CONTEMPLATIVE - KIDNEY YIN: nourishes kidney *qi* and *yin*

246   RELAXED WANDERER - STAGNANT LIVER QI:
       invigorates liver *qi*
247   WISE JUDGE - LUNG YIN AND QI: tonifies lung *yin* and *qi*;
       cough

APPENDIX 2
NATURE'S SUNSHINE CONSTITUTIONAL THERAPY

248   TIAO HE: liver congeston affecting digestion
249   BU XUE: liver blood deficiency
250   AN SHEN: disturbed *shen*
251   YANG XIN: deficiency of heart *yin*, *qi*, and blood
252   XIAO DAO: food stagnation and stomach phlegm
253   WEN ZHONG: deficiency of spleen *qi* with damp
254   XUAN FEI: lung phlegm-damp
255   FU LEI: deficiency of lung *yin* with heat and phlegm
256   QU SHI: edema
257   JIAN GU: deficiency of kidney with sore back
258   QING RE: dispels wind-heat and toxic heat
259   BU YIN: nurtures *yin*
260   JIE YU: for liver congestion affecting menstruation and
       digestion
261   SHENG MAI: general tonic for *qi* and blood, *yin* and *yang*

APPENDIX 3
CHINESE TRADITIONAL FORMULAS
(HEALTH CONCERNS)

262   ASTRA EIGHT: *qi* and *wei qi*; natural immune system
263   ASTRA GARLIC: detoxifies blood, anti-parasitic
264   CIR-Q: blocked blood vessels
265   EASE PLUS: disturbed *shen* affected by liver *yang*
266   EASE 2: stagnant liver *qi* affecting digestion
267   MOBILITY 1: dispels wind-damp rheumatism
268   MOBILITY 2: wind-damp rheumatism, sciatic pain
269   NASAL TABS: sinus congestion
270   REJUVENATE 8: kidney *qi* and *yang*
271   RESP: dispels lung phlegm-damp
272   STOMACH TABS: poor digestion due to food stagnation

GLOSSARY OF TRADITIONAL CHINESE MEDICAL TERMS

BLOOD HEAT - a pathology where the blood heats up due to liver or heart fire, or systemic fever. The main symptom is non-traumatic bleeding, including nose-bleed, uterine bleeding, and internal hemorrhaging.

BLOOD STAGNATION - a condition where the blood congeals, moves slowly, or forms clots. Due to cold, heat, deficiency or trauma.

BURNERS- the upper burner is the area above the diaphragm and includes the lungs, heart and head; the middle burner is the area between the diaphragm and the naval, and includes the organs stomach, spleen, liver and gallbladder. It often relates to digestion in general. The lower burner is below the naval, and includes the kidneys, bladder, small and large intestines, uterus and genital organs. It also includes the liver and gallbladder channels.

CENTER - can refer to either the middle burner in general, or the stomach and spleen specifically.

DAMP - refers to exogenous invasion affecting the musculo-skeletal system (wind-damp), or endogenous weakness of the spleen leading to watery accumulations in organs or cavities.

DAMP-HEAT - a pathological condition combining both excess damp and excess heat. It can affect the liver, gallbladder, intestines or uterus.

DEFICIENCY-HEAT - excess heat which has its basis in deficiency of *yin*. It can affect the body systemically or appear isolated in the lungs, heart, stomach-spleen, liver, or kidneys.

EXOGENOUS INVASION - any sickness whose origin is outside the body; includes wind invasions (colds), and toxic invasions (bacterial and viral) including measles, flu, encephalitis, meningitis, etc.

JING - condensed essence of congenital *qi* which is stored in the kidneys and circulates in the 8 Extra Channels. Related to sperm and ova production, as well as nurturing the fetus. Provides the basis for strong or weak constitutions.

LIVER FIRE - pathological fever in the liver, with symptoms rising upwards to include headache, eye burning, ear-ringing, etc.

LUO CHANNELS - secondary acupuncture channels dispersed from the primary channels.

ORIFICES - the sense organs of the head, namely, eyes, ears, nose and mouth. In pathologies where the orifices are "closed", unconsciousness ensues.

PHLEGM - congealed mucus formed by excesses of damp and heat. Often originates in the spleen and stomach, and accumulates in the lungs, sinuses, intestines, uterus, or the acupuncture channels. Includes fatty deposits in the heart and blood vessels.

PHLEGM-DAMP - chronic phlegm which is clear or white, and affects primarily the lungs, uterus or digestive tract. Distinguished from phlegm-heat.

PHLEGM-HEAT - acute phlegm, yellow and odorous, found primarily in the lungs, sinuses, stomach or uterus.

QI - (pronounced "chee"), the energy that flows through the acupuncture channels, is responsible for invigorating all organs, tissues and cells along its path. Also refers to the functional ability of individual organs, such as spleen *qi*, heart *qi*, lung *qi*, etc.

QI STAGNATION - *qi* moves under healthy circumstances. When the *qi* stagnates, dysfunction and pain ensue. Can refer to either impaired circulation in the channels due to trauma, or congested energy in specific organs, particularly the stomach and spleen (the center), or liver.

SHEN - often translated as "spirit", it includes the concepts of mind, consciousness, and higher spiritual connection . It is located in the heart. Disturbed *shen* manifests as insomnia, restlessness, muddled thinking, poor memory, uncomfortable dreaming, and manic disorders.

SPLEEN - includes the function of both spleen and pancreas, and is responsible for converting food to energy and blood, as well as regulating digestion.

SPLEEN-DAMP - in deficiencies of spleen *qi*, damp accumulates. This leads to water retention in the abdomen, loose or watery stools, and incomplete digestion; it is often the basis for phlegm congestion in the lungs.

SURFACE (Exterior) - the surface, rich in *wei qi*, is responsible for maintaining the body's internal homeostasis against a changeable environment. Exogenous invasions initially affect the surface, and the herbal approach is to dispel energetic invasions out through the skin, if the invasion has not proceeded too deeply into the body.

TOXIC HEAT - refers to exogenous toxic attacks (bacterial and viral) which can affect the body systemically with fever, attack specific organs, or affect the skin as inflamed boils.

WEI QI - the most energetic aspect of *qi*, which circulates from the main channels to the exterior of the body. It is responsible for repulsing exogenous wind or toxic invasions, as well as contributing to the body's immune defense system.

WIND - climatic disturbances in the air can induce pathogenic invasions if the *wei qi* is deficient. It attacks the surface of the body, further debilitates *wei qi*, and allows preponderance of toxic factors, causing the symptoms associated with flus and colds.

WIND-COLD - the body's response to a wind invasion exhibiting chills, nasal congestion, headache and body aches. Can occur as a response to over-exposure to wind and cold.

WIND-DAMP - in susceptible persons, exposure to wind in a damp environment or a preexisting internal damp excess will cause rheumatism and joint pain in the surface. Accounts for various musculo-skeletal complaints.

WIND-HEAT - in wind invasions affecting people with pre-exisiting heat or deficiency-heat, colds are marked by fever, sore throat, and restlessness.

WIND, INTERNAL - refers to an endogenous wind generated by liver fire. Symptoms include convulsions, muscle spasms, tics, severe headache, pressure behind eyes, or stroke. May follow a high fever.

WIND, LIVER - see Wind, Internal.

YANG - the functional aspect of kidney *qi* which warms the body, and invigortates digestion, excretion, and sexual function. Deficiencies of *yang* allow the predominance of cold and hypo-function of the organs.

YIN - the material and functional aspect of kidney *qi* which moistens and cools the liver, stomach, spleen, lungs, heart, throat, eyes and nose, and provides the basis for semen and vaginal fluids. Deficiencies of *yin* produce dryness and heat.

YING QI - the *qi* that circulates in the acupuncture channels, and which nourishes the organs.

ZANG-FU - as a group it refers to organs (in distinction from acupuncture channels). The *zang* organs are considered to be more *yin* and solid (storing and slowly transforming) and include the heart, spleen-pancreas, lungs, kidneys and liver. The *fu* organs are considered more *yang* (functionally active) and hollow. They include the small and large intestines, gallbladder, stomach, and urinary bladder.

INDEX OF PRODUCTS BY SYMPTOM

Number refers to product number

-A-

ABDOMINAL PAIN
  Deficiency with cold 124, 226, 253
  Due to liver stagnation 123, 129, 134, 135, 260
  Due to stagnation of *qi* 123, 125, 129, 132, 139, 226, 260
  Due to ulcer 52
  With bloating 127, 139, 252, 260
  With food stagnation 130, 131, 133, 139, 252, 260, 272
  With leukorrhea 56
  With spleen damp 137, 138

ABSCESSES 36, 38, 40, 43, 48, 50, 97, 233

ACNE 43, 55, 80, 108

ALLERGIES
  Food 123, 246, 248, 266
  Hayfever and nasal 2, 9, 123, 246, 248, 266
  Skin 10, 38, 40, 43, 55, 108, 233

AMENORRHEA 96, 138, 145, 148, 151, 161, 162, 239, 241

ANAL ITCHING OR PAIN 99

ANEMIA Group 7-B; 38, 56, 62, 81, 159, 160, 172, 196, 202, 239, 241

ANGINA 100, 101, 103, 105, 264

ANXIETY Group 8; 208, 211, 212, 213, 215, 237, 250, 251

APPETITE, POOR Group 6; Group 7-E; 232, 234, 244, 253

ARTERIES, hardened 100, 101, 105, 117, 209, 210, 221, 222, 229, 242, 264, 270

ARTHRITIS Group 4-A; 206, 267, 268,
  Rheumatoid 72, 258, 267

ASCARIASIS, roundworms in bilary ducts 59

ASTHMA
  Chronic 14, 16, 18, 23, 205, 206, 230, 247
  Cough 18, 23, 25, 33, 254
  Due to or aggravated by exogenous invasion 14, 20
  Due to kidney-lung weakness 23, 110, 165, 169, 170, 171, 172, 226, 243, 257

ATHEROSCLEROSIS (see ARTERIES, HARDENED)

-B-

BACKACHE, LOWER 164, 165, 169, 171, 177, 188, 228
  Due to cold Group 7-C; 164, 165, 176, 177, 243
  Due to deficiency of kidney *qi* or *yang* 69, 71, 155, 164, 166, 192, 198, 199,
      205, 257, 259, 270
  Due to prostate inflammation 93
  Due to trauma Group 5-C; 110, 111, 113
  Due to wind-damp Group 4; 56, 62, 71, 79, 164
  With numbness 173, 178
  With weakness 155, 164, 165, 192, 198, 199, 205

BEDSORES 108

BELCHING 123, 129, 133, 134

BELL'S PALSY 104, 106, 107, 224

BI SYNDROME (see JOINT PAIN)

BLADDER STONES 61

BLEEDING 88, 94, 95, 97, 157, 163

BLISTERING 108

BLOOD
  Clots 94, 95
  Deficiency Group 7-B; 38, 56, 62, 81, 159, 196, 202, 204, 241, 261
  Deficiency due to deficient spleen *qi* 144, 146
  Deficiency due to loss Group 7-B; 194, 241, 261
  Heat 36, 37, 43, 47, 138, 148, 161, 162
  In stool 99
  Reducing cholesterol 94, 95, 221, 222, 242, 264, 270
  Stagnation following childbirth 94, 95
  To invigorate circulation and remove stagnation Group 5; 28, 37, 43, 55, 74,
      76, 77, 79, 80, 82, 86, 103, 105, 138, 148, 151, 161, 162, 170, 171, 230,
      241, 248, 264
  Vessel hardening 100, 101, 105, 221, 229, 242, 264, 270

-D-

DELIRIUM, due to fever 35, 37, 41, 45, 46, 47, 49, 51

DEPRESSION 123, 208, 227, 246, 248, 260

DERMATITIS (see SKIN DISORDERS)

DIABETES 188, 191

DIARRHEA OR LOOSE STOOLS
   Acute 120
   Chronic 140
   Due to cold or deficiency of *yang* 121, 168, 171
   Due to spleen deficiency 118, 119, 124, 125, 128, 133, 144, 253, 256
   In children 64, 65, 66, 133

DIET SUPPLEMENT 237

DIGESTION, POOR   Group 6; 123, 140, 142, 144, 146, 193, 206, 232, 252, 272
   Acute 120
   Due to deficiency of liver blood 129
   Due to deficiency of spleen *qi* 118, 119, 124, 125, 127, 128, 133, 139, 140,
       144, 222, 232, 244, 253
   Due to deficiency of *yang* 165, 170, 171, 174, 226, 243, 270
   Due to liver congestion 123, 129, 134, 135,140, 248, 260, 265
   With food stagnation 19, 119, 120, 124, 125, 128, 129, 130, 131, 132, 134,
       135, 136, 137, 139
   With undigested food in stool 121, 165, 170, 171, 176, 244, 252

DIZZINESS
   Due to deficiency of blood or *yin* 149, 156, 163, 182, 185, 196, 223, 224,
       225, 245
   Due to deficiency of *jing* 157
   Due to disturbed *shen* 209, 214, 216, 218, 250
   Due to liver congestion 123, 156
   Due to liver fire or wind 35, 44, 45, 46, 47, 49, 211, 219, 220, 221, 222
   Due to phlegm 20, 128
   Due to wind 3, 21
   With fever 35
   With stomach flu 120

DREAMING, excessive 209, 213

DRUG WITHDRAWAL 227, 233, 265

DYSMENORRHEA 89, 151, 161, 162, 203, 246, 248

-E-

-F-

FACE, red 219, 220, 221

FACIAL PARALYSIS 106, 107, 224

FATIGUE Group 7-A, 7-E
　　Due to childbirth 151, 153, 161, 162, 169, 174
　　Due to deficiency of blood 149, 159, 163, 223, 241
　　Due to deficiency of heart *yin* 193, 200, 229, 251
　　Due to deficiency of kidney *yang* 201, 226, 243, 270
　　Due to deficiency of *qi* 143, 145, 157, 236, 240, 261, 262
　　Due to disturbed *shen* 216
　　Due to liver congestion 123
　　Due to menstruation 138, 241
　　Following ejaculation 170
　　General weakness 167, 172, 178, 194, 196, 205, 210, 240, 261, 262
　　Pregnancy 202

FEVER Group 3-A
　　Due to deficiency of *yin* 181, 183, 187, 259
　　Due to infection 40, 46, 51, 258
　　Due to liver fire 17, 45, 46, 47, 48, 49, 50,51, 54, 234, 258
　　Due to wind-invasion Group 1; 25
　　High Group 3; 35, 37, 46, 49, 50, 51, 54, 233
　　In children Group 3-C 35, 51

FEVER BLISTERS 42

FLATULENCE Group 6
　　Due to deficient spleen 119, 124, 125, 127, 128, 134, 232, 244, 252, 260, 266
　　Due to heat and stagnation 91, 98

FLU (see COLDS AND FLUS)

FLU, STOMACH 125, 130, 131

FRACTURES 88, 111, 114, 116

FUNGAL INFECTION 74, 80

FURUNCLES 36, 38, 40, 43, 48, 50, 97, 233, 258

-G-

GALLBLADDER
    Purge damp-heat 58
    Reduce heat 42, 58, 59, 60

GALLSTONES 58, 59, 60

GASTRITIS (see DIGESTION, POOR)

GASTROINTESTINAL LESIONS 38

GLAUCOMA 180, 186, 218

GOUT 81, 268

GUMS
    Bleeding due to heat 17
    Inflammed due to liver fire 45, 46
    Swollen due to wind invasion 5
    Swollen in babies 68

-H-

HEADACHES
    Due to blood stagnation 89
    Due to deficiency of blood 149, 156, 157, 158, 223, 224, 225, 241
    Due to deficiency of *yin* 185, 188
    Due to indigestion or food stagnation Group 6; (see DIGESTION, POOR)
    Due to liver congestion 48, 123, 156, 248
    Due to liver fire Group 9; 42, 45, 46, 47, 190, 258
    Due to restless *shen* 218
    Due to wind Group 1; 258
    Due to wind-damp Group 4-A; 79, 82

HEALTH, General improvement Group 7-E; 150, 196, 197, 206, 236, 235, 240,
        261, 262

HEARING DISORDERS (see EAR DISORDERS)

HEART
　　Attack 101
　　Chronic heart disease 101, 105
　　Congestive heart failure 169, 176
　　Deficiency of blood 149, 157, 200, 241, 242, 250
　　Deficiency of *qi* Group 7-A, 7-E; 239
　　Deficiency of *yin* 232, 233, 250, 251
　　Pain 101, 105
　　Phlegm 101, 103, 105, 106, 112, 229
　　Prevention of disease 103, 117
　　Stagnation of blood Group 5-B

HEART PALPITATIONS
　　Due to deficiency of blood or *yin* 179, 200, 250, 251
　　Due to deficiency of *yang* 201
　　Due to kidney deficiency 167, 169, 193, 198, 199
　　Due to liver fire 220, 233, 260
　　Due to restless *shen* 218, 250
　　Due to stagnation of blood or phlegm Group 5-B; 264
　　Due to systemic deficiency 176, 200, 211, 212, 213, 216
　　With nightmares 211
　　With restlessness 215

HEMIPLEGIA 104, 107

HEMORRHOIDS
　　Due to blood stagnation and heat 90, 99, 108, 109, 140

HEPATITIS 57, 60, 233

HERNIA 110, 140, 253

HERPES 42

HICCUPS 123, 134

HIVES 40, 43, 55, 108, 233

HOARSE VOICE 34

HYPERTENSION Group 9; 237

HYPERTHYROID 42

HYPOGLYCEMIA, due to liver-spleen disharmony 36, 37, 123, 134,140,143, 144,
　　246, 248, 265

-I-

IMMUNE SYSTEM, to strengthen Groups 7-A, 7-C, 7-E; 150

IMPOTENCE
  Due to deficiency of blood and *jing* 152
  Due to deficiency of *qi* and *jing* 141, 157, 170, 172, 175, 176, 178, 257, 261
  Due to deficiency of *yang* 171, 174

INFECTIONS
  Chronic 263
  Fungal 74, 80, 263
  Ulcerated abcesses 36, 38, 40, 43, 48, 50, 55, 233, 258

INFERTILITY
  Due to deficiency of blood 151, 154, 161, 162
  Due to deficiency of *jing* 157
  Due to deficiency of *qi* 141
  Due to deficiency of *yang* and cold 145, 171, 174, 243

INFLAMMATION, TOXIC 6, 36, 37, 39, 53, 234, 258
  With fever 40, 46, 51, 258

INFLUENZA 7

INJURY, TRAUMATIC Group 5-A, 5-C; 88, 94, 95, 112, 116

INSECT BITES 97, 108

INSOMNIA Group 8
  Due to deficiency of blood 163, 241, 250
  Due to deficiency of *qi* 193, 196, 197, 198, 199, 200, 205,
  Due to deficiency of *yang* 169
  Due to deficiency of *yin* 181, 185, 187, 188, 231, 233, 241, 245, 250
  Due to disturbed *shen* Group 8; 250, 265
  Due to excess heat 183, 190
  Due to liver congestion 123, 260, 265
  Due to wind invasion 5

INTESTINES
  Bleeding 61
  Moisten 189

IRRITABILITY 123, 208, 227, 246, 248, 260

-J-

JAUNDICE   57, 60, 233, 249

JING, tonify   76, 157

JOINT PAIN
    Due to blood stagnation   88, 89, 92
    Due to deficiency   155, 196
    Due to stroke   104
    Due to wind-damp   Group 4;   70, 72, 73, 75, 77,79, 81, 82, 85, 224, 256, 267, 268

-K-

KIDNEYS
    Clear damp-heat   62
    Clear heat   56
    Deficiency of *yin* with heat   181, 183, 187
    Pain or burning   177, 181
    Tonify kidney *qi*   23, 68, 76, 77, 78, 81, 156, 167, 257
    Tonify kidney *yang*   Group 7-C;   164, 165, 169, 170, 174, 175, 176, 178, 177, 226, 243, 257, 270
    Tonify kidney *yin*   Group 7-D;   156, 181, 188, 191, 231, 245, 259

KIDNEY STONES   61

KNEES, weak due to wind-damp-cold   70

-L-

LARYNGITIS   39, 41

LAXATIVE, in babies   68

LESIONS, skin   36, 37, 38, 40, 43, 48, 50, 97, 233, 258

LEUKORRHEA
    Due to deficiency heat   62
    Due to deficiency of *yang*   168
    Due to liver and gallbladder damp-heat   42
    Due to wind-damp   80
    Hot or cold   56, 110

LIGAMENT, torn   114, 116

LIMBS
    Cold   72, 165, 170, 171, 172, 176, 201, 226, 243, 257, 270
    Hot   187, 188
    Numb   Group 4   85, 225
    Sore   Group 4;   84
    Weak   68, 174, 177, 198, 199, 204, 205

MENOPAUSE
    Hot flashes 181, 183, 187, 245

MENSTRUAL DISORDERS
    Cramps 89, 94, 95, 96, 97, 138, 145, 148, 161, 162, 202, 246, 248
    Deficiency of blood (amenorrhea or scanty) 96, 138. 148, 149, 151, 153, 154, 156, 158, 159, 161, 162, 241, 249
    Depression 227
    Dysmenorrhea 89, 96, 151, 161, 162, 202, 246, 248
    Excessive bleeding 97, 148, 158, 163, 193
    Fatigue 138, 236
    Irregular 96, 148, 149, 151, 161, 162, 246, 248
    Premenstrual syndrome 123, 151, 153, 161, 162, 227, 233, 246, 248, 249, 260

MENTAL AGITATION Group 8; 128, 198, 210, 233

MISCARRIAGE, habitual or threatened 31, 87, 140, 174

MORNING SICKNESS 124, 125, 130, 136, 203

MOTION SICKNESS 115, 125, 130, 131

MOUTH SORES 17
    Due to liver fire 42, 45, 46
    Due to toxic wind-heat 53

MUMPS 39, 41

MUSCLE
    Poor tone 104
    Rheumatic aches due to wind-damp 73, 77, 78, 79, 80, 83, 114, 116, 267
    Spasms with high fever 35
    Strain 76, 114, 116
    Weak 192

-N-

NASAL CONGESTION 2, 3, 7, 8, 9

NAUSEA 20, 115, 118, 119, 120, 121, 124, 125, 128, 131, 137, 139
    In pregnancy 119, 124, 125, 130, 203
    Due to food stagnation Group 6; 119, 124, 125, 126, 128, 129, 134, 136
    Due to wind-damp Group 4-A; 79

NECK, STIFF
    Due to wind invasion 4, 10, 11, 12
    Due to liver fire 219

NEURALGIA 111, 113

NIGHTMARES Group 8; 216, 250

-U-

ULCERS
With bleeding 91, 97
Without bleeding 52, 272

UPPER BURNER (see BURNERS)

URINARY TRACT INFECTIONS 38, 42, 61, 93

URINATION
Blood 94, 95
Concentrated or scanty 17, 42, 44, 48, 166
Incontinence 166, 169, 170, 171, 172, 177, 257
Painful 42, 61, 93, 184
Profuse 165
Promote in babies 68

UTERINE BLEEDING 94, 95, 97, 148

UTERUS
Benefits 56, 235
Bleeding 140, 163, 193
Cold 145, 174, 202
Damp discharge 62

-V-

VAGINAL DISCHARGE 174

VAGINAL INFECTIONS 56

VARICOSE VEINS 140

VERTEBRAL CALCIFICATION 173

VERTEBRAL DISK SUBLUXATION 75, 173

VERTIGO (see DIZZINESS)

VIRAL INFECTION 36, 45, 50

-W-

RECOMMENDED READING

Chinese Herbal Medicine Materia Medica by Dan Bensky and Andrew Gamble, Eastland Press, 1986

Chinese Herb Medicine and Therapy by Hong-yen Hsu and William Peacher, Oriental Healing Arts Institute, 1976

Chinese Tonic Herbs by Ron Teeguarden, Japan Publications, Inc. 1985

Essentials of Chinese Acupuncture by Foreign Language Press, Beijing 1980

Handbook of Chinese Herbs and Formulas, Volumes I and II by Him-che Yeung, Los Angeles 1985

Synopsis of the Pharmacoepia by C.S. Cheung and U Aik Kaw, American College of Traditional Chinese Medicine, 1984

Traditional Therapeutic Classifications of Chinese Herbs by Hong-yen Hsu and M.M. Van Benschoten, Bulletin of the Oriental Healing Arts Institute, Volume 8, No, 4, June 1983.

The Web That Has No Weaver by Ted Kaptchuk, Congden and Weed, 1983

Your Nature, Your Health by Subhuti Dharmananda, Institute for Traditional Medicine, 1986

Most of the above are available from:

> Redwing Books
> 44 Linden Street
> Brookline, Massachusetts 02146

DISTRIBUTORS OF PRODUCTS

Chinese herbs and patent medicines:

MAYWAY TRADING COMPANY
622 Broadway
San Francisco, California 94133
Telephone (415) 788-3646

Turtle Mountain and Jade Pharmacy Products:

K'AN HERB COMPANY
339 Rio Del Mar Bld
Aptos, California 95003
Telephone (408) 662-2894

Constitutional Therapy
(Nature's Sunshine Products):

NATURE'S SUNSHINE PRODUCTS
P.O. Box 1000
Spanish Fork, Utah 84660
Telephone (801) 798-9861

Chinese Traditional Formulas
(Health Concerns):

HEALTH CONCERNS
2318 Second Ave
Seattle, Washington 98121
Telephone (206) 622-7972

BIOGRAPHICAL INFORMATION

JAKE FRATKIN, Dipl. Ac., Lic. Ac. has been a full time practitioner of Traditional Chinese Medicine since 1978. He studied acupuncture for seven years with Dr. Ineon Moon, and herbal medicine with Dr. Guo, Zhen-gang and Dr. Pak-leung Lau, all in Chicago, Illinois.

Mr. Fratkin has taught acupuncture and herbal medicine since 1981 at the following institutions in the United States: Midwest Center for Oriental Medicine, Oregon College for Oriental Medicine, Northwest Institute for Acupuncture and Oriental Medicine, and the Southwest College of Acupuncture. He served as a commissioner on the National Accreditation Commission for Schools and Colleges of Acupuncture and Oriental Medicine for two years.

Until recently, he was the chairman of the Department of Oriental Medicine at the John Bastyr College of Naturopathic Medicine in Seattle, Washington. Mr. Fratkin currently resides in Santa Fe, New Mexico where he is on the faculty of the Southwest Acupuncture College, where he serves as chairman of the Department of Herbal Medicine.

SUBHUTI DHARMANANDA, Ph.D. is director of the Institute for Traditional Medicine, with offices in Portland, Oregon, Santa Cruz, and Oakland, California. He received his Ph.D. from the University of California in biology. Dr. Dharmananda has been a writer and lecturer on Chinese herbal therapy for the last eight years, during which time he has been a frequent visitor and guest in the People's Republic of China.

He is the editor of *Update on Herbs*, the journal of the Institute of Traditional Medicine, as well as the author of numerous articles for professional journals. He has recently published *Your Nature, Your Health*, a book on herbal constitutional therapy. Besides writing a special chapter for *Chinese Herbal Patent Formulas*, Dr. Dharmananda commented and advised throughout the writing of this book.